WADSWORTH PHILOSOPHERS SERIES

D1476568

ON

PHILOSOPHY IN CHINA

Hyun Höchsmann
New Jersey City University

THOMSON

™

WADSWORTH

Australia • Canada • Mexico • Singapore • Spain • United Kingdom • United States

For more information about our
products, contact us at:
**Thomson Learning Academic
Resource Center
1-800-423-0563**

For permission to use material from
this text, contact us by:
Phone: 1-800-730-2214
Fax: 1-800-731-2215
Web: www.thomsonrights.com

Asia
Thomson Learning
5 Shenton Way #01-01
UIC Building
Singapore 068808

Australia/New Zealand
Thomson Learning
102 Dodds Street
Southbank, Victoria 3006
Australia

Canada
Nelson
1120 Birchmount Road
Toronto, Ontario M1K 5G4
Canada

Europe/Middle East/South Africa
Thomson Learning
High Holborn House
50-51 Bedford Row
London WC1R 4LR
United Kingdom

Latin America
Thomson Learning
Seneca, 53
Colonia Polanco
11560 Mexico D.F.
Mexico

Spain/Portugal
Paraninfo Thomson Learning
Calle/Magallanes, 25
28015 Madrid, Spain

Contents

Acknowledgement

I wish to thank the editor of the series, Daniel Kolak, for his encouragement and advice throughout the project. Raziel Abelson, Larry Carter, Marie Friquegnon, Xiaoli Fang, Trinity Martinez, John-Paul Gorgoroso, Sky Liu, William Mayne, and Richard Pare have provided indispensable assistance. I have been most fortunate to receive Paul Mustacchio's insightful comments on the entire manuscript.

I owe Yang Guorong an immense debt of gratitude for his stimulating ideas and his generosity. I am grateful to Yu Lizhong and Yang Guorong for the invitation to be a visiting scholar at East China Normal University. I am indebted to Huang Yong, the editor of the journal *Dao, A Journal of Comparative Philosophy* and Jiyuan Yu for their insightful criticism of an earlier version of the Confucius chapter. The chapters on Confucius and Mozi are based on the papers read at the conferences held at East China Normal University in Shanghai and at Zhongshan University in Guangzhou. Zhai Zhenming and the members of the philosophy departments as well as the students of both universities engaged me in stimulating discussions. I thank Samuel Natale and Parviz Morewedge for their invitation to read a paper on Daoism at the Conference on Social Values at Oxford University. Pan Derong's invitation to read a paper on Zhuangzi at the Conference on Ontology and Hermeneutics at Anhui Normal University enabled me to complete the book at the foot of the mountains at Huangshan. Tong Shijun's thoughtful advice put things into a broader perspective. William McBride who led the Philosophy Delegation to China expanded my horizon. I am indebted to Cheng Chung-ying for his comments on the Zhuangzi chapter. Saul Kripke, with his passion for all things philosophical, has been a constant and an abiding source of inspiration. Chen Lisheng's deep and broad learning has enhanced my understanding of the subject and his reading from the *Book of Odes* provided a poetic momentum. At a decisive moment, David Wiggins encouraged me with his exhortation, "Follow your passions!" and Callimachus' words, "Big book, big bad" (μέγα βιβλίου, μέγα κακόυ – *Mega biblion, mega kakon*) saved me from the quandary of whether to present the writings of the philosophers with resolute fidelity by following the main arteries of literal exposition or to embark on intriguing and perilous paths suggested by interpretive analyses of the texts. I strove to exercise a certain restraint in poetic license pursuing the ideas of the ancient sages of China.

Peter Singer, when he suggested *Changing Harmonies – Ways of Thought in China* as a possible title for the book, provided me with a unifying theme for this study. His contribution to the book from its inception to its final expression has been vital.

Note on translation and texts

I have drawn extensively from the following texts. Richard Wilhelm's German translations of Zhuangzi, Laozi, Mencius and the *Yijing* are illuminating. Fung Yu-lan's *A History of Chinese Philosophy* is still the most comprehensive study of philosophy in China. James Legge's *The Chinese Classics Series* is one of the standard authoritative translations of the major thinkers. A. C. Graham's *The Disputers of the Tao, Philosophical Argument in Ancient China*, is one of the most stimulating books on the classical period of philosophy in China. Graham's translation of Zhuangzi is lively and engaging. Arthur Waley's translations of *Dao De Jing* and *The Analects* are illuminating. Jacques Gernet's *A History of Chinese Civilization* is a vivid illustration of the magnitude of the civilization of China. Recent interpretations of the classics include works by Yang Guorong, David S. Nivison, Roger Ames, Huang Yong, and Cheng Chung-ying.

There is an initial uncertainty about whether the ideas of the philosophers of China can be translated accurately and how correct our understanding of the texts can be. When Zhuangzi's imagination takes us beyond the metaphysical heights reached by philosophers of all times even the most prolific of the translators of the classical texts of China, James Legge, mentions that he welcomed a commentary from the 13th century: "If you cannot understand one or two sentences of Zhuangzi it does not matter." But the case is not radical translation. There is no indeterminacy of translation and no principle of charity is needed for us to be able to grasp the meaning of the philosophical concepts. The frame of reference is essentially the same.

To convey the vigorous directness and terseness of expression characteristic in the philosophical writing of China I have avoided paraphrases and quoted from the original sources to let the philosophers speak for themselves. I have frequently reformulated the translations of the texts rather than reproducing them verbatim for the sake of clarity of meaning and the flow of ideas. For instance, in the *Great Learning*, "*ming ming de*" is translated as "manifesting clear character" (by W.-T. Chan) and "manifesting illustrious virtue" (D. Bodde's translation of Fung Yu-lan's exposition). *Ming ming de* might be rendered, "light, light, virtue," or "making virtue to shine forth." It is more of an exclamation arising from an encounter with virtue rather than a somber requirement. I have sought to strike a balance between the wish to give a broad general survey brought within small compass and the urge to delve deeper into a topic with accuracy and intensity. While finding my way through the complex and intricate passages, I hope not to have been too inventive.

Preface

Hold all things in your love, favouring and supporting none specially. This is called being without any local or partial regard; all things are equally regarded; there is no long or short among them. Be large-minded like space, whose four terminating points are illimitable, and form no particular enclosures (*Zhuangzi* 17).

Love of knowledge and the search for the best way to live have led to the invention of philosophical thought in China. The moral, aesthetic, and political ideal of China is harmony: harmony of the individual, the family, the state, and ultimately with all of nature. The historic civilization of China, one of the oldest and the most varied of living civilizations, developed over more than four millennia. It has a tradition of poetry reaching beyond 1,700 BCE and philosophical thought which is imbued with high moral idealism and is at the same time vigorously practical, providing effective ethical principles for private and public life. It has endured with a social organization that made it possible for more human beings to exist together than any other known to history.[1]

This study is an introduction to the major philosophical traditions of a complex and diverse civilization where all that has been thought and imagined seems to have been discovered, developed, practiced, and found a clear and lasting expression. We begin with the period of classical philosophy from the sixth century BCE and conclude with a sketch of the philosophical movements in the early twentieth century.

At present there are two divergent approaches to the study of classical philosophy of China: historical and comparative. In the historical approach philological fidelity to the original texts becomes the focus of study and what the texts really mean becomes the main subject of the debate. Philosophical writing in China from the classical period does not comprise of a systematic exposition of a body of doctrine. Several interconnected ideas are expressed simultaneously in one context. The first sustained philosophical work is *Dao De Jing*, written in poetic form and language. Confucius' *Analects* is full of epigrammatic and elliptical sayings. Zhuangzi's writings have been celebrated for the poetic inventiveness as well as for the originality of his insight.

In the explication of the philosophers' ideas when we reconstruct the order of arguments we may convey the impression that their expositions are more systematic than they really are. It is frequently necessary to engage in an interpretive analysis of the ideas of a particular philosopher to guess at the intended meaning and to place their ideas in a broader context of philosophical traditions. This leads us to the comparative approach. In the comparative approach the theories of philosophers are interpreted in the context of analogous systems of thought from the Western tradition. For instance, viewing the Confucian school of thought as primarily rationalistic and the Daoist school of thought as empirical, brings out the focal point of the clear contrast between the two schools and links the development of philosophical thought in China with the philosophical traditions in the West.

There is a common task of both the historical and comparative approach: to explain the ideas of the philosophers, insofar as possible, without relying on a technical vocabulary familiar only to the scholars in the field, in a language free of philosophical presuppositions. But in a comparative study of philosophers working from distinct traditions a neutral vocabulary is not ready at hand. One task of comparative philosophy then is to discover the core concepts underlying the different frames of reference. When the two approaches are integrated we recognize that there are no irreducible concepts for which there are no counterparts in other systems of thought. When we read the philosophical writings of China, what is noteworthy is that the same issues about human nature (whether it is good or bad), the conflict between universal love and partial love and our duty to assist all keep coming up.[2] The ideas are expressed differently and presented in a different form but the basic issues are the same. We find that there are clear points of convergence of ethical values and beliefs. Philosophical ideas, insofar as they are discoveries and inventions of the human mind, resonate across the ages and geographical and cultural boundaries.

When we study the philosophical thought of China we are able to grasp in one long sustained breath the entire range of ideas produced by intense and persistent endeavours of the life of the mind which have originated nearly three thousand years ago and are vibrantly alive in our present. Philosophy inhabits supracelestial realm of ideas beyond the confines of place and time.[3] The immediacy of the topics and the continuity of the philosophical exploration of ideas make it possible for us to engage in the ongoing dialogue with the philosophers from the sixth century BCE to the twentieth century. This brief excursion is but an invitation for further adventures in philosophy. The only mandate we need to follow is the Mandate of Heaven.

When it sometimes seemed too drastic and reckless to sum up the splendour of philosophy in China in two hundred pages, the galloping pace of the book too heady, and the cascade of ideas too overpowering for brief and fleeting encounters, remembering that we live in borrowed time, I drew consolation from the motto, "Everything we have heard can be said in three words."[4] In the West these words might be *Truth*, *Beauty*, and *Goodness*. In China there might be four words: *Dao, De, Ren,* and *He* – Way, Virtue, Love, and Harmony.

Introduction

The Rise of Philosophical Thought

How ceaselessly heaven revolves! How constantly it abides at rest! And do the sun and moon contend about their respective places? Who presides over and directs these things? Who binds and connects them together? Who is it that, without trouble or exertion on his part maintains them? Is it perhaps, that there is some secret spring, in consequence of which they cannot be but as they are? Or is it, perhaps, that they move and turn as they do, and cannot stop of themselves?

How do the clouds become rains! And the rain again forming clouds! Who is it that effortlessly produces this elemental enjoyment? The winds rise in the north; one blows to the west and another to the east. By whose breathing are they produced? Who affects their undulations? I venture to ask their cause (*Zhuangzi* 14).

The origin of the universe came about at 2,229,000 BCE with Pan Gu who worked, not for six days resting on the seventh, but unceasingly for 18,000 years. As he worked his breath became the wind and the clouds, his voice thunder, his veins the rivers, his flesh the earth, his hair the vegetation, his bones the metals, his perspiration the rain, his eyes the sun and the moon, and at last the insects that clung to his body became the human race.[1] This myth sketches the continuum of human life and the whole of nature. The creation myth in China is distinct from the myths of other ancient civilizations: there are no gods, elemental forces, or a mortal combat among the titans and the gods; nor does inanimate matter turn into animated spirit. In place of a deity who

1

makes man in his own image giving his creation a dominant role, there is Pan Gu, a proto-human who creates the world though his own *work* until his body becomes part of all that exists. The evolution of myth further unfolds the deeds of five celestial emperors.

The writers of history in China recorded facts and legends, interweaving them with myths. The legend relates that emperor Fu Xi (2,852 BCE) taught, music, writing, painting, fishing, domestication of animals, growing silk worms, and marriage. The emperor Shen Nung taught people agriculture, invented the plow, established markets and trade, and developed the science of medicine from plants. The next emperor, Huang Di, a warrior, invented the magnet and the wheel, built an observatory, revised the calendar, and redistributed the land. Shun, a paradigm of filial piety controlled the floods. The sage emperor, Yao, who was venerated in the Confucian tradition, put a drum outside his palace gates for people to call upon him and a tablet to write their advice to the government. The *Book of History* relates that "he was kind and benevolent as Heaven, wise and discerning as the gods. From afar his radiance was like a shining cloud and approaching near him he was as brilliant as the sun."[2] No wonder then that even Confucius gives credence to the legend that people became virtuous simply by looking at him.

What was the society like when philosophical thought first emerged? The development of systematic philosophy from Laozi and Confucius coincided with the search for a new political rule and social order following the dissolution of the feudal society which resulted in the Warring States Period (403-221 BCE). It was an age of transition, uncertainty, and divergence. It was a time of the dissolution of the established beliefs and values and social change during which the hierarchy of ruling families was replaced by the rise of enterprising men who attained positions of power. In the armies of Qin, the most ruthless of the Warring States, the courtesies of feudal warfare were abandoned. Cities were taken by assault and the entire populations were often annihilated. Philosophy as a sustained and systematic rational inquiry into the ultimate structure of the universe and the way to aspire to the life worth living did not begin in wonder and lofty contemplation but in bewilderment, as things began to fall apart and the center could no longer hold. As in ancient Greece, philosophy arose amidst conditions of disunity and chaos. While the epoch of the Warring States was at its most terrible stage and tyrants and adventurers ruled the day, philosophers forged moral theories and sought to restore the ways of the sage rulers and create a state based on an ethical order.

2

Introduction

The history of philosophy in China is generally divided into three main periods. The first is the classical period (from the sixth to the second century BCE); the second period (from the first to the tenth century) is marked by the introduction and ascendancy of Buddhism; and the third period (from the eleventh century to the sixteenth century) is the renaissance of philosophy in China, Neo-Confucianism.

When we enter the classical period of philosophy, we encounter a world of excited debate generated by the Hundred Schools of philosophers. The vigour of philosophical thought in the classical period led to forceful and original conceptions of morality. The major schools of thought during the classical period of philosophy were Confucianism, Daoism, and Mohism. Confucius sought to cultivate ethical conduct of benevolence and righteousness as opposed to profit. The key figures in the Confucian tradition after Confucius were Mencius and Xunzi. Following Confucius, Mencius advocated cultivation of benevolence and righteousness. Mencius built a system of ethics based on his conviction that human nature is inherently good, while Xunzi put forward the contrasting view of the evil nature of man. Laozi launched Daoism with a single text consisting of eighty-one verses, *Dao De Jing* (*The Way and Its Power*). Zhuangzi expanded the idea of the *dao* to embrace freedom and spontaneity and called for living in harmony with all beings. Laozi, Zhuangzi and the philosophers in the Daoist tradition sought to return to the earlier stage of simplicity free of rituals and institutions. Mozi envisaged universal love to end all strife and conflict. Among the other influential movements were the Legalists, the Logicians, and the Yin Yang school. The Legalists criticized and opposed the ancient traditions and sought to establish new institutions in their place. The Logicians' enthusiasm for debate over language could be summed up in a phrase, "Glorious is the power of the art of contradiction!"[3] The Yin Yang school postulated that there are two complementary cosmic forces *yin* (earth, receptive and yielding) *yang* (heaven, creative and dominant).

The second period was marked by the entry of Buddhism in the first century from India via the Silk Routes to China. Buddhism influenced the whole spectrum of society from the people to the emperors as well as the poets, painters, and scholars. By the fifth century Buddhism became firmly established in northern China, and by the seventh century it became the third main philosophical and religious tradition in China. Daoism influenced Buddhism deeply and led to *Chan* (Zen) Buddhism.

In the third period, from the eleventh century to the sixteenth cen-

3

tury, Neo-Confucian philosophy emerged as a formidable synthesis of the insights of the Confucian tradition, Daoism, Mohism, and Buddhism. The major Neo-Confucian philosophers were Zhou Dunyi, Zhang Zai, the Cheng brothers, Zhu Xi, Lu Xiangshan, and Wang Yangming. In the late nineteenth century Kang Youwei put forward a revolutionary ethical perspective reinvigorating the insights of Confucius and the Neo-Confucian philosophers advocating political and social reform.

The philosophers of China sought to understand the ultimate structure of reality and bring about harmony in all spheres of human action amidst constant change. Ethics and political and social philosophy have been the foremost concerns of the thinkers in China from the beginning. They interpreted the question "What is the way?" in practical terms, as they were seldom concerned with speculation for its own sake. The urgent moral questions were "How shall we live?" and "How should the Empire be governed?"[4] Laozi, Zhuangzi, and Mozi condemned war. They advocated the best government as the one which seeks to bring about the well-being of the people. While the conception of human nature, proposals, strategies, and the specific aims varied greatly, there was a common goal among the philosophers of the classical age. The central tenet of Daoist thought, being in harmony with the whole of existence, formed the common core of all philosophical thought. The various schools of thought explored the *dao* as the way of reality and the ethical way of living and debated what the life of virtue consists in.

1

The Legacy of Confucius

Confucius

Love of Learning

> I make no complaint against Heaven, nor blame men, for though my studies are lowly my mind soars aloft (*Analects* 14.37).

With his love of learning Confucius sought to guide all people, from the emperor to the people of the land to live ethically. Confucius (551-479 BCE), the most renowned of all philosophers in China, was a person of deep intellectual and moral humility. Through the sheer range and clarity of his ideas Confucius was able to bring together the ways of thought and connect the customs of a vast and complex civilization with moral principles acceptable by all. Confucius' ideas have shaped the moral values and practices and formed the foundation of political thought and institutions in China and East Asia. It might be argued that it was not the intrinsic merit of his ideas but the force of an imperial edict which established the ideas of Confucius as a state religion. In the Han Dynasty during the reign of Emperor Wu (141-87 BCE) as the Confucian scholar officials gained political power, Confucianism became established as state orthodoxy. But a way of life and a moral perspective accepted by the people are unlikely to be the result of laws enforced by political authority especially when "the mountains are high and the emperor is far away."

At the center of the power of his philosophy and achievement was his great ability to bring to a synthesis the entire learning and art up to his time. Drawing upon his intensive study of the classics, Confucius provided the one universal standard with which philosophers and rulers sought to reconcile conflicting claims and interests.

The life of Confucius, Kong Fuzi (Kongzi, Master Kong) is well documented in the *Historical Records*. Born in the state of Lu, Confucius began his political career as a keeper of grain stores and eventually became a chief magistrate in 501 BCE. He resigned the office when the state of Qi sent a present of eighty dancers and musicians to the ruler of Lu who became negligent of his duties. Confucius set out with his disciples in 497 to wander from state to state for thirteen unsettled and difficult years. Retiring to his native state, he spent his last years studying and teaching. There is some uncertainty about whether he visited Laozi to learn about ancient rites and ceremonies. Confucius taught rites, music, odes, and history to his disciples, who numbered about 3,000.[1] Believing that "in teaching there should be no class distinctions," and taking a completely egalitarian approach to teaching, Confucius initiated the dissemination of learning among the general population.

Confucius was a pioneer in philosophical thought. There was no established tradition of systematic schools of thought when Confucius began his philosophical activity. All Confucius had before him were the *Book of Changes* (*Yijing*), the *Book of Odes*, the *Book of History*, and the *Book of Music*. The *Book of History* is a collection of documents, speeches, prayers and lectures given on various historical occasions from the time of the legendary emperor Yao (2357-2198 BCE) to the early Zhou dynasty (1100-770 BCE). Given the significance of these classics which became the corpus of all subsequent Confucian learning, we can briefly trace in outline the main ideas of the *Book of Changes* (*Yijing*) and the *Book of Odes* before embarking on the study of Confucius' philosophy.

Yijing is the earliest book of antiquity; the recorded history of philosophical thought in China begins with this work. Like most texts of ancient China it is a work of many writers over several centuries (1200-249 BCE). The text of the *Yijing* consists of sixty-four hexagrams composed of a combination of continuous and discontinuous lines and judgments on them. (Sixty-four is the total number of possible combinations of continuous and discontinuous lines of hexagrams.) The specific meaning of each line is determined by its relation to the others in a particular hexagram. The interpretation of the meaning of the hexagram is given in the judgement which is an analysis of each line in relation to the rest. Each hexagram is intended to be a symbolic representation of

6

natural phenomena and the laws governing their occurrences. The sixty-four hexagrams symbolize all possible situations in the universe and in human relations. Pythagoras, who postulated that the universe is governed by mathematical relations and assigned values to numbers, would have been fascinated by the possibility of interpreting the whole of reality with the sixty-four combinations of hexagrams.

Within the sixty-four hexagrams two central themes which run through all philosophical thought in China are developed. One theme is that the universe is a well-ordered state of existence in which all things are correlated and man and nature form a unity. The other is that the universe is a process of continuous change, as things are combined and intertwined ceaselessly. The universe and the human world are in a constant state of change, and all occurrences are incorporated as parts of the organic whole. The concept of change in the *Yijing* is formed by the observation of nature and human relations: like the course of the sun and the colour of the sky, the waves of the ocean and the change of seasons human relations are constantly changing. Confucius remarked one day, standing by a river, "Like this river, everything is flowing on ceaselessly, day and night" (*Analects* 9.16).

The thinkers of the classical period of philosophy in China were surrounded by the uncertainty of theology, the relativity of morals, and the imperfections of the government. Turning to the *Yijing*, they found a formal philosophical structure with which they sought to explain and unify all science and history. The metaphysics of the *Yijing* is an ontology of process, not of substance. In real space and time everything is in a state of transformation. Only when we isolate the objects in abstract thought is there static existence.[2] But the constant flow of things is not random: there are laws that govern the continuous transformation. The underlying assumption of *Yijing* is that the universe and man's actions are governed by moral purposiveness. The basic outlook of the *Yijing*, that only the accurate understanding of the physical world can lead to right actions in the human realm, is far from superstition. The belief on which the *Yijing* is based is that there are general patterns and principles of physical and human reality which can be grasped. The underlying view of reality is that it is rational, and that it can be comprehended by applying systematic reasoning.

The philosophical interest *Yjing* held for all schools of thought in China for many centuries up to the present lies in its metaphysical and ethical implications. It has exerted a deep and wide influence as a text in the tradition of literature of wisdom and in everyday life as a book of divination. Laozi's profound aphorisms were inspired by it, and it was held in high regard by the Daoists. It continued to be a constant source of inspiration from Confucius to the later Neo-Confucian philosophers. Leibniz, who was interested in constructing a universal concept language in which ideas can be expressed with directness and clarity long before the invention of the formal notations of symbolic logic, responded enthusiastically to the mathematical implications of diagrammatic representations of philosophical ideas in the *Yijing*. As a collection of reflections on the course of ethical values and actions, it continues to retain its popularity as a source of practical counsel and decision-making.

The hexagram called "Inner Truth" presents this image.

> Wind over lake: the image of Inner truth.
> Thus the superior man discusses criminal cases
> In order to delay executions.

The hexagram combines the image of wind (which has the characteristic of being gentle and penetrating) with that of the lake (which has the characteristic of being joyful). As wind moves over water the power of inner truth can guide the actions of men. The inner truth of the sage is that the highest form of justice consists not in the punishment of wrong actions but in reaching the desired goal of justice: to prevent the destruction of lives. This principle of benevolence governed the administration of justice in ancient China.

In 1692, when a bibliography on the classics was published, approximately two thousand titles were on the *Yijing*. It occupies an important place in the history of China in two ways. Because of the authority of the book, it could serve as a means whereby an imperial whim could be checked and enabled individuals who consulted the book to interpret their circumstances for themselves to determine the course of actions and hence remain masters of their own fate.[3] During the entire course of subsequent history in China, great reformers have drawn inspiration from this book. The concept of change which forms its foundation was a vital and stimulating counterpoint against the conservative tendency of the established orthodoxy of institutions.

The *Book of Odes* consists of three hundred and five poems ranging over a thousand years from the ancient compositions of the Shang dynasty (1600-1100 BCE) to the time of Confucius. According to tradition Confucius selected the poems from three thousand. Most of the verses written before Confucius' time have not survived. Here is one ode Confucius might well have sung accompanying himself on the

Zither in the grove of apricots while his disciples were studying.

> The morning glory climbs above my head,
> Pale flowers of white and purple, blue and red.
> I am disquieted.

> Down in the withered grasses something stirred;
> I thought it was his footfall that I heard.
> Then a grasshopper chirred.

> I climbed the hill as the new moon showed,
> I saw him coming on the southern road,
> My heart lays down its load.

Love poetry is abundant in the *Book of Odes*. The themes of the *Book of Odes* address deep and fervent love and longing, the transience of passions, the hope and despair of desire, the solitude of man and the search for tranquility, the brevity of life, the vanity of terrestrial agitation, and the tragedy of war (*Book of Odes*, I. x. 8).

> How free are the wild geese on their wings,
> And the rest they find on the verdant Yu trees!
> But we, ceaseless toilers in the king's services,
> Cannot plant our millet and rice.

> What will our parents have to rely on?
> O distant and azure Heaven!
> When shall all this end? ...
> What leaves have not turned purple?
> What man is not torn from his wife?
> Mercy on us: – Are we soldiers not also men?

In the age of disorder the basis of language, literature, art and philosophy was laid. In the *Book of Odes* carefully considered inferences produce the effect of a spontaneous overflow of powerful feelings and emotions recollected in tranquility.[4] The language of compactness captures delicacy of sentiment, refined sensibility, and frank expression of deeply felt emotions. But the emotions expressed are not the lava of the imagination which forestall volcanic eruptions.[5] In reading the poems with their simplicity of subject matter and directness of expressive language an unequalled light is cast on our interior life. Poets and philosophers of China expressed what the people of the land felt and experienced deeply. From the ancient songs in the *Book of Odes* to the poems of the Tang and Ming dynasties, the poets turned to nature and were nourished in their aesthetic sensibility and moral imagination. They were stimulated by constancy and limitless expansiveness of nature.

The poems in the *Book of Odes* are not explicitly moral or didactic. The poems include songs from ceremonial state occasions and popular themes from the various states of the early Zhou period. There are verses of gratitude and homage to sage rulers of the past. Some odes are celebrations of the plentitude ("Abundant is the year, with much millet and much rice...") and the abundance of blessings. The theme of virtue as keeping what is natural which develops into many variations among the Daoist and Confucian philosophers is noteworthy. What did Confucius value in poetry?

> The odes can stimulate the mind, can train the observation, can encourage social intercourse, and can alleviate the vexations of life. From them one can learn how to fulfill one's more immediate duties to one's father, and the more remote duties to one's ruler. And in them one may become widely acquainted with the names of birds, beasts, plants and trees (*Analects* 17. 9).

The lyric poetry in the *Book of Odes* is interpreted by Confucius with a moral meaning. He states: "Though the Odes number three hundred, one phrase can cover them all, namely, 'with uncorrupted thoughts'."[6]

In studying the writings and recorded conversations of Confucius, we encounter directly the classics of Chinese thought. He refers to the *Book of History* for moral instruction and wishes that he could devote fifty years to the study of the *Book of Changes*. He studied the *Book of History* to re-assemble and restore it, carrying his research into the study of the rites of the three dynasties, Xia, Shang, and Zhou. He is also believed to have written the *Spring and Autumn Annals*, a chronicle of the history of the state of Lu from 722-484 BCE which came to be known as the Period of Spring and Autumn.

During the period of the decline of the traditions, there was a movement to preserve the lessons of antiquity, and there arose philosophers who proposed a wide range of solutions to restore justice and end conflict. Confucius differed from these later philosophers who focused on specific doctrines of the particular schools. Setting the goal of education to be the cultivation of the whole person for the whole of life,

Confucius taught his disciples a wide range of subjects. This broad range of knowledge is reflected in the differing interests of Confucius' disciples. A disciple says of him, "He has broadened me by culture and restrained me by the usage of good conduct" (*Analects* 9.10). Confucius was the first to methodically study the classics and make them into the foundation of systematic learning and the basis of education for the common people.

What was the general state of human knowledge before the time of Confucius? Natural phenomena and human affairs were viewed as being under divine and supernatural control. Besides the multitude of ordinary spirits, Heaven (*Tian*) or God (*Di*) was supposed to exist. The wide-spread belief in the Sovereign on High (*Shang Di*) as the highest authority presiding over an elaborate hierarchy of spirits is evident. The *Book of Odes* and the *Book of History* make reference to the Supreme Emperor (*Shang Di*) as a source of justice. The celestial order was maintained by August Heaven (*Huang Tian*) or *Shang Di*. In the same way, order on earth was regulated by the ruler, invested for this purpose with the Mandate of Heaven (*Tian Ming*) which made him the Son of Heaven (*Tianzi*). *Tian* was thought to determine earthly rule and existence. The political and social institutions were construed as being in accordance with the will of *Shang Di*. This belief in the divine origin of the institutions of the state was also held by the ancient Greeks regarding the city-states. They believed that fate ruled the mortal destiny and even the gods. However, in contrast to this supra-human view of laws and institutions, there was also the view in ancient China that laws were established by human beings for their well-being. The distinguishing feature of philosophy in China is the rationalism in the attitude regarding spirits. A historical commentary on the events of 622 BCE report several speeches which espouse a sceptical view regarding the supernatural.

> It is when a state is about to flourish that its ruler listens to his people; when it is about to perish, he listens to the spirits. The Way of Heaven is distant, while that of man is near. We cannot reach to the former; what means have we of knowing it? The state of Xie makes its appeal to men, while that of Song makes its appeal to spirits. The offence of Song is great.[7]

Confucius adopts a similarly sceptical attitude toward spirits and asks "when you are unable to do your duty to men, how can you do your duty to the spirits?" Confucius believes that "to devote oneself ear-

11

nestly to one's duty to humanity, and, while respecting the spirits, to keep away from them, may be called wisdom." He "sacrificed to [his ancestors] as if they were present, and sacrificed to the spirits as if they were present" (*Analects* 3.12). When he was asked about death, Confucius answered: "Not yet understanding life, how can you understand death?"

When Confucian philosophy became the state doctrine and Confucius was eventually elevated to the status of a divine being in the popular imagination, it was contrary to his own modest view of himself as one who seeks virtue and wisdom. Confucius describes himself as "A transmitter and not a creator, and a lover of antiquity striving unwearingly [in study] and teaching others without flagging" (*Analects* 7.1). Given the inherent characteristic of Confucius' philosophy which is syncretic, it can be argued that the establishment of the Confucian tradition as the dominant doctrine was not entirely detrimental to development of freedom of thought and investigation. The most creative among the later Neo-Confucian philosophers embodied the same lively interest in examining all ideas and in incorporating the insights of opposing points of view to amalgamate them into highly original theories.

Confucius' ideas are recorded in the *Analects*. It is a simple and abbreviated record of Confucian sayings and conversations with the disciples. Confucius' moral and political philosophy is clearly set forth in the *Analects*. What were the ideas conceived in the mind of Confucius that came to be developed into a continuous unbroken tradition from his time, spanning over two thousand and five hundred years from the sixth century BCE to the present? The familiar view of Confucius portrays him as contentedly conforming to the conventions. But this overlooks the innovations which are at the core of Confucius' philosophy: moral perfectibility of all men and the ideas *ren* (love), *de* (virtue), and *li* (right action). We begin with love.

Love in Ancient China and Confucian Love

Love *all* men (*Analects* 12.22).

This is Confucius' reply when he is asked, "What does being moral consist in?" What is the origin of love in ancient China? We do not find love among the oracle bones of 2000 BCE (also known as "dragon's bones," in which we have the earliest writings written on bones or shells used in divination). In the *Book of Odes*, *ren* occurs more than once in conjunction with *mei*, "handsome and *ren*" – in the sense of "handsome and strong," or "handsome and noble." When a lady sings admiringly of a man riding out to hunt, an aesthetic ideal rather than someone endowed with moral virtue is being praised as a perfectly satisfactory lover.[8] Laozi declares that (*Dao De Jing* 5):

> Heaven and earth do not act from *ren*. They regard all things as grass dogs destined for sacrifice. The sages do not act from *ren*.

Ren, in the sense of benevolence, is not a virtue for the sage of Laozi who, as a true man of the *Dao*, does not seek deliberate cultivation of the virtues of benevolence or righteousness but lets all things come to fruition following their course.[9]

The word "*ren*" is made up the characters for "man" and for "two." It derives from the relation between two people and so is the basis of all relations between one man and another. *Ren* is frequently used as the term for human virtue in its entirety including benevolence, beneficence, good will, goodness, and love. Among Confucian literature, there is a considerable range of interpretations regarding the meaning of *ren*.[10] In taking "love" as encapsulating the essential meaning of "*ren*", we focus on what "*ren*" means in its most direct and encompassing sense: all levels of affection in human relations. Confucius' conception of love begins as an individual human relation in the family and expands as the sum of social relations in the state. *Ren* stands for love between parents and children, rulers and people, and good will in the broadest sense. Conscientiousness (*zhong*) and altruism (*shu*) are the expressions of *ren* in social contexts. Only occasionally the expression "*ren*" is found in texts before Confucius, and in all cases it denotes a particular virtue of kindness, the kindness of a ruler to subjects.[11] Confucius' innovation was to transform *ren* into the essential virtue of all men. Confucius is the first philosopher to expound love as the essence of man and to derive from love moral guidelines for personal conduct and public morality.

Ren is the most important concept in Confucius' moral philosophy. The development of *ren* in all spheres of human action is the goal of moral education and political life. In the *Analects*, 158 of 499 chapters concern *ren*. Given the conversational and informal structure of the *Analects* Confucius' ideas are presented as a persistent inquiry into the nature and practice of *ren* rather than a systematically ordered argumentation. The most fundamental moral principle, the love of humanity is introduced by Confucius as he elicits from a disciple a sceptical view of the extent of his knowledge. Confucius approaches a disciple saying,

13

"Perhaps you regard me as a man of multifarious study who retains all in mind?" As expected, the response is "yes," and then the disciple adds, "but maybe it is not so?" Confucius replies, "No, but I have one principle connecting all" (*Analects* 15.3). What is that principle? *Ren*.

The duty of love is carried out by developing what is natural to all men. For Confucius *ren* is inherent in human nature: it is the essence of humanity. "*Ren* has its source in oneself, and cannot be derived from others" (*Analects* 12.1). Morality consists in the full development of the potential to love. The duty common to all men is to love humanity. *Ren* from the beginning is love in the sense of respect, reverence, beneficence, good will, or benevolence. Love becomes the basis of all ethical relations and the basis of justice as benevolence and harmony in the state. *Ren* generates moral commitment and establishes the ethical foundation of individual and social life in the state.

How do we begin to put *ren* into practice? There is a persistent search for a precise understanding of *ren* in the *Analects*. When asked about the meaning of *ren*, Confucius replies that it is to practice five things: "They are respect, magnanimity, sincerity, earnestness and kindness. With respect you will avoid insult, with magnanimity you will win over everyone, with sincerity men will trust you, with earnestness you will have success, and with kindness you will be well fitted to command others" (*Analects* 17.6). The five virtues are related to specific beneficial consequences for the person who practices them. The previous explanation of *ren* emphasized its origin in human nature and its value for ethics, family, and society and thus *ren* is explained both as an individual and a social virtue as it benefits both the individual and society. *Ren* as a term for virtue in its entirety includes loyalty, altruism, courage, and wisdom (*Analects* 14.5; 5.18).

A disciple inquires: "Suppose there were one who conferred benefits far and wide upon the people, and able to assist all. Could this be called *ren*?" Confucius replies: "It would no longer be a matter of *ren*. He would no doubt be a Sage" (*Analects* 6.28). *Ren* is a very high but not an impossible ideal to fully realize since Confucius believes it to be rooted in human nature. Confucius exclaims, "Is *ren* indeed far off? If we really wanted *ren* we should find that *Ren* was at our very side" (*Analects* 7.29). We put *ren* into action by coming to know humanity. In order to love, one requires knowledge. When asked what knowledge consists in, Confucius replies: "Know *all* men" (*Analects* 12.22). Confucius expounds the highest knowledge as the study of man – not as an abstract discipline but as a way of practicing the principle of humanity.

When love is broadened to altruism, is self-sacrifice called for?

Confucius does not call for self-sacrifice. A disciple who is sceptical about the value of altruism tests Confucius: "A man of *ren* if someone said to him, 'There is a man in the well,' would, I suppose, go in after him?" Confucius retorts: "Why should he act like that? The highest type of man might be imposed upon but not utterly hoodwinked" (*Analects* 6.24). What if there is no sight of love but only vice? From Confucius' statement about the connection between our virtues and vices we may find a way: "A man's faults all conform to his type of mind. Observe his faults and you may know his virtues (*ren*)" (*Analects* 4.7). Understanding our deficiency can be a beginning of ethical development.

Then what of the competitive or aggressive instincts and tendencies which lead us to promote our own interests at the expense of others? This position of self-interest and egotism no doubt exists prior to the first stage of moral development and is often the way of the world. Confucius' purpose, however, is not to describe the way of the world but to prescribe the way of morality. He criticizes calculating self-interest and actions motivated by profit as marks of an inferior person in the moral sense. For Confucius the origin of ethics resides in the capacity for love in human nature and in human relations. Is giving a free rein and spontaneous expression to human nature the best way of putting *ren* into action? That would be the way of Zhuangzi.[12] But being aware of the general predilection toward excessive self-interest, Confucius emphasizes that "*ren* is subduing oneself and responding to the right and proper (*li*)" (*Analects* 12.1).

Love and Propriety

Confucius launches ethics from a new point of departure. For Confucius *li* (propriety, right actions or rules for appropriateness of actions) and *ren,* as love which is the essence of humanity, form the basis of ethics simultaneously. Prior to Confucius morality was a matter of emulating the actions of particular revered personalities upheld as moral paradigms for all occasions. *Li* meant something entirely external and objective applying to acts which are concordant with circumstances, in compliance with tradition and custom.[13] The rites, *li*, are the ordering principles of human relations from birth to death. They are the rules that guide human interactions. The connection between *li* and *ren* is clear. *Li* is the set of rules governing the appropriate expression of *ren.*

The meaning of "*li*" in ancient China was wide, signifying everything from courtesy to right conduct in political and social institutions. Throughout the explanation of the place and function of *li* as constituting the standard of Heaven, the principle of earth, and the conduct of men, the interconnection between the state of nature and the human life is emphasized. There is a pervasive belief that the rites are laid down by the pattern of Heaven and Earth for the purpose of the regulation of impulses.[14] *Li* gives the fineness of form to the chaos of experience. *Li* in the aesthetic sense means ceremony or ritual; in the ethical sense it is rule or duty. The function of rites, ceremony, and music is to inspire reverence and awe. In creating order and giving form to human relations rites, *li*, guide the actions by determining the boundaries of appropriateness. *Li* is not ceremony or ritual in the sense of refinement or decorum.

The high regard Confucius has for rites has frequently been viewed as an excessive attachment to orthodoxy and social conventions. However, Confucius focuses on the sincerity of will and not the observation of ceremony as the distinguishing mark of a moral person. "Artful speech and ingratiating demeanor rarely accompany *ren*" (*Analects* 1.3). "The firm of spirit, the resolute in character, the simple in manner, and the slow of speech are not far from *ren*" (*Analects* 13.27). In a society where convention and decorum were stressed to an extraordinary degree, Confucius emphasizes the moral character and good intentions underlying outward behavior. *Li* also is a way of setting the boundaries of uprightness, *zhi*: "Uprightness, *zhi*, uncontrolled by the rules of good taste becomes rudeness" (*Analects* 8.2). In Confucius' conception, *li* becomes an internal moral sense which can be cultivated and called upon in action. Confucius invents the inner moral life of man. Confucian revolution was to set the course of the moral life in society on the development of the moral character and action of the individual.

Li, conceived as the rules of right conduct, guides our actions as objective criteria of ethics. Confucius sees the interconnectedness of human development. *Li* is not restrictive but expands the individual as well as others. By developing ourselves we create an environment in which others may also flourish. In Confucius' thought the two pillars of ethics, *ren* and *li*, build the bridge between the individual and the world. *Ren* and *li* permeate the individual moral life and social relations. The five relations among all human beings – parent and child, husband and wife, friends, old and young, ruler and subject – are associated both with *ren* and *li*. Each relation is guided by *li* as an expression of *ren* appropriate to it. Acting in accordance with *li* creates social order and acting from *ren* creates kindness and charity.

From the point of view of ethics, the difficulty with *li* is that on one hand there is a danger of adhering to rigid rules of propriety and on the other hand if we admit that in each circumstance a different interpretation of what is appropriate may be required, then all values disintegrate into subjective preferences. *Li* can only give general rules. Each particular circumstance calls for a new interpretation of the universal. For Confucius righteousness is generated from human relations and not dictated by abstract rules. Confucius takes account of each particular circumstance as well as the individual character of each of his disciples. Confucius' ethical beliefs were the result of continual reflection about human beings and were not built on abstract moral imperatives.[15]

What of Confucius' emphasis on the observation of rites and the duty of filial piety – are they not imposed as unvarying external measures? The standards of human conduct, benevolence, and righteousness come from human nature, since benevolence is human essence. They do not emanate from the will of heaven or an external law. From the ruler to the people of the land all have the duty of *ren* and filial piety. But since individual nature varies, the application of moral standards varies. Confucius takes into account that human relations vary according to the propensities of the individuals; he allows for modification and does not adhere to immovable ceremony. It is the great achievement of Confucius and, later, the Neo-Confucian philosophers that by building on *ren* and *li* as the core of all moral actions, they laid the foundation of universal ethics.

Li, as right action, can be linked to Confucius' theory of rectification of names, *zheng ming*. It refers simply to the doctrine. "Let the ruler be ruler, the minister, minister; let the father, father, and the son, son" (*Analects* 12.11). Confucius' insistence that the names be applied accurately is not a theory of language but a theory of ethics. It is about the significance of the discourse based on an accurate use of the meaning of the words which teaches the ethical way of living. It is a discussion of the important connection between ethical concepts and ethical conduct. What makes the ruler a ruler, in Confucius' view, is his love of the people; what makes the son a son is his filial piety. In the absence of the essential characteristics of the ruler, the minister, the father, and the son, the names are not rectified. Confucius maintained that when we do not fulfill our function designated by the name or title we bear, disorder ensues.

Confucius includes the rectification of names as an integral part of moral education, together with the study of the classics, poetry, history, rites, and music. He would not go as far as Laozi to propound, "The *dao* that can be expressed is not the real *dao*. The name that can be named is not the eternal name." But he is acutely aware of the deficiency of language to express truth. Confucius bursts out, "I wish I could do without speaking." To the response "If you did not speak, what should we disciples pass on to others?" Confucius replies, "What speech has Heaven? The four seasons run their course and all things flourish; yet what speech has Heaven?" (*Analects* 17.19) But below in the fallen world, during the period of chaos of the Warring States, when the possessors of names no longer corresponded to their appropriate names – when the ruler was not a ruler, the minister not a minister – Confucius stressed the importance of definitions and correct usage of language. Like Confucius Socrates also emphasized the central place of definitions and clear understanding of language. Confucius matches Socratic tenacity in his persistence in seeking to clarify the meaning of the fundamental ethical concepts.

Confucius redefines what a virtuous person is. He transforms the concept of "the superior person," *junzi*, designating the son of a ruler or a person of social rank and privilege conferred by birth to apply to all who are capable of moral action. Confucius' idea of a morally excellent being amounts to a social revolution.[16] This conception of "the superior person" and the worthwhile life emphasizes the development of moral character and virtue rather than the conventional display of decorum and refinement in ceremony.

The strength of Confucian ideals emerged in their ability to set clear guidelines for the rulers and the people. Confucius' view of the role of the emperor is not that of a supreme ruler with absolute power. Nor is it that of the world-historical individual who carries out the grand schemes of history outside the bounds of ordinary moral standards. From the moral point of view, equality prevails. The moral obligations of the emperor to his parents are the same as that of the people to their parents. Confucius has a remarkably egalitarian view of virtue: from the people to the ruler, all have the same duty of benevolence and righteousness, and the same virtues of altruism and conscientiousness are to be cultivated. Confucius believed that all can acquire virtue through knowledge and emphasized that all are to abide by the same standard of righteousness. Confucius does not value knowledge for its own sake but for its practical application.

> A man may be able to recite the three hundred Odes, but when given a post in the administration, he proves to be without practical ability, or when sent on a mission he is unable himself to

answer a question, although his knowledge is extensive, of what use is it? (*Analects* 13.5)

Do *ren* and *li* ever come into conflict as love and propriety? If they do, which should take precedence? In his own personal conduct Confucius protests against the conventional interpretation of propriety. When Hui, his favourite disciple dies, Confucius' grief is deemed to be excessive and brings down the censure of his disciples. Confucius protests that his grief is thought to be against propriety and that he is not permitted to mourn as a father may mourn the death of a son. There are other indications of how unconstrained Confucius was by custom and propriety. Defending a man who had been in prison as being a worthy person, Confucius accepts him into his family as a son-in-law.

Which is higher, *ren* or *li*? Is it morally justifiable to go along with unethical actions out of love? Here Confucius takes filial piety to the utmost limit. Confucius' example of uprightness, *zhi*, is that of a son shielding a father who has stolen a sheep (*Analects* 13.18). Upon hearing that in one province it is considered to be upright for the son to bring the matter into the court of law, Confucius exclaims that where he comes from it is upright for the son to shield the father. We should gently try to persuade our parents to be virtuous, but when we fail we should still act with respect. What tells us that shielding our parents is a right action and revealing their wrongdoing is not? Confucius' reply would be that the natural relation between father and son establishes the duty of filial piety and affection in all circumstances and determines the course of righteous action. For Confucius what is of higher moral priority is filial piety stemming from *ren*.

Can this view of uprightness be extended to all human relations? Building on this explanation of *ren* we can put forward an interpretation of the Confucian view as an amalgamation of two distinct approaches to justice: benevolence and fulfilling one's function. When *ren* is applied in the family it is love of parents and filial piety; when it is applied in society it is the love of the ruler for the people and justice as benevolence. *Ren* is the basis of moral excellence in personal life and justice in political life. There is also a sense of justice as the performance of one's proper function which leads to harmony in the family and in the state. This sense is related to *li*, propriety. Confucius' idea of *ren* as love of humanity, altruism, beneficence, and benevolence leads directly to the conception of justice as fulfilling one's function. In Socrates we also have a view of justice as performing one's proper function. A just individual is a just citizen. In Confucius individual morality and the civic and social morality are interconnected.

The Common Good as the Goal of Morality

The philosophers of the classical period believed that there is a moral order of the universe which connects individual actions with the common good. Civic order is a reflection of the cosmic order.[17] Confucius places the good of the whole state above individual honour. When Duke Huan (683 BCE) was murdered by his brother, one of the two ministers of the murdered Duke committed suicide, while the other minister asked only to be imprisoned and later took office under the new ruler. When one of the disciples criticizes this as conduct lacking in virtue, Confucius praises the ability of the second minister for having saved lives through his intervention and for having brought about peace. What characterizes moral goodness for Confucius is not what was conventionally regarded as honour but the ability to sacrifice one's honour for the common good (*Analects* 14.17).

With its emphasis on filial piety, reverence of ancestors, and performance of rites, it has been frequently observed that in China the individual is subsumed in a social matrix of relations and obligations. It is nevertheless true that Confucius' emphasis on the cultivation of personal life is a clear indication of the importance of the individual. Confucius does not regard it as the aim of moral education to produce a duty-bound citizen or a member of a committee. *Junzi*, a moral person, has inner qualities of honesty, self-criticism, self-reflection, sincerity of will, and rectitude of mind.

Confucius is often thought of as emphasizing loyalty to family. Is there an excessive emphasis on filial piety in Confucius? Does Confucius put more significance on personal obligations than public duty? Drawing from the *Book of History*, Confucius defends himself against these objections. When he is asked: "Why are you not in public service?" Confucius replies, "What does the *Book of History* say about filial duty? One's duty as a son and friendliness to one's brothers are shown forth in the public service" (*Analects* 2.21). Confucius implies that carrying out personal obligations develops into fulfilling public duty. Individual moral life and communal life are seen as a continuum. When asked, "If a man refrains from ambition, boasting, resentment and desire, it may ... be counted to him for *ren*?" Confucius replies, "It may be counted as difficult, but whether for *ren*, I do not know" (*Analects* 14.2). Self-regarding virtues of modesty, self-discipline, and mild disposition are undoubtedly praiseworthy but not equivalent to *ren*, which

has a wider sphere of influence.
As an explanation of *ren*, Confucius elaborates:

> When abroad, behave as if interviewing an honored guest; in directing the people, act as if officiating at a great sacrifice; do not do to others what you do not like yourself. Then neither in your state nor in your private home will there be any resentment against you (*Analects* 12.2).

Conscientiousness (*zhong*) and altruism (*shu*) are the expressions of *ren* in social contexts. The virtue of *shu* is described by the Principle of Reciprocity: "Do not do to others what you do not like yourself." In not doing to others what we do not wish for ourselves, we exercise moral empathy. The first step in ethical thinking is to expand the sphere of concern beyond our own domain of interests. If we decide what is right by calculating whether an action would harm us or whether it would harm only other people our actions cannot be regarded as moral. The Principle of Reciprocity requires that in our actions we take into consideration our well-being as well as that of others.

Ren can be generated from the desire to maintain oneself and what one wishes for oneself.

> Developing oneself one develops others, and maintaining oneself one maintains others. For the man of *ren* is one who desiring to maintain himself sustains others, and desiring to develop himself develops others. To be able from one's own self to draw a parallel for the treatment of others: that may be called the way to practice *ren* (*Analects* 6.28).

This is a variation on the theme of the Principle of Reciprocity. Confucius is convinced that in developing oneself, one develops others. What Confucius means by developing oneself and others is clearly set forth in the explanation of *ren*. Confucius' explanation of *ren* as a simultaneous development of oneself and others offers a solution to the central and difficult question in ethics, "Why act ethically?" Confucius transforms *ren* from a particular individual experience to an activity with a broader and deeper moral function. Confucius values the cultivation of personal life not in isolation or as ends in themselves but as a part of the good of the whole. There is a continuum and a unity of life – all draw one breath.

21

The Most Perfect Sage

> The man who bare-armed would beard a tiger, or rush a river,
> dying without regret.

When asked what perfection in man consisted in, this was Confucius' reply. For all his reserve, Confucius was a person of considerable fire. He writes that at seventy he was able to follow what his heart desired without transgressing what was right (*Analects* 2.4). What did Confucius think of his own effort?

> ... simply a man so eager for improvement that he forgets his
> food, so happy in doing so that he forgets his sorrow, and so
> does not realize that old age is at hand (*Analects* 7.18).

Confucius confesses that he has not succeeded in treating his brothers as he would like to have been treated himself. He has not succeeded in putting the Principle of Reciprocity into action: "In literature perhaps I may compare with others, but as to my living the noble life, to that I have not yet attained" (*Analects* 7.32). Who then is the Confucian Sage? A student of philosophy, a lover of knowledge, and not an authority.

> Am I indeed a man with innate knowledge? I have no such
> knowledge; but when an uncultivated person, in all simplicity,
> comes to me with a question, I think out its pros and cons until I
> fathom it (*Analects* 9.7).

Confucius stresses the constant awareness of his own moral imperfection and ignorance and the need for persistent effort in correcting his mistakes through critical self-examination and the "unwavering pursuit of wisdom" (*Analects* 7.3).

> The thought that I have my moral power unattended, my learn-
> ing unperfected, that I have heard of righteous men, but been
> unable to go to them; heard of evil men, but unable to reform
> them – it is these thoughts that disquiet me.

Confucius' view of himself as the "one who is fond of learning" and Socrates' characterization of a philosopher as a lover of knowledge are parallel. There is a striking similarity between Socrates' view that wisdom begins with knowing that one does not possess knowledge and Confucius' view of knowledge. Confucius announces (*Analects* 2.17):

> Shall I teach you the meaning of knowledge? When you know a thing, to recognize that you know it; and when you do not, to know that you do not know, – that is knowledge.

Confucius' humility is akin to Socratic humility. Confucius believed that he is a transmitter and not an originator of knowledge.

> I am not one who was born in the possession of knowledge. I am one who is fond of antiquity and earnest in seeking it there (*Analects* 2.17).

Socrates confesses that he has no knowledge of his own to impart and that he is like a "mid-wife" who assists in the birth of knowledge. While Confucius sought to preserve and restore what he regarded as great and true, Socrates inquired and strove to create a new conception of the life worth living since there were no precedents which satisfied his search for truth.

There is a general impression that philosophy in the East is less philosophical in the sense that it emphasizes the preservation of scholarly tradition, whereas philosophy in the West is practiced as an independent rational inquiry. Not only in the field of knowledge but also in the moral and political realms, the Eastern sensibility may appear to be more prone to veneration than to disputation. Confucius' prominence in the history of philosophy and the vast influence of his thought frequently led to an uncritical admiration of the man and his ideas. Confucius is almost always seen as an upholder of tradition, and his assertion that he is "a lover of antiquity" reinforces the received view. But Confucius emphasizes the study of classics not as ends in themselves but as an approach to achieving moral and intellectual virtue.

Unlike the writings of Plato, the *Analects*, which is a discursive record of Confucian sayings, is neither a consummate literary composition nor a series of compelling arguments sustained in a philosophical dialogue. Its fragmentary nature and the conversational style have been compared to pre-Socratic writing. We need to piece together the statements and the questions to construct arguments. But once such a reconstruction is made the similarity in the flow of thought and expression to the Socratic dialogues emerges. Socratic method and Confucian method are similar. Initially both are destructive. There is a common core of scepticism in their approach regarding the reliability of general experience and sense perception. Confucius is described as being entirely without preconceptions. Neither Socrates nor Confucius can resist the urge to question what is customarily taken for truth. The sophists, relativists, and subjectivists of ancient China and Greece questioned the objectivity of knowledge while being certain of the relative merits of each individual's claim to knowledge. The scepticism of Confucius and Socrates, on the other hand, is about their own individual ability to know the truth. Both Socrates and Confucius are certain about the possibility of objective knowledge and the mind's ability to acquire it. Socratic doubt and Confucian uncertainty are about the unreliability of the general claim to knowledge based on individual experience and not about the capacity of human mind, reason, and intellect to know the nature of things.

The epithets, "the most perfect sage," "the first teacher," and the subsequent veneration of Confucius was detrimental to an open-minded inquiry and also contrary to Confucius' own view of his arduous attempt at learning. Confucius as the historical personage is distinct from the legendary and idealized representative of the Confucian school of thought. If Confucius came to be revered not as a mortal but as though he were born of a dragon, certainly it is contrary to his view of himself.

What then does Confucius think of his own work? (*Analects* 5.6)

> My doctrines make no progress. I will get upon a raft and float away upon the sea! If anyone accompanies me will it not be Yu? ... Yu is fonder of daring than I; he also exercises no discretion.

Confucius relishes the company of Yu (Tzu Lu), a soldier, who was the boldest of his disciples.

Once when an attempt on his life was made by a minister who was a brother of one of his disciples, and a tree was cut where he was resting during his exile, Confucius merely remarked that not much harm can come to him, as he seeks to follow the way of heaven. Throughout the reported sayings of Confucius, we catch a glimpse of a person of daring, courage, and sympathy. The sage of ancient China is not an unrecognizably lofty being but of a certain international type.[18] Plato's view of the good man as someone who fulfills his proper function and seeks wisdom would characterize Confucius' *junzi*, the morally accomplished person.

If Confucius came to be venerated as sage and serious and his utterances were subsequently engraved into stone tablets in later centuries, these developments do not reflect the frank scepticism and the challenge of the disciples in the *Analects*, who were not unthinking followers but active participants in an ongoing dialogue. When Confucius was in exile, many of the followers became so ill that they could no longer sustain themselves. One disciple, completely overwrought, cries out "Does a man of the higher order also have to suffer?" Confucius calmly replies, "The superior man bears wants unshaken, the inferior man in want becomes demoralized" (*Analects* 15.1). This courage and fortitude and firm resolve are shared by Socrates who serenely maintains that "no harm can come to a good man." The moral idealism of Confucius and Socrates compelled them to question the practices of those who wielded power without the knowledge of virtue. But above all it is in their commitment to living an ethical life that there is a significant parallel. Socrates saw his task as combating the pretenders to authority and the mercenaries of rhetoric, the sophists. He believed that it was his divine mission to be the conscience of Athens. Socrates valued virtue more than self-preservation and chose to die rather than to act dishonourably. Confucius sought to rectify the world, urging the rulers to cultivate virtue and spent years in perilous exile rather than serve corrupt rulers.

What was the view of Confucius by later Confucian thinkers? Mencius compares Confucius with the paragon of a virtuous ruler, the Duke of Zhou, (*Mencius* 3. II.9). Mencius, the foremost advocate of the view that human nature is inherently good, builds his ethics on the Confucian foundation of *ren*. Xunzi (fl. 298-238 BCE), the second major Confucian thinker after Mencius, expresses a deep regard for Confucius.[19]

> Confucius possessed the qualities of human-heartedness and wisdom, and was not prejudiced. Hence his scholarship and mastery over all teachings were sufficient to be those of the early kings. He possessed the whole of the Way; he brought it to people's notice, and he used it; he was not prejudiced in the carrying out of it. Hence his virtue was equal to that of the Duke of Zhou, and his reputation was abreast of that of the Three Kings.

Confucius' confidence in the human ability to acquire moral knowledge reverberates in the Neo-Confucian philosophy of Wang Yangming who held that "all men originally pursue an intuitive knowledge so that throughout the streets everyone is a sage."[20] If human nature were allowed to flourish and intuitive knowledge were followed, there would be goodness everywhere.

Mencius

The Willow of Human Nature and the Cup of Morality

> The superior man ... loves all things (*Mencius* 7. I.45)
> Benevolence is man's mind and righteousness is man's path
> (*Mencius* 6. I.11).

Benevolence (*ren*) and righteousness (*yi*) are the two central tenets of Mencius' moral philosophy. *Ren* brings people together forming a bond and righteousness is needed to make distinctions and determine the right course of conduct. The concept of *ren* in Mencius is essentially the same as in Confucius. While Confucius' emphasis in the *Analects* is on how *ren* can be practiced in all spheres of action, Mencius inquires into the origin of *ren* seeking to establish the basis of morality in human nature. Confucius conceives *ren* as a passion for goodness, a moral quality of an individual to be developed through learning. In Mencius the meaning of *ren* has evolved to become a general virtue of benevolence and is constantly associated with *yi*, righteousness.

Mencius (Mengzi, 371-289 BCE) was born near the state of Lu (Confucius' birthplace), a renowned center of Confucian learning. Having received his education from the disciples of the grandson of Confucius, he set out to visit the rulers of various states with the aim of rectifying men's hearts and the world in accordance with Confucian teaching. Confucius has been compared to the jade that is truly precious, while Mencius has been likened to a mirror which glitters.[21] Mencius' philosophy reflects the ideal of living an ethical life most vividly conceived first in Confucius' mind: the love of the classics, the abiding dedication and readiness to put the moral goals of bringing about a better world before all else and seeing the most worthwhile life of personal fulfillment as being continuous with the development of all of humanity. Mencius' achievement consists in creating the consummate Confucian philosophical perspective. New truths emerge as the doctrines of the sage take on more than a tinge of his mind as they pass through it.[22] It could be said of Mencius that if he saw further than other men it was because he was standing on the shoulder of a giant (as Newton said of Bacon).

It is in his political ideas that Mencius reaches a new height. Men-

26

cius affirms the function of philosophy as providing practical guidance to the rulers and the people. The most original contribution of Mencius is his theory of the inherent goodness of human nature and his political philosophy. The main ideas of Mencius are found in the *Book of Mencius, Mengzi,* which consists of seven books, each subdivided into two parts. It is thought to have been compiled by his disciples posthumously. Some of the exchanges are reminiscent of the conversational style of the *Analects* but on the whole there is more thematic organization of the subjects in sustained arguments and criticisms of various philosophical schools of thought as well as practical advice on political topics.

Mencius was resolutely committed to the Confucian cause of renovating the world in the time of moral turpitude and political disintegration. With a sense of urgency he calls out "If there is a desire that the world should enjoy tranquility and good order, who is there today, besides myself to bring it about?" (*Mencius* 2. II.13). Mencius declares his goal: "Now what I desire to do is to study to be like Confucius." Mencius believed that the mantle of Confucius had fallen upon him and that there was no one else in the empire but him on whom it devolved to live and labour for the good of the world. [23] As he faces the task of teaching the princes and the people the moral way of living he goes beyond Confucius who had a certain reserve and decorum in regard to those who had authority (*Mencius* 7. II.38).

The relation of human nature to morality became a topic much debated among the philosophers in Mencius' time who sought to understand and eliminate the causes of continuous warfare, devastation, and suffering in the world by finding the ways of restoring the rulers and the people to live ethically. We find in the *Book of Mencius* the most comprehensive discussion of human nature entertained up to his time as he explores the topic in a dialogue with his opponents and disciples. A perplexed disciple inquires of Mencius (*Mencius* 6. I.6),

> The philosopher Gao says, "Man's nature is neither good nor bad." Some say, man's nature may be made to practice good, and it may be made to practice evil ... Some say, "The nature of some is good, and the nature of others is bad ... And now you say, "The nature is good." Then are all those wrong?

Mencius criticizes Gaozi's view that man's nature is neither good nor bad and that morality or righteousness is something external to man.

Gaozi said, "Human nature is like the willow tree, and right-eousness is like a cup or a bowl. To turn human nature into be-nevolence (*ren*) is like turning the willow into cups and bowls."

Mencius said, "If you must do violence and injury to the willow in order to make cups and bowls with it, on your principle you must in the same way do violence and injury to humanity in or-der to fashion from it benevolence (*ren*) and righteousness! Your words, alas! would certainly lead all men on to reckon be-nevolence and righteousness to be calamities" (*Mencius* 6. I.1).

Mencius pursues energetically the topic of the innate goodness of hu-man nature. But why is it of a great moment whether righteousness and benevolence are innate or acquired? Mencius seeks to build the basis of morality from an accurate understanding of human nature and experi-ence. His discussion of human nature engages the central questions of ethics: "What motivates us to act morally?", "What makes morality possible?" and "What are the grounds of morality?" Mencius argues that if human beings were completely lacking in goodness, it would not be possible to make people act with kindness and good will through "violation of their nature." For Mencius the inherent goodness of hu-man nature is the foundation of the moral life. Morality is possible only if there is a moral capacity within man. Morality does not stem from pre-existing external moral laws or our experience of the physical world but from the inherent goodness in human nature.

Mencius builds up the thesis of the innateness of morality by closely arguing for what all men have in common. He maintains that we pos-sess the moral sense in common as we possess the sense of beauty, taste, hearing, and sight (*Mencius* 6. I.7). But surely it is precisely in ordinary sense experience and in the matters of what is pleasing to the senses that there is most frequent disagreement? Mencius is less im-pressed by differences than by similarities. "All things of the same kind are similar to one another. Why should there be any doubt about men? The sage and I are the same in kind"(*Mencius* 6 I.7). Like stalks of wheat, the differences between individuals are not significant since they belong to the same natural kind. Mencius' attention is repeatedly drawn to explaining the differences between human beings as regards their achievement. To the question, "We are all human beings, why is it that some men become great and others become small?" Mencius re-plies:

> Those who follow the greater qualities in their nature become great men and those who follow the smaller qualities in their nature become small men. ... If we first build up the nobler part of our nature, then the inferior part cannot overcome it. It is simply this that makes a man great (*Mencius* 6. I.15).

In these passages Mencius asserts that human beings possess "the nobler part" and "the inferior part" and "greater qualities" as well as "lesser qualities." For Mencius human nature is a composite of good and bad qualities, the rational and the irrational. To affirm that human nature is *inherently* good does not commit Mencius to the view that we are *entirely* good.

If there is inherent knowledge of the good why is the exhortation to vigorously exercise altruism necessary? What is innate is the capacity for morality which has to be developed by continuous effort. To possess the capacity is necessary but not sufficient to bring about moral actions. Mencius relates a story of a man who was anxious that his corn was not growing and told the people that he helped the corn to grow by pulling it up. When his son ran to look at it, the corn had already withered. This is an illustration of Mencius' dictum, "Always be doing something without expectation. Let the mind not forget its objective, but let there be no artificial effort to help it grow" (*Mencius* 2. I.2).

Mencius is convinced that not only do we have innate knowledge of the good but also the "innate ability" to act morally.

> The ability possessed by men without their having acquired it by learning is innate ability, and the knowledge possessed by them without deliberation is innate knowledge. Children carried in the arms all know to love their parents. As they grow, they all know to respect their elder brothers. To have filial affection for parents is benevolence, and to respect elders is righteousness. These feelings are universal in the world (*Mencius* 7. I.15).

Mencius points to ordinary instances of human affection in the family as certain indications of benevolence and righteousness.

But how widespread are such feelings? Mencius does not overestimate the human ability for moral wisdom, nor indiscriminately praise the general practices: "To act without understanding and to do so habitually without examination, following certain courses all their lives without knowing the principles behind them – this is the way of the multitude" (*Mencius* 7. I.5). Mencius recognizes that human nature evolves with adapation to the environment (*Mencius* 6. I.7-8). He describes what happens to the nature of human beings in different societies as they undergo various stages of change with a simile of a mountain which was once covered with trees. "Once the trees have been hewed with axes and hatchets, is the mountain no longer beautiful? And if the trees are cut down day after day, can a mountain retain its beauty?" The same holds for the human mind. With "proper nourishment and care everything grows, without proper nourishment and care everything decays."

Anticipating the objection that people might perform altruistic acts for motives of gain, Mencius illustrates genuine concern for others with an example (*Mencius* 2. I.6):

> Now, when men suddenly see a child about to fall into a well, they all have feeling of alarm and distress, not to gain friendship with the child's parents, nor to seek the praise of their neighbours and friends, nor because they dislike the reputation [of lack of humaneness if they did not rescue the child].

With this celebrated illustration of a child about to fall into a well, Mencius concludes that it is indisputable that all human beings have sympathy for the suffering of others.

> The feeling of commiseration is found in all men, as is that of shame and dislike, and that of respect and reverence, as well as that of right and wrong. The feeling of commiseration is what we call benevolence (*ren*); the feeling of shame and dislike is what we call righteousness (*yi*); the feeling of respect and reverence is what we call propriety (*li*); and the feeling of right and wrong is what we call wisdom (*zhi*) (*Mencius* 6. I.6).

For Mencius the origin of morality is specifically in the feelings of commiseration, like and dislike, respect, and right and wrong which develop into the corresponding virtues of *ren, yi, li,* and *zhi*. Mencius believes that we can develop the virtues of benevolence and righteousness not from the lofty ideals of the sage but by not doing to others what we ourselves cannot bear (*Mencius* 7. II.31).

> All men have some things which they cannot bear. Extend that feeling to what they can bear, and benevolence will be the result. All men have some things which they will not do. Extend

30

that feeling to the things that they do, and righteousness will be the result.

In his explanation of benevolence as extending to others one's own feeling of not wishing to be harmed, Mencius connects *ren* and the Confucian Principle of Reciprocity.

> Try your best to treat others as you would wish to be treated yourself, and you will find that this is the shortest way to benevolence.

For Mencius there is one essential virtue necessary for all other virtues: being true to oneself.

> There is no greater joy for me than to find, on self-examination, that I am true to myself (*Mencius* 7. I.4).

But surely being true to oneself is not necessarily a virtue by itself? A kind as well as a cruel person can both claim to be true to himself and to have acted sincerely. Mencius can be interpreted as asserting that only with an understanding of what is good and the readiness to practice the Principle of Reciprocity being true to oneself is a virtue. Mencius regards sincerity as the source of all ethical and political relations.

> There is a way to be sincere with oneself. If one does not understand what is good, he will not be sincere with himself. Therefore sincerity is the way of Heaven, and to think how to be sincere is the way of man. There has never been a person who was completely sincere and yet did not move others. Nor has there been a person who was not sincere and yet could move others (*Mencius* 4. I.12).

The sage "fulfills the way of Heaven" through self-knowledge. "He who knows his nature knows Heaven" (*Mencius* 7. I.1). "To preserve one's mind and one's nature is the way to serve Heaven." By "Heaven" Mencius does not mean a supernatural authority but an objective ethical standpoint beyond fluctuating moral preferences. We come to know and develop our individual nature fully not in subjective isolation but by being engaged in the objective domain of values and actions.

If human nature is inherently good, do we become moral simply by letting nature take its course and relying on our senses to lead us to the discernment of right from wrong? "The wise man does not say that [the satisfaction of the senses] is man's nature" (*Mencius* 7. II.24). We do not turn to excavate the wisdom of the sage emperors, nor do we gaze upon the doctrines of scholars, nor to externally imposed laws, but to the inherent moral ability and the capacity of the mind to think. The origin of morality is in human feelings but developing our moral nature requires that we call upon the mind's ability to think. Mencius explains that if we rely on our senses, which are influenced by material objects we go astray.

> When our senses of sight and hearing are used without thought they are obscured by material things which act on the senses and lead them astray. The function of the mind is to think. By thinking, it gets the right view of things; by neglecting to think, it fails to do this. (*Mencius* 6. I.15).

Mencius makes explicit the connection between the mind's ability to think and the ability to act ethically. Confucius launched the idea that the cultivation of our moral nature requires a broad knowledge of a wide range of subjects. Intellectual virtue and moral virtue are on a continuum. From Mencius' development of this idea it became one of the central tenets in the moral philosophy of the Confucian tradition: the search for the good is simultaneous with the search for knowledge of the world.

> Heaven is high and the stars are far away. But if we investigate the facts, we may go back to the solstice of a thousand years while we sit (*Mencius* 4. II.26).

We turn to Mencius' conception of the good life achievable by all.

The Good Life

What kind of life is thought to be worth living by Mencius? The life of pleasure and the gratification of the senses? When a ruler admits that his desire for wealth is a weakness, Mencius reassures him, "If your Majesty loves wealth, let your people enjoy the same, then what difficulty will there be for you to become the true ruler of the empire?" (*Mencius* 1. II.5). When the ruler further confides, "I have a weakness. I love beauty," Mencius calmly responds, "If you love beauty, let the people enjoy the same. What difficulty will there be for you to become the true ruler?" Love of wealth and beauty is not necessarily bad nor do they prevent us from being moral. But the unequal treatment of the people in not allowing them to have the same pleasures is wrong. Mencius shows a readiness to accept the physical nature of man with equanimity. There is no dual conception of man's physical nature as being inimical to his moral conduct. Mencius recognizes that the nourishment of passions is not contrary to cultivating a moral life. But Mencius is far from being a hedonist for he believes that in the nurture of the heart there is nothing better than to have few desires.[24] Mencius rejects the worldly goods acquired disregarding ethical considerations as being worthless.

> What good does a salary of ten thousand bushels do me if I accept them without any consideration of the principle of propriety and righteousness? (*Mencius* 6. I.10)

What prevents us from pursuing our desires without restraint, Mencius argues, is the innate moral sense present in every person.

> I like life and I also like righteousness. If I cannot have both of them, I shall give up life and choose righteousness. I also hate death, but there is something I hate more than death, and therefore there are occasions when I will not avoid danger.

Confucius also stated: "Do not seek life at the expense of *ren*. Some even sacrifice their lives to complete their *ren*" (*Analects* 15.8). Mencius is not urging that we ought to give up life for the sake of worthier causes but simply pointing out that we already value something more than preserving life and that avoiding death at all cost is not actually our chief motivation. It is not only the sage who values morality more than life.

Since the life of pleasure or wealth were deemed to be incomplete, does the pursuit of honour constitute an ethical life? Mencius distinguishes virtue from honour. Virtue, or "Nobility of Heaven," consists of "benevolence, righteousness, loyalty, faithfulness, and the love of the good" (*Mencius* 6. I.16). Human nobility or honour on the other hand, is "to be a grand official, a great official, and a high official." Contrasting the ways of the ancients that placed the nobility of Heaven above human ambition with the tendencies of his time, Mencius laments the delusion of forsaking virtue to pursue honour. What Mencius says of honour parallels Aristotle's view in the *Nicomachean Ethics*:

honour cannot be the supreme good we seek, for it is not conferred on the basis of our achievements but on reputation and appearance and is therefore superficial.

> The desire to be honoured is shared by the minds of all men. But all men have in themselves what is really honourable. Only they do not think of it. The honour conferred by men is not true honour. Whoever is made honourable by Zhao Meng can be made humble by him again (*Mencius* 6. I.17).

We have what is worthy of honour within us without waiting to receive it from others. A kinder view of human beings than this is rare.

How far does Mencius extend the concerns of an ethical community? Mencius does not advocate that we extend the affection we have for our family to all people. He maintains that there must be distinctions in love (*Mencius* 7. I.45-6). Parents are at the foundation of life and therefore our moral obligation to them is the greatest. Is our feeling of sympathy restricted to human suffering only or does it include other sentient beings? The true possessor of *ren* feels sympathy for the pain inflicted on animals. King Xuan of Qi on one occasion admits that he could not tolerate having an ox sacrificed for a ceremony: "I could not bear to see its frightened appearance, like an innocent person going to the place of death." Mencius tells Xuan that his kindness to animals is a clear indication that he possesses the ability to cultivate the virtue of "the love and protection of people."

> The superior man is so affected by animals that, having seen them alive, he cannot bear to see them die; having heard their cries, he cannot bear to eat their flesh (*Mencius*. 1. I.7).

Mencius calls for extending kindness to all creatures while not insisting that we treat them with equal consideration which we should have for people.

> In regard to inferior creatures, the superior man is kind to them but not benevolent. In regard to people generally, he is benevolent to them, but not affectionate. He is affectionate to his parents and to people generally. He is lovingly disposed to all people generally and kind to all creatures (*Mencius* 7. II.45).

A central topic in ethics is whether there are universal standards. In politics as well as in personal ethical conduct, Mencius believes that there are objective moral standards and rules just as there are rules in geometry. "The compass and square are the ultimate standards of the circle and the square. The sage is the ultimate standard of human relations" (*Mencius* 4. I.2). But Mencius is not Spinoza, who conceived ethics as a deductive system analogous to Euclidean geometry and sought to derive the entire foundation of ethics from a set of *a priori* axioms. While Mencius emphasizes the virtuous conduct and observation of the rules of propriety he does not determine what is ethical by following rules in all circumstances but by recognizing that the rules need to be adapted to individual natures.

> The love between father and son, righteousness between ruler and minister, ceremony (propriety) between guest and host, knowledge among the wise, and fulfilling the heavenly course by the sage – these are the appointment of Heaven. But there is an adaptation of our nature for them.

Love, righteousness, propriety, fidelity, wisdom, and following the way of Heaven are the entire ensemble of the central virtues for Mencius. But how they are to be cultivated varies with individual nature and circumstances. A celebrated debater challenges Mencius on the subject of propriety:

> "Is it a rule of propriety that men and women should not touch hands when they give or receive things?" Mencius replied, "It is a rule of propriety." "If someone's sister-in-law is drowning, should he rescue her with his hand?" Mencius replied, "He who does not rescue his drowning sister-in-law is a wolf. It is a rule of propriety for men and women not to touch hands when giving or receiving things, but it is a matter of expediency to rescue one's drowning sister-in-law with hands. A drowning empire must be rescued with moral principles. Do you wish me to rescue the world with my hand?" (*Mencius* 4. I.17)

Saving drowning women justifies breaking the rule of propriety. The particular examples of rules are of Mencius' time in China, but his argument that rules exist to ensure harmonious relations in society, and that when more harm results from obeying the rules it is ethical to break them, engages the central debate among moral philosophers on the subject of rules from Plato to the present.

How are the moral principles with which Mencius sought to rescue the empire arrived at? Simply by extending the same virtues in the cultivation of personal life to the broader social and political domain (*Mencius* 1. II.1-5). Mencius is confident that we can build on the individual virtue of filial piety as the foundation of political peace.

> Ever since there has been mankind, none has succeeded in leading children to attack their parents. Thus such a ruler will have no enemy in the world, he will be an official appointed by Heaven (*Mencius* 2. I.5).

The duty of the ruler is to provide the government under which all people can flourish.

The Mandate of Heaven

The Mandate of Heaven is conferred on the ruler on the basis of virtue. There is an essential connection between the conduct of the ruler and good government: the ruler governs through moral example. Only by cultivating in himself an exemplary moral character and acting with the common good as his goal can the ruler's power to govern be justified. The emphasis that only the virtuous are entitled to govern is evident in Laozi, Confucius and all the major thinkers of Confucian and Daoist traditions and has formed the foundation of political philosophy in China. There is a sense in which the Mandate of Heaven is equivalent to the idea of natural law: both are based on the belief that there exist in nature objective laws which determine what is right. Mencius' daring innovation was to identify the Mandate of Heaven with the judgment of the people and the will of Heaven with the will of the people. For Mencius to say that the Mandate of Heaven is given to the ruler is tantamount to saying that people's consent is given.

> It was Heaven that gave the empire to him. It was the people that gave the empire to him. Therefore, I said, "The emperor cannot give the empire to another person" (*Mencius* 5. I.5).

The Mandate of Heaven is the mandate of the people. The sole criterion of legitimate rule is the possession of morally upright character and the people's acceptance of the conduct of those who rule. The Mandate of Heaven does not confer the divine right of kings to rule. Heaven is the objectification of people's choices, convictions and decisions. Mencius

36

does not believe that he is radically revising political thought but drawing from the *Book of Odes* and the reflections on the topic from the Zhou period recorded in the *Book of History* (*Mencius* 4. I.1). Mencius quotes from the *Book of History*: "Heaven sees as my people see; Heaven hears as my people hear."[25] Endorsing humane government, he persistently sought to overcome the "way of a despot" (the way of force) by the "kingly way" (the way of moral power). The guiding principle of the just ruler is righteousness; that of a despot, profit. This distinction is frequently in the foreground of Confucian thought on politics (*Mencius* 2. I.3).

> A ruler who uses force to make a pretense at benevolence is a despot. Such a despot requires a large kingdom. A ruler who practices benevolence with virtue is a true king. To become a true king does not depend on a large kingdom. When force is used to overcome people, they do not submit willingly but only because they have not sufficient strength to resist.

In his reply to a ruler who inquires how the state can be united, Mencius states that if there were a person "who took no pleasure in killing men," "all the people of the nation will unanimously" support him and "the people will flock to him as water flows downwards with a rush which no one can repress" (*Mencius* 1. I.6).

The duty of the ruler and the ministers consists in ensuring that laws and institutions make it possible for benevolence and propriety to be the foundation of public life. Mencius is convinced that the people are more important than the ruler or territory.

> The people are the most important in the state; the spirits of the land and grain are the next; the ruler is the lightest. When a feudal lord endangers the spirits of the land and grain, he is removed and replaced (*Mencius* 7. II.14).

Mencius is not calling for a violent revolution to overthrow the ruler who abuses political authority. Mencius consistently advocates peace and he is generally interpreted as being opposed to violence of any kind. Mencius' discussion brings to the foreground the dichotomy between political obligation to obey the law and moral responsibility to disobey the laws of an unjust government – a topic of central concern in Western political thought from Plato to the present.[26] What are the legitimate means of bringing about a change in government? Mencius does not wait in attendance to Heaven for guidance but urges those who take on political power to turn to the people. The decisions of the ruler should be based on the judgement of the people (*Mencius* 1. II.7).

> When all your immediate ministers say that a man is worthy, it is not sufficient. When all your great officers say so, it is not sufficient. When all your people say so, look into the case, and if you find him to be worthy, then employ him.

Believing that with proper guidance all people are capable of engaging in the same moral endeavour, Mencius calls for the participation of the people in determining who should be given political authority. Mencius is generally regarded as the most democratic of philosophers from the classical period.

How far does Mencius carry the idea of equality? When it is said that the way for the ministers to govern is to "cultivate the field with the people for food, and prepare their own meals while they carry on the government," Mencius retorts,

> Why does Master Hsu not do the work of the potter and the founder, and supply himself with the articles which he uses solely from his establishment?

> When can the government of the empire alone be done along with farming? There is the work of great men and there is the work of small men. ... It is said, "Some labour with their minds and some labour with their strength. Those who labour with their minds govern others; those who labour with their strength are governed by others. Those who are governed by others support them; those who govern them are supported by them." This is a principle universally recognized (*Mencius* 3. I.4).

This particular passage has been criticized as adhering to a hierarchy of class distinctions. How does this fare with Mencius' view of the equality of people? Mencius accepts the distinction in the abilities of the people to carry out specific tasks and the division of labour based on interest and need. Mencius would concur with the formulation of justice as "From each according to his capacity, to each according to his need." The distinction between who should govern and who should work in the fields is not based on differences in wealth, social status, or birth but solely on knowledge and ability to act for the good of the people. To this end Mencius advises the rulers to "establish seminaries, academies, schools, and institutes to teach the people" (*Mencius* 3. I.3).

Mencius argues that it is poverty which leads to vice and urges the rulers to "practice a humane government to the people, reduce punishments and fines, lower taxes" (*Mencius* 3. I.3).[27] Mencius tells the rulers that making provisions for the "most destitute of the people" should be "the first objects" of the government and refers to the *Book of Odes*. "The rich may get through *life well*. But alas! for the miserable and solitary!" (*Mencius* 1. II.5). Inculcation of virtue is possible only with the regulation of agriculture and commerce which reduce hardships caused by poverty and promote secure living conditions. Mencius lists the measures for reducing taxation to promote free-trade, to increase cooperation, and to diminish competition: not to tax the traders and the goods that are brought into the state, not to tax farmers who work on the common public field for "mutual aid," and not to fine "the family that fails to meet certain quotas." A great officer of Song, expecting Mencius' approval, declares that he is ready to comply with what Mencius urges: "With your leave I will lighten the tax and the duties until next year, and will then make an end of them. What do you think of such a course?" Mencius replies with an analogy.

> Here is a man, who appropriates some of his neighbour's strayed fowls every day. Some one says to him, "Such is not the way of a good man," and he replies "With your leave I will diminish my appropriations, and will take only one fowl a month, until next year, when I will make an end of the practice." If you know the thing is unrighteous, then use all dispatch in putting an end to it. Why wait till next year? (*Mencius* 3. II.8)

The forthrightness with which Mencius responds is characteristic of his forceful way of addressing those who hold political power to implement policies for the benefit of the people.

What are the significant differences between Confucius and Mencius? Mencius had acquired a deep and wide learning characteristic of the Confucian scholars. As Confucius stressed Mencius also saw the study of the classics as a foundation of the cultivation of virtue. Both Confucius and Mencius draw philosophical insight from the *Book of Odes* and the *Book of History*. However, Mencius is critical of the *Book of History* since it presents violent conquest as a part of the sage ruler and declares that "It would be better to have no *Book of History*, than to believe all of it". Wisdom and violence are incompatible in Mencius' view. In Mencius' philosophy, a man of humanity has no need of violence since people move to him as water flows downward.

Maintaining the balance in the relation between the individual and society was the topic of importance throughout the history of Confucianism. While Confucius upholds the importance of the balanced relation between society and the individual, Mencius frequently focuses on the importance of the individual. In this he is closer to Laozi and Zhuangzi (*Mencius* 2. I.9; 3. I.1; 5. II.1). Mencius was deeply influenced by Daoism, especially the idea of the inherent goodness of human nature and the belief that the right way to live is a full development of what is naturally good.[28] Mencius builds on Confucius' view of human nature: "By nature, men are close together. In practice they grow wide apart" (*Analects* 8.2). This belief in the equal moral ability of all is shared by the Daoist and Confucian philosophers. Mencius carries the moral egalitarianism of Confucius further. "It is not only the worthies alone who have this moral sense. All men have it, but only the worthies have been able to preserve it" (*Mencius* 6. I.10). Mencius states that "All things are complete in us" (*Mencius* 7. I.4). In his view of the completeness of things in themselves, Mencius' views are close to that of Laozi and Zhuangzi.[29] There are further similarities between the Mencius and the Daoist philosophers. The Confucian scholar is learned in the classics and the rites. But Mencius also recognizes the value of innocence devoid of worldliness. Mencius' statement that "The great man is one who does not lose his child's heart" recalls Laozi's sage who is like an infant without guile (*Mencius* 4. II.12). Laozi and Zhuangzi are critical of the excesses of the scholars. Mencius calls out impatiently:

> What I dislike in your wise men is their forced conclusions. ...
> If wise men would act without any special effort their wisdom
> would also be great (*Mencius* 4. II.26).

What is Mencius' view of the sage?

> ... one who practices virtues along with the people when he is
> successful, and practices the Way alone when he is disap-
> pointed; one whose heart cannot be dissipated by the power of
> wealth and honours, who cannot be influenced by poverty or
> humble stations, who cannot be subdued by force and might –
> such a person is a great man (*Mencius* 3. II.2).

A great man has intellectual and moral courage. "He preserves benevolence and propriety" and "loves and respects others" (*Mencius* 4. II.28).

How effective was Mencius in rescuing the empire with his principles? For a brief period under the rule of Wang Mang (9-22 CE), a reign a political reform spread, based on the principles advocated by the Confucian scholars. Emulating the principles of Mencius, each family was granted a property for cultivation and landowners with large properties were made to distribute their holdings. The state was declared the sole proprietor of the land and all sale of land was prohibited. Mencius inspired a spirited defense of virtue when his appellation for the ruler who fails to respect his ministers, "robber and enemy" incited the indignation of the founder of Ming dynasty who ordered that Mencius be demoted from his place in the temples of Confucius. Unflinching in the face of the consequences of defying the imperial will, the president of the Board of Punishments declared "I will die for Mencius, and my death will be crowned in glory."[30] The emperor not only relented but after having studied the *Book of Mencius* issued a proclamation in the following year reinstating his place as the second sage.

Mencius' clear delineation of what human nature consists in, what is internal to man, and what is due to external factors has influenced all subsequent philosophical discussions of human nature. Confucian teaching by the middle of third century BCE was divided into various sects. The journeying philosophers visited various courts each with advice on the art of ruling. Regardless of the differences among the various views, the main common concern of the philosophers was what constituted the best way of eliminating harm and strife and how this goal could be achieved, whether by stern laws enforced by powerful rulers or by reforming the rulers to govern with benevolence. Mencius' philosophy eclipsed the rival sects and emerged as the direct transmitter of the teachings of Confucius establishing the legacy of the Confucian tradition. But one philosopher working in the Confucian tradition, only next in importance to Mencius, was not convinced by Mencius' arguments. That was Xunzi (Hsun Tzu, ca. 312-238 BCE), who held a diametrically opposite view of human nature. Where Mencius saw in man kindness and good will, Xunzi saw a rough and envious disposition which must be restrained by laws and sanctions through reward and punishment.

Xunzi

The Nature of Man is Evil

Mencius said, "The nature of man is good; it becomes evil because man destroys his original nature." This is a mistake. By nature man departs from his primitive character and capacity as soon as he is born and he is bound to destroy it. From this point of view, it is clear that man's nature is evil (*Xunzi* 129).[31]

Xunzi's theory of human nature is the point of departure for his ethics. Mencius and Xunzi represent the two divergent tendencies of idealist Confucianism and naturalist Confucianism in ancient China.[32] Mencius sought to bring about the ideals of morality, benevolence, and righteousness attainable by all. Xunzi on the other hand looked to the realities of human experience within the limits of what can be practiced. The *Book of Mencius* contains mostly dialogues, while Xunzi's writings consist of explanations and arguments. Xunzi investigates the subjects of moral psychology and logic more extensively and systematically than Mencius. The *Xunzi* consists of thirty-two chapters on topics such as "Against Physiognomy," "Against the Twelve Philosophers," "National Wealth," "The Kingly Way versus the Despot's," "On Confucius," "A Discussion of Mozi," "Improving Yourself," and thorough critiques of philosophers in ancient China. Xunzi was one of the most eminent scholars of his time and his ideas exerted a considerable influence up through the Han period (206 BCE – 220 CE). However, the *Xunzi* has not played a significant role in the development of the Confucian tradition. It was Mencius and not Xunzi who was considered to be in the direct line for the transmission of Confucius' ideas. There were no commentaries on Xunzi's work until the ninth century, and very few since then. His realism, emphasis on logic, belief in progress, stress on law, and critical discussions of the various philosophical schools have generated more interest in contemporary China.[33]

Philosophical debate about the nature of man in China tended to be focused on the broad concerns of the ability of man to acquire knowledge and habits conducive to a moral way of life. There is little attention paid to philosophy of mind or the aspects of moral psychology in probing the recesses of the mind to discern motivation, intention, deliberation, choice, and will. In Laozi, Confucius, Zhuangzi, and Mencius the views of human nature tend to be on the whole benign while Mozi is more neutral. But with Xunzi we have a sharp contrast. Xunzi argues that human nature is inherently evil: left to follow its own course the excessive indulgence in the pursuit of pleasure will lead to turmoil, strife, and violence. Xunzi argues that "It is the original nature and feeling of man to love profit and seek gain" (*Xunzi* 130). "If they follow their natural feelings, they will love profit and seek gain and these will do violence to each other and grab the property."

> Mencius said, "The nature of man is good." I say that this is not true. By goodness at any time in any place is meant true principles and peaceful order, and by evil is meant imbalance, violence, and disorder. This is the distinction between good and evil. Now do we honestly regard man's nature as characterized by true principles and peaceful order? If so, why are sages necessary and why are propriety and righteousness necessary? What possible improvement can sages make on true principles and peaceful order? (*Xunzi* 131)

But Mencius would have a ready reply to this objection. Mencius more than acknowledges the state of affairs where there is violence and disorder: the sages have their work cut out for them in setting the world right with their principles and exemplary conduct. Mencius' view of human nature does not commit him to the thesis that this is the best of all possible worlds or to deny the existence of evil. When Mencius' view is interpreted as asserting that the inherent moral ability and nature need to be nurtured for the potential goodness to be fully realized in actuality, the existence of evil can be explained as the failure to fully develop human nature.

Xunzi argues that Mencius fails to understand the distinction between human nature and human activity.

> Mencius said, "Man learns because his nature is good." This is not true. He did not know the nature of man and did not understand the distinction between man's nature and his effort. Man's nature is the product of Nature; it cannot be learned and cannot be worked for. Propriety and righteousness are produced by the sage. They can be learned by men and can be accomplished through work. What is in man but cannot be learned or accomplished through work is what can be achieved through activity. This is the difference between human nature and human activity. Now by nature man's eye can see and his ear can hear. But

43

the clarity of vision is not outside his eye and the distinctness of hearing is not outside the ear. Clear vision and distinct hearing cannot be learned (*Xunzi* 129).

But surely the eye and the ear can be trained and clear vision and distinct hearing can be learned? If they were not, education in art and music would not be possible. Mencius does make a distinction between what is inherent in man's nature and what can be achieved by effort. By the goodness of human nature Mencius means that the feeling of sympathy, propriety, and righteousness are what can be achieved by effort. Both the feeling of sympathy and ability to develop it in all human relations are inherent but unless they are maintained by individual effort and guided by the principles of benevolence and righteousness, they will deteriorate.

For Xunzi human beings stand in need of laws and institutions of enforcement to restrain their pursuit of pleasure. Xunzi appeals to evidence from his present, history, "ancient matter" and the physical nature of man. Xunzi argues that the senses desiring satisfaction, "the heart desiring gain, and the body desiring pleasure and ease – all these are products of man's original nature and feelings" (*Xunzi* 130).

> Now, man's inborn nature is to seek for gain. If this tendency is followed, strife and rapacity result and deference and compliance disappear. By inborn nature one is envious and hates others. If these tendencies are followed, injury and destruction result and loyalty and faithfulness disappear. By inborn nature one possesses the desires of ear and eye and likes sound and beauty. If these tendencies are followed, lewdness and licentiousness result, and the pattern and order of propriety and righteousness disappear. Therefore to follow man's nature and his feelings will inevitably result in strife and rapacity, combine with rebellion and disorder and end in violence (*Xunzi* 128).

What Xunzi means by the "evil nature" of man is the feelings of envy and hatred, the desires of the senses, and the propensity to pursue material gain which can result in violence. When allowed to follow their natural inclination human beings will turn out to be self-interested hedonists. "The nature of man is evil; goodness is the result of his activity" (*Xunzi* 128). This is a puzzling assertion, for if the nature of man is evil, how can his activity produce good? Xunzi distinguishes between what natural inclination of the senses and the needs of the body lead us to do and what our awareness of right and wrong guides us to do.

> Now by nature man desires repletion when hungry, desires warmth when cold and desires rest when tired. These are man's natural feelings. But now when a man is hungry and sees some elders before him, he does not eat ahead of them but yields to them. When he is tired, he dares not seek rest because he wants to take over the work [of elders]. The son is yielding to or taking over the work of his father, and the younger brother yielding to or taking over the work of his older brother – these two lines of action are contrary to original nature and violate natural feeling. Nevertheless, the way of filial piety is the pattern and order of propriety and righteousness. If one follows his feeling, he will have no deference or compliance. Deference and compliance are opposed to his natural feelings. From this point of view, it is clear that man's nature is evil and that his goodness is the result of his activity (*Xunzi* 129-130).

What Xunzi describes as the instances of "natural desire" for the satisfaction of physical needs is indisputable. But couldn't it be argued that altruism is also a "natural desire" and not instilled by moral education? Just as the senses and the body have the desire for satisfaction and gratification, the mind also has concern for the well-being of others. Where is the evil that Xunzi regards as inherent in human nature? It could be argued that it is not in the sense organs or functions of the body. They are not in themselves morally deficient or proficient but would appear to be neutral. There are further difficulties with Xunzi's thesis of the evil nature of man. If human nature is evil, from where do moral values originate? If self-interest and gratification of the desires of the senses and satisfaction of the needs of the body underlie all human actions, how can any laws or education possibly succeed in altering the given nature of human beings? If by human nature he means the traits which cannot be altered, ten thousand sages could not hope to transform human beings.

Xunzi is aware of these difficulties and reinforces his argument with illustrations reminiscent of Gaozi's analogy of the cup and the willow tree to argue that morality is external to man's nature (*Xunzi* 130).

> Someone may ask, "If man's nature is evil, whence come propriety and righteousness?" I answer that all propriety and righteousness are the results of the activities of sages and not pro-

duced from man's nature. The potter pounds the clay and makes the vessel. This being the case, the vessel is the product of the artisan's activity and not the original product of man's nature.

Xunzi explains the origins of moral values.

> The sages gathered their ideas and thoughts and became familiar with activity, facts and principles, and thus produced propriety and righteousness, and instituted laws and systems (*Xunzi* 130).

Moral laws do not exist as natural laws prior to human construction; nor do they originate from human nature. This is a radical departure from the prevailing belief in natural law or the will of Heaven and a rejection of the Confucian view that to develop our nature is to cultivate virtue. We can see how the Legalist School of thought which advocated the institution of law as the only means of governing the empire and the people grew directly out of Xunzi's philosophy.[34] It may be asked how at the conference of the sages ethical values were first generated and gathered.

> As activity was aroused, propriety and righteousness were produced and as propriety and righteousness were produced, laws and systems instituted (*Xunzi* 130).

The sages transform human nature by stimulating us to moral activity. Guided by the moral percepts of righteousness and propriety our natural impulses can be restrained and our actions can become altruistic. Xunzi is convinced that it is possible to "transform man's nature" as the sages have done. This transformation of man's nature from self-interest to righteous conduct is the origin of ethical activity (*Xunzi* 128).

> The sage-kings of antiquity, knowing that the nature of men is evil, and that it is unbalanced, off the track, incorrect, rebellious, disorderly, and undisciplined, created the rules of propriety and righteousness and instituted laws and systems in order to correct man's feelings, transform them, and direct them so that they all may become disciplined and conform with the Way (*dao*).

Xunzi stresses the importance of moral education and laws.

> There must be the civilizing influence of teachers and laws and

the guidance of propriety and righteousness, and then it will result in deference and compliance, combine with pattern and order, and end in discipline (*Xunzi* 128).

The task of laws of civil society and institutions is to keep man from becoming unbalanced and to keep him from going off the track.[35] Xunzi regards propriety as the measure of all human conduct and that "without propriety and righteousness there will be rebellion, disorder, and chaos." Xunzi's understanding of propriety (*li*) emphasizes the formal and social aspects of active intervention of laws and rules. This is in sharp contrast to the conception of *li* in Confucius and Mencius who believed that the ethical person has an understanding of *li* as an objective moral standard which is not necessarily identical with the prevalent rules of conduct in society. For Confucius and Mencius *li* is not a set of moral codes based on tradition or laws of the society at a particular time or place, but a universal standard which is applicable to all circumstances.

For Xunzi, living in accordance with *li* as a moral guideline requires a correct understanding of language. The ancients recognized the important connection between language and morals. This was a central field of inquiry among the philosophical schools. We have seen how Confucius regards the rectification of names to be essential in moral education. Xunzi also stresses the ethical implications of the clarification of meanings of words: inculcating moral character through laws and institutions requires a correct understanding of language. Xunzi believes that arbitrary and incorrect uses of language lead to strife and social conflict. He argues that "when sage-kings instituted names, the names were fixed and actualities distinguished."

> Therefore, the practice of splitting terms and arbitrarily creating names to confuse correct names ... brought much litigation and was called great wickedness. It was a crime, like private manufacturing of credentials and measurements and therefore the people dared not rely on strange terms created to confuse correct names. Hence the people were honest (*Xunzi* 124).

While the schools of philosophy which discussed the rectification of names were mainly interested in social and moral implications, Xunzi develops the inquiry further into a systematic account of the relation between language and the domain of reference, or "actuality." There is a sustained effort at formulating a theory of meaning and truth.[36]

Xunzi asks whether the values of righteousness and propriety are excessively demanding and can only remain remote ideals. Building on the idea of the equal moral ability of all first clearly stated by Confucius Xunzi argues that it is possible for everyone to become a sage. Mencius also held the view that all men can become sage emperors.

> "Any man in the street can become (sage ruler) Yu." What does this ancient saying mean? I say that Yu became sage ruler Yu because he practiced benevolence, righteousness, laws, and correct principles. This shows that these can be known and practiced. Every man in the street possesses the faculty to know them and the capacity to practice them. This being the case, it is clear that every man can be Yu (*Xunzi* 132).

The sages are not born with a different moral constitution from the common people. Only with their "accumulated effort" in pursuit of propriety and righteousness to "the fullest extent," and not giving rein to their natural feelings did they excel others. To what extent are we free to shape our characters?

> As to cultivating one's will, to be earnest in one's moral conduct, to be clear in one's knowledge and deliberations, to live in this age but to set his mind on the ancients (as models), that depends on the person himself (*Xunzi* 119).

Xunzi emphasizes that we can bring about change through our effort. "Instead of obeying Heaven and singing praise to it, why not control the Mandate of Heaven and use it? ... to neglect human effort and admire Heaven is to miss the nature of things" (*Xunzi* 122). Good government does not depend on natural causes or events but on human endeavour. It has been remarked that the idea of controlling nature, which is forcefully expressed by Xunzi, did not lead to a development of natural science, because Xunzi's idea of overcoming nature was overshadowed by the prevalent doctrine of the harmony of man and nature which he also accentuates.

We conclude the study of the Confucian legacy with a discussion of the *Great Learning* and the *Doctrine of the Mean*, which comprise the Four Books of Confucian learning with the *Analects* and *Mencius*.

The Great Learning

The way of learning to be great consists in manifesting illustrious virtue, loving the people, and abiding in the highest good. [37]

The *Great Learning* (Education of Adults) is originally a chapter from the *Book of Rites*. It has been variously attributed to Confucius, his disciples and his grandson which would make it date from the fifth century BCE but more recent scholarship dates it from 200 BCE. The substantive part of the book addresses the education of those who are to govern the state and specifies the conditions of just rule. We find the Confucian educational programme applied to the individual and political life. It was regarded as one of the foremost Confucian classics by the Neo-Confucian philosophers from the eleventh century, who wrote commentaries on it. With the *Analects*, the *Book of Mencius* and the *Doctrine of the Mean*, it exerted a considerable influence as the basis of civil service examinations from 1313 to 1905.

The aim of great learning is to teach the way to act with illustrious virtue, to renovate the people and to achieve highest excellence. There are seven steps to realizing these goals: the investigation of things, extension of knowledge, sincerity of thought, rectification of the mind, cultivation of the personal life, regulation of the family, and order in the state and world peace. The worth of the *Great Learning* has been celebrated by writers in China and in the West. [38] But it has also been criticized as consisting of general rules for the maintenance of a good government. The criticism that the *Great Learning* addresses the sovereigns only overlooks the aim of the book which focuses on the perfecting of self, and of the practice of virtue by all men. The common goal of personal cultivation is emphasized: "From the Son of Heaven to the people, all are to consider the cultivation of the person to be the root of everything." Regarding the seven steps in realizing the goal of great learning it has been remarked that it is not clear how one stage leads to the next and that it asks for what is of inordinate difficulty. The seven stages leading to the attainment of the great learning appear to be as arduous as the seven labours of Hercules. Zhuxi's commentary that knowledge must be perfected before we can achieve the sincerity of our thoughts and rectifying of hearts, provoked the objection that "This learning would not be for adults only but even Methuselahs would not be able to compass it." Zhuxi can be interpreted as explaining that the means to personal cultivation requires constant effort to inquire into the nature of all things and not resting in received opinions. Sincerity of thought is an attitude of the inquiring mind. Rectification of the heart can be understood as setting one's mind and directing the will to set things right. No doubt this learning for adults is difficult but as Zhuxi states, of any person who perseveres we might be able to say that "After exerting himself for a long time, he will suddenly find himself possessed of a wide and far-reaching learning."

To the objection that there is no philosophical argument but only injunctions the following response may be made. The significance of the *Great Learning* is not in "severity of its logical processes, or the large-minded prosecution of any course of thought." We find in them the announcement of certain seminal principles which could be beneficial in government and in personal conduct. What are these principles? The goal of government consists in providing for the well-being of the people, and that those who govern act not for their gratification but for the good of the people. The view that the rulers have no divine right but only what springs from the discharge of their duty is forcefully stated. "The decree does not always rest on them. Goodness obtains it and the want of goodness loses it." The requirement that all who have authority in the family and the state are to cultivate personal excellence has an important political and social implication. These principles are familiar and perhaps commonplace but they are "eternal verities."

Manifesting illustrious virtue is not a matter of possessing an excellent character but acting ceaselessly to reform oneself with the aim of bringing about peace throughout the world. "The superior man tries at all times to do his utmost in renovating himself and others." The distinguishing characteristic of a moral person is his sincerity and his tireless effort in renovating himself.

> What is meant by "making the thoughts sincere" is allowing no self-deception ... Therefore the superior man will always be watchful over himself when alone.

Only with complete sincerity is it possible to rectify the mind. To set the mind right means investigating the nature of things. To know the truth about the nature of the things one has to be sincere in his will. In the investigation of the principles of things only those who have the sincerity of thought can grasp the truth about the nature of things. The cultivation of personal life depends on the rectification of the mind. The mind cannot be set right if we are swayed by powerful emotions and desires. "When one is affected by wrath, fear, fondness, worries and anxieties, his mind will not be correct."

The cultivation of virtue in the individual is the basis of social and political harmony.

> Therefore the superior man must have the good qualities in himself before he may require them in other people. He must be free of the bad qualities in himself before he may require others not to have them. There has never been a man who does not cherish altruism (*shu*) in himself and yet can teach other people.

The family life cannot be harmonious unless personal life is cultivated. The goodness and right actions of the individuals lead to harmony in the family and to order in the state and ultimately to peace in the world.

> Only when one is good and correct to one's elder and younger brothers can one teach the people of the country.

> What is meant by saying that peace of the world depends on the order of the state is this. When the ruler treats the elders with respect then the people will be aroused toward filial piety. When the ruler treats the aged with respect, then the people will be aroused toward brotherly respect. When the ruler treats compassionately the young and the helpless, then the common people will not follow the opposite course.

The *Great Learning* continues the Confucian exhortation to the ruler to uphold a just and benevolent course of government and to provide for the well-being of the people. In the *Great Learning*, more than in any other of the Confucian classics, the poems from the *Book of Odes* are given ethical interpretations and cited as illustrations of the moral life. Benevolence, reverence, filial piety, love, and faithfulness are upheld as the high moral achievement of wise rulers. "The common people enjoy what they enjoyed and benefited from their arrangements." The people admire the moral accomplishments of the perfectly virtuous prince who embodies "the pursuit of learning, self-cultivation, eminent character, and perfect virtue" as they celebrate the beauty of nature: "The *Book of Odes* says, 'Look at that curve in the Chi River. How luxuriant and green are the bamboo trees there! Here is our elegant and accomplished prince'." The rulers are warned that "if they deviate from the correct path, they will be cast away by the world." The Confucian Principle of Reciprocity is emphasized as an essential aspect of bringing about peace in the world.

> What a man dislikes in his superiors let him not show it in dealing with his inferiors. What he dislikes in those in front of him, let him not show it in preceding those who are behind. What he dislikes in those behind him, let him not show it in following those in front of him.

The connection between investigating the principles of all things which operate in the universe and acquiring the knowledge of virtue necessary for living in the right way forms the core of the *Great Learning*.

> If we wish to extend our knowledge to the utmost, we must investigate the principles of all things we come into contact with, for the intelligent mind of man is certainly formed to know... It is only because all principles are not investigated that man's knowledge is incomplete. The first step in the education of the adult is to instruct the learner, in regard to all things in the world, to proceed from what knowledge he has of their principles, and investigate further until he reaches the limit. After exerting himself in this way for a long time, he will one day achieve a wide and far-reaching penetration.[39]

The laws of human reasoning can uncover the laws by which the universe operates. "Were the eyes not sunlike, how could we see the light?"[40] As the mind discovers the order of the cosmos inherent in its operations, with a continuous and an interconnected effort in all spheres of action we begin to cultivate the moral life.

The Doctrine of the Mean

> Where there is anything not yet studied, or studied but not yet understood, do not give up. Where there is any question not yet asked, or asked but its answer not yet known, do not give up. Where there is anything not yet thought over, or thought over but not yet apprehended, do not give up.

> When there is anything not yet practiced, or practiced but not yet earnestly, do not give up. If another man succeeds by ten ef-

forts, we will use a thousand efforts. If we really follow this course, though unintelligent, we will surely become intelligent, and though weak, will surely become strong (*Doctrine of the Mean* 20).

The *Doctrine of the Mean* is a chapter from the *Book of Rites*. With the *Great Learning*, it exerted a significant influence for over eight hundred yeas as a required text for the civil service examination. It is a Confucian treatise in the tradition of Mencius.[41] It was commonly attributed to Zi Si (491-431 BCE), the grandson of Confucius, but most likely it was composed at two different times. The first section purports to describe Confucius' views by specific references to the *Analects* and shows close similarities to Confucius' ideas. The later section shows the influence of Mencius. The Daoist and Buddhist thinkers who wrote commentaries on it from the fourth century to the eleventh centuries as well as the later Neo-Confucian philosophers were drawn to its ideas on human nature and the Way of Heaven. The central themes are cultivation of the person and sincerity.

Throughout the *Doctrine of the Mean* the emphasis is on the universal aspects of human relations, virtues, and purposes.

Wisdom, humanity, and courage are the three universal virtues.

The way by which they are learned is one. Some are born with the knowledge of these virtues. Some learn it through study. Some learn it through hard work. But when the knowledge is acquired, it comes to the same thing. Some practice them naturally and easily. Some practice them for their advantage. Some practice them with effort and difficulty. But when the achievement is made, it comes to the same thing.

The Confucian regard for the moral ability of all to achieve virtue is emphasized. In the varying human relations and endeavours there are universal standards. The emperor is not above the law and there are universal standards that apply to all rulers.

As in the *Great Learning*, the Confucian doctrine of reciprocity is advocated. "Conscientiousness (*zhong*) and altruism (*shu*) are not far from the Way. What you do not wish others to do to you, do not do to them." All people are to cultivate the personal life through developing *ren*.

The cultivation of the person is to be achieved through the Way, and the cultivation of the Way is to be achieved through benevolence, *ren*. *Ren* is the distinguishing characteristic of man... Righteousness (*yi*) is the principle of setting things right and proper, and the greatest application of it is in honouring the worthy.

In urging us to cultivate *ren* and *yi*, and to follow the rules of propriety which arise from them, the *Doctrine of the Mean* upholds Confucian virtues. However, the emphasis on cultivating the way can be related to a Daoist perspective.

What Heaven imparts to man is called human nature. To follow our nature is called the Way (*dao*). Cultivating the Way is called education. The Way cannot be separated from us for a moment. What can be separated from us is not the Way.

Sincerity is regarded as the foundation of all knowledge and moral life. Only with complete sincerity can we develop the nature of others. The Confucian idea of the development of the individual as being continuous with the development of others is expanded to developing the nature of all things. This idea is taken up by the Neo-Confucian philosophers and fully expanded to an ethical point of view.[42]

Sincerity means the completion of the self, and the Way is self-directing. Sincerity is the beginning and end of things. ... Sincerity is not only the completion of one's own self, it is that by which all things are completed. The completion of the self means humanity. The completion of all things means wisdom. Sincerity is the Way of Heaven. To think how to be sincere is the way of man. He who is sincere is one who hits upon what is right without effort and apprehends without thinking. He is naturally and easily in harmony with the Way. Such a man is a sage. He who tries to be sincere is one who chooses the good and holds fast to it.

This characterization of the sage as the one who can harmonize naturally and easily without effort describes the man of the dao. This view of sincerity is linked to the perspective of Laozi and Zhuangzi: the *dao* as infinite, lasting and accomplishing its ends without effort.

2

Dao

The Way of Reality

It is heavy as a stone, light as a feather.[1]

The idea of the *dao* is first distinctly formulated by Laozi in the *Dao De Jing* as a subject of a sustained inquiry and developed further by Zhuangzi in his view of reality as a dynamic process. The Daoist philosophy is a persistent search to understand the way of reality and derive a way of life from the knowledge of the way things are. The *dao* literally means the way. It also means a road or path. Applied to human action, it is the way in which one does something: this is the *dao* of man. The *dao* is also the way in which all life takes form: this is the *dao* of nature. The *dao* of nature is then the aggregate, the collection, and the sum total of all the individual entities. The *dao* is furthermore the way in which the universe and everything within it – man, nature, and the ten thousand things under all of heaven – unfold, develop their nature, and come to be what they are. All things that exist form one continuum and one great chain of being. The *dao* is infinite potentiality which coincides with actuality: this is the *dao* of heaven. The *dao* of heaven is a single perspective from which the totality of all existing things can be seen and comprehended. The knowledge that all undergoes constant transformation is from the standpoint of the *dao* of heaven. The view of the totality of all phenomena given by the *dao* is that reality is a flux, transformation, and an eternal process.

Does the concept of the *dao* relate to any central philosophical ideas in the West? The first translations of *Dao De Jing* by Jesuit scholars

55

imbued the *dao* with religious significance.[2] The *dao* as the origin of all things was seen as being analogous with the idea of a creator or "Primordial Reason" or "the Sublime Intelligence which created, and governs the world." However, in the concept of the *dao* of Heaven there is no connotation of a personal God. Heaven stands for an objective source of universal morality, the standpoint of just and fair perspective rather than a personal deity who can be placated with sacrifices and prayers and dispenses justice or oversees the salvation of individual souls.[3]

Dao has been called many things by many interpreters. Here is a partial list from which a judicious selection might be made. It has been described as a principle at once transcendent and immanent. Other variants include "cosmic substance before all determination and a unique substance in which *yin* and *yang* are only modes", logos and nature. Contemporary explanations include the following: "the unity underlying plurality", and "the unchanging unity underlying a shifting plurality and at the same time the impetus giving rise to every form of life and motion."[4] Each of the phrases captures only an aspect of the meaning of the idea of the *dao*. The meaning of the *dao* remains illusive when it is taken as a metaphysical concept. It has been suggested that the *dao* is a way of reality or being. The *dao* is not a collection of existing objects but the way in which actions take place in accordance with the inner nature of things. This way of seeing the *dao* as the inner workings of nature is akin to the view of the Romantics. Thus imagination for Coleridge is an intuitive power to grasp the inwardness of nature.

The *dao*, or "way," the path along which all things move, is a concept shared by all the philosophical schools of China.[5] The expandability of the concept of the *dao* makes it possible to be taken up by widely differing schools of thought. In their energetic opposition to the Confucian doctrine, the Daoist thinkers set the life of the *dao* in sharp contrast to Confucian virtues of benevolence and righteousness. However, the idea of the *dao* is one thread of continuity throughout the various opposing branches within Confucian and Daoist philosophy. Historically, the *dao* is seen as the way of the sage emperors that the philosophers throughout the subsequent ages sought to recover.

The *dao* as an ethical concept connects human actions with the whole of the universe. The conception of the *dao* as the ultimate source of morality forms the common core of widely divergent schools of thought from Daoism, Confucianism, Mohism, and Buddhism to Neo-Confucianism. What are the main differences in the approaches to the *dao*? "The Way of Confucianism is primarily a system of government

56

and a moral code, mastered by study, thought and discipline."[6] The significance of the *dao* in Confucian political thought is related to the objectivity of laws. To follow the Way of Heaven is to follow objective laws that govern all human actions rather than the particular preferences determined by a partial judgment of a ruler. For Confucius, propriety, *li*, is not determined by convention or custom but aligned with the Way of Heaven. It resembles the idea of natural law. "For Taoists, man occupies the humble position of the tiny figures in Sung landscape paintings, and lives rightly by bringing himself into accord with a non-human Way which does not favour his ambitions, tastes and moral principles." [7]

Laozi

The Old Master as an Infant

I am like an infant who has not yet smiled (*Dao De Jing* 20).

The smile on the face of a tiger and the smile of an infant are alike: they both signify a satisfied desire or an anticipation of gratification. The image of the man of the *dao* is an infant without guile. The infant Laozi (ca. 604-531 BCE) who has not yet smiled exists in the realm of being free from the constraints of desire. He is not yet conscious of the gulf between the objects of desire and fulfillment.

The multitude of men look satisfied and eased; as if enjoying a full banquet, as if mounted on a tower in spring. I alone seem listless and still, my desires having as yet given no indication of their presence (*Dao De Jing* 20).

He stands apart from the multitude because his mode of life and thought are not the way of the world which is taken in by all that glitters on the surface. To be without an awareness of one's desires one would make no demands on the world for their gratification that generate conflicts of interest. The world is still an undifferentiated continuum without individuation. All beings are regarded equally. To perceive the whole of existence as the unity of all that exists is the moral goal Laozi sets forth in the *Dao De Jing*.

Legend surrounds the person of Laozi ("Old Master"): that he was born of a shooting star and that he was sixty years old when he was born and immediately began demonstrating filial piety by bowing to his parents. The historian Sima Qian (163-85 BCE) wrote of Laozi that "He strove towards self concealment and remaining without name." He is believed to have held the office of archivist at the court of Henan Province in the North. He was about fifty years older than Confucius, who was said to have visited him. The meeting between the two philosophers became established in the popular imagination as recorded in a tomb sculpture of the second century BCE, where Confucius is offering a pheasant to Laozi.

Laozi is believed to have set down his ideas in the *Dao De Jing* at the request of a border warden when he was on his way to retreat from the turbulent state. *Dao De Jing* is the foremost text of Daoist thought. It is a collection of aphorisms of varying length and subjects but unified under the theme of the book itself: the way and its power. It consists of eighty-one short stanzas. Each stanza expresses a philosophical reflection in bold summary, often drawing upon well-known proverbs to make a fresh point. The brief text of *Dao De Jing* has exerted a significant influence. Daoism was a favourite subject of study with many of the Han Emperors and their court. In the West since its first translation in 1788, the knowledge of Laozi's writing has become widespread. *Dao De Jing* (literally, "way – virtue – a work of standard authority, a classic") has been translated as *The Way and Its Power*, *The Book of Tao*, and *The Book of the Way*. It is the most frequently translated text of the classics of China.

The *Dao De Jing* is not a systematic philosophical treatise. Unlike the Confucian texts where lucidity prevails throughout, there is a penchant for paradoxes and contradictions. This is a distinct characteristic in the writings of the Daoist philosophers in which the intended meaning is shrouded in an elliptical expression inviting us to penetrate the cryptic constructions. The Daoist thinkers do not conceive the task of philosophy as showing the fly its way out of the fly-bottle but to entice and bewilder the mind and to take us into the labyrinth of philosophical imagination at the center of which we find the way to soar above with the *dao*.[8] If the text is on occasion less than transparent, it is not because there is a deliberately enigmatic hidden meaning to be deciphered or esoteric teaching open only to the initiates. The epigrammatic sayings in the *Dao De Jing* are frequently new renderings of inherited maxims whose initial clarity has been blurred by time. Laozi glides effortlessly from one stanza on the metaphysics of the *dao* to concrete objections against war, violence, and retributive justice.

In the Beginning is the Dao Beyond the Word

> All things are produced by the *dao* and nourished by its outflowing operation (*de*). They receive their forms according to the nature of each, and are completed according to the circumstances of their condition (*Dao De Jing* 51).

The *dao* is eternal and present everywhere. Laozi places the *dao* as being earlier than all else. What Laozi means by the *dao* has fascinated the philosophers in the East and the West. Does the world have a beginning? Laozi is occupied with a topic of metaphysical magnitude entrancing to philosophical minds from Plato to the present. What is the origin of the *dao* itself?

> I do not know whose son it is. It might appear to have been before God (*Dao De Jing* 4).

Laozi explains the *dao* as the source and the origin of all things. *De*, virtue, is the operation of the *dao* (*Dao De Jing* 51).

> Thus it is that the *dao* produces all things and nourishes them to their full growth, completes them, and sustains them. It produces them and makes no claim to the possession of them. It carries them through their processes and does not vaunt its ability in doing so; it brings them to maturity and exercises no control over them. This is called its mysterious operation.

Laozi's main concern is not the metaphysics of the *dao* but the *dao* as primarily a moral concept. When combined with *de*, virtue, the *dao* represents the essential ordering principle behind nature, society and the individual. The *dao* is analogous to *logos* as the principle which creates order. Seen in this light, the *dao* is demystified. The *dao*, as it constitutes the essence of an individual object, is the source of that object's *de*, its power, or virtue, or its ability to carry out its right function. *De* is a characteristic of the *dao* from the ethical point of view. There is a close parallel here between *de* and *areté*, virtue, in Greek philosophy: both refer to the excellence of a thing in fulfilling its function.

The *dao* itself is not perceivable by the senses or the mind. It is ineffable. *De* is the manifestation of the *dao* in the world. The *dao* and *de* are related as essence and function of an entity. The *dao* of a particular entity is that which makes it what it is: the necessary and sufficient conditions for the existence of the object. It is the essential characteristic without which the object would not be what it is but something else. The *de* of an individual object is its activity. The *dao* of man could be "featherless biped," and his *de*, rationality; the *dao* of man is his nature and his *de*, *ren* (love or benevolence). The way to comprehend what *dao* is through its effects or by observing the events in nature and human actions. By comprehending the *dao* in all things, the way in which things develop and function, we come to know the *de*, the power or the excellence of everything and what makes them function. The *dao* is the force of nature and *de* is how the *dao* operates in the world.

The Confucian sage is the man of *de* and the Daoist sage is the man of *dao*. *De* is not more difficult to comprehend than *dao* but more difficult to be in possession of as we are constantly straining to attain it. The ethics of the *dao* is concerned with how to live well. The *dao* of man is essentially a guide for living, not for a life of refinement, rites, and decorum, or as a noble savage in the wilderness as opposed to the civilized life of the court, but in harmony with all of nature. *De* from the perspective of Laozi and Zhuangzi is not an assiduously acquired virtue in accordance with a code of conduct but moral power to comprehend the *dao* and to act in unity with the way of reality.

The celebrated opening of the *Dao De Jing* announces the extent of the *dao* and the limitation of our effort in describing it as well as the unbridgeable gap between words and what they aim at (*Dao De Jing* 1).

> The *Dao* that can be expressed is not the eternal *Dao*.
> The name that can be named is not the eternal name.

The order of the *Dao De Jing* is logically coherent. It begins with the explication of the central concept, the *dao*. Laozi declares that by definition the *dao* is undefinable. Words describe objects and their properties by drawing boundaries around the objects. But if we have a process whose characteristics are infinite, like the *dao*, there are no finite sets of words that can fully capture its meaning. The *dao* cannot be circumscribed within the boundary of words and things. All that is written about it in the *Dao De Jing* and other texts are at best only approximations.

There is a tension in Laozi's effort to confront that which is beyond conceptual formulation and beyond description in words. On the one hand, *Dao De Jing* begins with the observation about how the *dao* is beyond language, beyond full comprehension and full realization in actions. On the other hand, throughout the entire *Dao De Jing* Laozi's explanation of what constitutes reality, knowledge, and values directly invokes our understanding of the *dao* and acting in accordance with the knowledge of the *dao*.

The relation between language and reality is at the foreground of *Dao De Jing*. The *dao* is beyond language in this sense. All efforts to understand the *dao* through language belong in the human world. But what there is to be known, all that there ever was and will be, extends beyond the human world, beyond the human mind. If it cannot be spoken of is it knowable? Words at best can lead to knowledge by description but not knowledge by acquaintance. The *Dao De Jing* abounds in positive characterization of the *dao*. It is unnamable but present in all things. The *dao* of Laozi is not transcendent but immanent. It can only be apprehended in its infinitely multiple aspects.

> Painfully giving it a name I call it "great."
> Great: that means "always in motion" …
> Thus *dao* is great, heaven is great, earth is great,
> and man too is great.
> There are in space four Great Ones,
> and man is one of them (*Dao De Jing* 25).

The *dao*, as the totality of all things, is indescribably great. To give it a precise name is to do injustice to its immensity. From the point of view of "the *dao* of Heaven" man is a microcosm.

Laozi is frequently regarded as a quietist urging renunciation of the world and finding consolation in solipsistic introspection. Daoism is taken as insisting that all values have only subjective and relative standards. Read in isolation there are passages from the *Dao De Jing* which might lead to such an interpretation. However, the whole point of Daoism is that there is a single underlying unity, the *dao* of all things. The *dao* is also the ultimate standard of truth in all things. All actions are measured in the light of conformity with it.

> Man conforms to earth.
> Earth conforms to heaven.
> Heaven conforms to *dao*.
> *Dao* conforms to itself (*Dao De Jing* 25).

Since there is also one moral way for all, the way of the sage who lives in accordance with the *dao*, and one supreme good, the knowledge of the *dao* and life according to the *dao*, Daoism is an affirmation of the ethical life based on the most comprehensive knowledge of reality.

To Know the Dao We Must Renounce Learning

When we renounce learning we have no troubles.

As an archivist of the royal library Laozi must have accumulated considerable learning he could afford to divest (*Dao De Jing* 19). Laozi seems to point to the antithesis of the Confucian love of learning. There appears to be much less searching and questioning regarding the nature of reality and our capacity to attain wisdom and virtue than in Confucius. In pronouncing a set of theses with certainty and not constantly engaging in rational debate, the text of *Dao De Jing* might appear to be less inviting as a philosophical investigation than the *Analects*. However, the ideas Laozi grapples with are profoundly philosophical and his speculations plunge us into the depth of philosophical inquiry. Laozi criticizes the excessive scholasticism of his day, which was not efficacious in changing the world for the better. The intent of the *Dao De Jing* is frankly didactic. For a text which calls for renouncing all learning, it insists on a more direct pedagogical approach and active strategy of learning than the *Analects*. Laozi urges that we seek knowledge until we reach the limit of our knowledge (*Dao De Jing* 71).

> To know non-knowledge is the highest good. Not to know what knowledge is is a kind of suffering. Only if one suffers from this suffering does one become free from suffering.

To know that we do not possess complete knowledge is the beginning of true knowledge – Socrates would concur with Laozi.

The suggestiveness of Laozi's remarks that the knowledge of *dao* is beyond language and is accompanied by silence since words cannot adequately express it has led to interpretations of Laozi and the Daoists as adherents of mysticism in contrast to the rational Confucians.[9] If by mysticism what is meant is a direct insight into depths as yet unspoken then Daoism is mystical.[10] But the purpose of philosophy is to rationalize mysticism: not by explaining it away, but to relate it to knowledge and experience without appealing to a special intuition to apprehend the realm of reality beyond ordinary experience. If Laozi had made the inexplicability of the *dao* the basis of his philosophy there would be more justification for attributing a mystical attitude to him. The *dao* is not a mystical notion in the sense of being directly grasped in an inspired moment of revelation or in union with the supernatural. Throughout the text of *Dao De Jing*, there is a persistent effort to explain the nature and working of the *dao* in terms of concrete and tangible experience. The explanations of the *dao* as a metaphysical and an ethical concept are linked with ordinary perceptions. Even when knowledge and excessive reliance on book learning are criticized by Laozi and Zhuangzi – as they are seen to stifle spontaneity and freedom of thought – it is by argumentation and not by jettisoning reason in favour of mystical insight that the man of the *dao* is upheld as the paradigm of virtue to be emulated.

Religious and philosophical Daoism share the desire to be completely free of physical constraints and limitations. Religious Daoism takes this impulse to develop techniques to prolong life by controlling the physical movements of the body. This aspect of religious Daoism, not the ideas of Laozi or Zhuangzi, is what the later Neo-Confucian philosophers criticize forcefully. Approaching the *dao* philosophically, the same impetus culminates in moral autonomy. In the *Dao De Jing* there are remarks about lasting forever, and in the *Zhuangzi* commentary regarding the control of breath reminiscent of the Yoga practices in India. But they do not occupy a central place in the philosophy of Laozi and Zhuangzi. On the contrary, it is the way of the sage not to cling to life.

> Heaven is long enduring and earth continues long. The reason why heaven and earth are able to endure and continue thus long is because they do not live of or for themselves. This is how they are able to continue and endure (*Dao De Jing* 7).

The promise of eternal life held out by religions of the West has not exerted the equivalent fascination among the philosophers in China.

Wisdom consists in self-knowledge and true strength consists in self- discipline.

> Whosoever knows others is clever; whosoever knows himself is wise. Whosoever conquers others has force; whosoever conquers himself is strong (*Dao De Jing* 33).

Laozi advocates action not discourse (*Dao De Jing* 23):

> Use words sparingly, then all things will fall into place ...

> If you set about your work with the *dao*
> You will be at one in *dao* with those who have *dao*,
> At one in life with those who have life,
> At one in poverty with those who are poor.
> If you are at one with them in *dao*
> Those who have *dao* will come to meet you gladly.

The aim of working with the *dao* is to be at one with all forms of life.

The Wisdom of the Sage in Action

> Weapons are instruments of bad omen: all beings, I believe, loathe them. Therefore, whosoever has the true *dao* does not want to know about them.

> Weapons are instruments of bad omen, not the instruments of the noble. He uses them only when he cannot help it. Quietness and peace are his highest values. He gains victory but he does not rejoice in it. Whosoever would rejoice in it would, in fact, rejoice in the murder of men. Whosoever would rejoice in the murder of men cannot achieve his goal in the world ... He who has killed a multitude of men should weep for them with the bitterest grief (*Dao De Jing* 31).[11]

The *Dao De Jing* is concerned with practical ethics – a subject as much in urgent need of philosophical reflection in the present as it was in Laozi's time. In Daoist thought it is taken as being self-evident that violence of any kind is contrary to the principle of *dao* which acts through its specific *de*, virtue. Laozi argues that putting people to death as a punishment for crimes does not work as a deterrent. When people are driven to desperation they do not fear death and it inevitably brings harmful consequences upon those who destroy lives to achieve their ends (*Dao De Jing* 74).

> If people do not fear death, how can one frighten them with death? But if I keep the people constantly in fear of death and if someone does strange things, should I seize him and kill him? Who dares do this? There is always a power of death that kills. To kill instead of leaving killing to this power of death is as if one wanted to use the axe oneself instead of leaving it to the carpenter. Whosoever would use the axe instead of leaving it to

the carpenter shall rarely get away without injuring his hand.

We may concede that the threat and the infliction of violent punishment make people prudent but not moral and incite impulses of retaliation. But since neither the individuals nor governments have yet succeeded in eliminating the causes of harmful actions what is the just way to remedy the ills of society? Laozi urges that we work to eliminate exploitation and poverty which cause crime (*Dao De Jing* 19).

> If we could renounce our artful contrivances and discard our scheming for gain, there would be neither thieves nor robbers.

Laozi calls for equality and not preferential treatment of people and discouraging the tendency to accumulate property (*Dao De Jing* 3).

> By not preferring the competent one brings about that people do not quarrel. By not treasuring precious things one brings about that people do not steal. By not displaying desirable things one brings about that people's hearts are not confused.

The way to lead people is not to put them to death for wrong actions but to reform the government.

> When the people go hungry, this comes from too much tax being devoured by the high and mighty ... When the people take death too lightly, this comes from life's abundance being sought too greedily by the high and mighty (*Dao De Jing* 75).

Laozi considers the best government to be one of least interference, which allows people to be free.

> If a great ruler rules, the people hardly know that he exists. Lesser men are loved and praised, still lesser ones are feared, and still lesser ones are despised. How thoughtful one must be in what is said. When the work was done [by the great ruler] all people think, "We are free" (*Dao De Jing* 17).

How simple is what Laozi proposes to put into action?

> My words are very easy to understand, and easy to carry out.

Why isn't everyone a Daoist sage then? Laozi replies in paradoxical terms (*Dao De Jing* 70).

> But no one on earth can understand them nor carry them out.
> Words have an ancestor. Deeds have a lord.
> Because they are not understood I am not understood.

The sage does not throw pearls of wisdom to the indifferent multitude.

> It is precisely in being so rarely understood that my value rests.
> Therefore the sage walks in haircloth but in his bosom he guards a jewel (*Dao De Jing* 70).

What is the value of *not* understanding what the *dao* is? The *dao*, in *not* being easily accessible and understood, arouses our fascination for the difficult, deepening our desire to seek to discover the laws underlying the transformation of things in the universe so that by knowing them we may arrive at a pattern of life in harmony with all things. Laozi invites us to delve deeper to seek ways of correcting the defects of the world. That which is common practice and general knowledge has little value in making things better as it does not stimulate our thinking and lead us to critically examine the established patterns of conduct. Does the sage have a special instinct or intuition to grasp the *dao*? The source of his wisdom, the knowledge of the *dao*, is not in his own mind but in listening to the people.

> The sage has no invariable mind of his own; he makes the mind of the people his mind (*Dao De Jing* 49).

> If we could renounce our sageness and discard our wisdom, it would be better for the people a hundredfold (*Dao De Jing* 19).

What is gained by living in the *dao*? Not blessedness or serenity but the possession of the ability to do good in the world. Laozi expounds:

> Whosoever holds fast to the great primal image [of the invisible *dao*] to him the world will come ... Music and allurement will make the wanderer linger for a moment. *Dao* seems insipid and seems not worth being looked at or listened to but its use is inexhaustible (*Dao De Jing* 35).

The explication of the *dao* as "the whole world" and having inexhaustible use leads us to conclude that it is the supreme good in the world. What is this supreme good? This passage has the title of *"Ren De,"* "the Virtue of Love." The *dao* is explained by *de ren*, the power to bring about beneficial consequences. The virtue of love is unlike what readily pleases the senses but for the good of the world its efficacy is boundless.[12]

The *Dao De Jing* is intent on making transparent "what you would want to do if you had the wisdom of the sage."[13]

> The *dao* occupies the place of the highest excellence not by seeking to extinguish all by its dazzling brilliance but by seeking the low place spurned by men.

The *dao* of Laozi is symbolized by the quietly flowing water which overcomes all in time by steadfastly enduring.

> The highest excellence is like water. The excellence of water appears in its benefiting all things, and in its occupying, without striving, the low place which all men dislike. Hence [its way] is near to the *dao* (*Dao De Jing* 8).

Water is the most ubiquitous symbol of the *dao*. The sage's way is to be like water which is higher than all else because it does not seek to be high but low (*Dao De Jing* 20).

> Ordinary men look bright and intelligent, while I alone seem to be benighted. They look full of discrimination, while I alone am dull and confused. I seem to be carried about as on the sea, drifting as if I had nowhere to rest. All men have their spheres of action, while I alone seem dull and incapable, like a rude borderer. I alone am different from other men.[14]

Being without ambition for power and influence and not dependent on the recognition of the world, one charts the course as on an open sea. But can this be a happy life? In Laozi there is an element of intellectual asceticism absent in the Confucian tradition. While the *Analects* is a record of Confucius' discourse as he is engaged in a continuous dialogue with close disciples, the *Dao De Jing* is "the soul's dialogue with itself."[15] From restless wandering and an awareness of confusion and doubt, clarity may emerge. The Daoist adept, like the Cheshire cat in

Alice in Wonderland, will console us, "If you do not know the way, the road will get you there." Through the persona of the sage, humble in haircloth and appearing to be clueless but nonetheless a sage by all measures of heaven, earth, and man, Laozi confidently sets forth the way of the sage in resounding declamatory tones. To have no fixed abode is to be completely free of attachment and possessions. One who can survive this way knows his own capacity and the meaning of his own life without the trappings and the props of conventional existence. Laozi paves the way to the beginning of philosophical inquiry.

> He does not want to shine, therefore will he be enlightened. He does not want to be anything for himself, therefore he becomes resplendent. He does not lay claim to glory, therefore he accomplishes his works. He does not seek excellence therefore he will be exalted. Because he does not engage in strife no one can cause strife for him (*Dao De Jing* 22).

The noblest action is to put another before us.[16] The sage does not seek to dazzle the world with his brilliance but remains in the unlit low place. Without applause or censure, the Daoist sage may be able to act more effectively, directly, and independently since being unnoticed he is not assisted or hindered. Why should an unnoticed act of kindness be of more value than a well-publicized action? If the moral worth of an action is judged from its consequences only, whether I rush to save a child who has fallen in the well having made sure that the entire village has gathered to witness my heroic deed or no one is watching should not make any difference. But if we seek to inculcate moral traits and develop moral character, this emphasis on the intentions and the purposes of actions is relevant. Being free of the desire for fame and profit characterizes not only Laozi's sage. We recall that Confucius also believes it to be a mark of the moral person to be without the motive of profit. In the Judaic tradition Laozi's sage would also be praised insofar as anonymous acts of charity have a higher moral value.

For Laozi it is not through vigorous inculcation of the virtues of benevolence and righteousness but by returning to our original goodness that filial piety and kindness are established (*Dao De Jing* 19).

> If we could renounce our benevolence and discard our righteousness, the people would again become filial and kindly.

It is when the natural way of being is lost and decadence sets in that there is much talk about morality and duty. Laozi upholds the same values of filial piety and kindness as in the Confucian tradition but the way of attaining these virtues is different.

It is with the arrival of Zhuangzi (Chuang Tzu, ca. 369-286 BCE) that the ideas of Laozi become imbued with a deeper philosophical significance. With Laozi, Zhuangzi is regarded as the founder of Daoism as a philosophical school. In advocating moral autonomy and a critical re-examination of the established authorities of learning and conventional values, Zhuangzi goes further than Laozi in provoking us to engage in the "transvaluation of all values".[17]

Zhuangzi

Leaping into the Boundless

> Forget the passage of time. Forget the differences. Leap into the boundless and make it your home (*Zhuangzi* 2, Legge I. 196).[18]

Going beyond the trajectory of the *dao* outlined by Laozi, we find ourselves with Zhuangzi leaping into the boundless – What happens when we leap into the boundless?

> Heaven and earth come into being with me together, and with me, all things are one (*Zhuangzi* 2).

We find ourselves at the beginning of all existence.[19] What awaits us is not an abyss but the infinity of existence. I discover that I exist not as an isolated individual but as an integral part of all things in the universe. Living in the *dao* begins with overcoming the boundaries of time and place and exploring the uncharted terrain. We question everything and dare to go beyond the traditions of ceremony, ritual, piety, and virtue.

> In his inquiries, he must not set to himself any limits, and yet he cannot be without a limit. Now ascending, now descending, then slipping from the grasp, the *dao* is yet a reality, unchanged now as it is in antiquity, and always without defect: – may it not be called what is capable of the greatest display and expansion? Why should we not inquire into it? Why should we be perplexed about it? With what does not perplex let us explain what per-

plexes, till we cease to be perplexed. So may we arrive at a great freedom from all perplexity! (*Zhuangzi* 24, Legge II. 113).

Aspirants of the *dao* leap into the boundless, you have nothing to lose but your inhibitions! You have freedom and clarity to gain. Investigate everything around you and within you without presuppositions and preconceptions to abide in the infinite. Unless we go as far as being ready to plunge into the precipice we have not really decided for ourselves what makes life worth living. The *dao* of Zhuangzi holds out for us infinite possibilities.

Zhuangzi is the most original of the philosophical minds in China. Zhuangzi's ideas enliven the philosophical imagination making it possible for us to examine our received ideas from a fresh threshold setting us free from the inherited traditions and the orthodoxy of the moment. With a poetic vision, Zhuangzi presents the entire universe of the *dao* from the minute to the most grand and seeks to comprehend the cause of all things (*Zhuangzi* 14, Legge I. 345). The impression we receive from Zhuangzi's writings is that he was a person of an active and ardent temperament. He is constantly in a state of wonder about the nature of all things and phenomena, seeking to know the ultimate reality underlying constantly changing appearance, and engaged in philosophical debates on various topics with considerable zeal. He is not an adherent of disinterested withdrawal from the affairs of the world, but an impassioned advocate of change, urging the rulers to rise up to the task of governing the state to bring benefit to the people.

The *Book of Zhuangzi* has been applauded as "one of the most entertaining as well as one of the profoundest books in the world."[20] The intense vitality and the originality of the ideas set it apart from the venerable theories of the sage philosophers and led the scholars in the West to hail the writings of Zhuangzi as a work of genius. The *Book of Zhuangzi* consists of thirty-three sections. Zhuangzi's main ideas are found in the first seven sections. These "inner books" are attributed to Zhuangzi. The remaining "outer books" are reputed to be compilations of his followers and disciples and are subsidiary and supplementary. There is a persistent inquiry regarding a wide range of subjects in metaphysics, epistemology, ethics, political philosophy, and philosophy of mind. Zhuangzi's writings reflect a deep awareness of the fundamental problems of philosophy: the nature of reality, the certainty of knowledge, the meaning of life, the just state, and the nature of the mind. He was known for his vast erudition and recognized as a formidable critic of the philosophy of the classical period. The *Historical*

Records states: "His literary and dialectical skill was such that the best scholars of the age were unable to refute his destructive criticism of the Confucian and the Mohist schools. His teachings were like an overwhelming flood which spreads unchecked according to its own will."[21]

There is a rapier's thrust in his ruthless criticism of all doctrines from the Confucian and the Mohist schools to the Logicians. He is at times not without a certain amount of rhetorical flourish when he takes up the arguments of the disputers of the world. But life is no argument, and as he is interested in capturing the living moment of the *dao*, he rarely resorts to argument to persuade. He quickens our thinking with juxtapositions of allegories, paradoxes, and startling analogies. There is a prevailing impression that Daoism is against the intellect, reason and knowledge. Some selected passages from Laozi and Zhuangzi do give this impression. But to the extent that they criticize certain theories, they also engage in rational debate and present a Daoist theory since, as Aristotle observed, in order to criticize theories we need to theorize. Zhuangzi does not rely on the power of anecdote to produce a conviction. Poetry when it consists of carefully constructed inferences is an expression of philosophical thought. To come upon the writing of Zhuangzi after Confucian thinkers may be compared to the emerging of the Romantic movement from the Enlightenment. "The intellectual dryness of the Enlightenment" is, to a certain extent, also a part of Confucian tradition with its emphasis on the observation of rites, and fulfillment of political and personal duty. Zhuangzi's writings have the spontaneity of an immediate response even as he relates a distant and imagined event. Zhuangzi's influence, not only as a thinker but as a poet, on the philosophy and literature of China has been profound: "he is someone with an absolutely fearless eye."[22] His inventiveness parallels Plato's imagination.

The most imaginative and metaphorical expressions in the *Dao De Jing* about the power of the *dao* are tame, compared with the language of Zhuangzi (Legge I. 128). Zhuangzi amplifies the depiction of the *dao* in a vivid and daring language. The *dao* is described as "the store of light." The virtue of the possessor of the *dao* will "exceed all suns"(Legge I. 190). The accomplished Daoist is a "spirit who covers himself with light as with a garment, who stretches out the heavens as a curtain, who lays the beams of his chambers in the waters, who makes the clouds his chariot, who walks on the wings of the wind," and "who inhabits eternity" (Legge I. 128).

Zhuangzi adds a completely new dimension to the *dao*. The *dao* of Laozi is exalted as *logos*, a guiding principle of morality and all that

71

exists. The *dao* of Zhuangzi is limitless. In the *Dao De Jing* water as the symbol of the *dao* was a constantly abiding force, always seeking the lowest place. Zhuangzi shows the vast expanse of a great ocean as the symbol of the *dao* (*Zhuangzi* 17). For Laozi the *dao*, as the origin of all things, is distant and remote. It is not fully comprehensible in thought or directly intuited but known only to the sage. Emptiness, vacancy, and tranquility are its characteristics. The *dao* of Laozi is the stillness of being. The *dao* of Zhuangzi is full of the activity of becoming. The *dao* is the movement and transformation in all things. It is the ceaseless revolution of the heavens, the vast expanse of the sea, the torrential autumn floods, the rising wind, and the bud as it opens silently (Legge I. 345).

Zhuangzi explains that the concept of the *dao* is a metaphor for the process of reality underlying all phenomena and thought beyond the limit of silence.

> The name *dao* is a metaphor, used for the purpose of description.

> The *dao* is the extreme to which things conduct us. Neither speech nor silence is sufficient to cover the notion of it. Neither by speech nor by silence can our thoughts about it have their highest expression (Legge II. 130).

The *dao*, because it is conceived in the broadest possible terms, is an infinitely expandable concept. In Zhuangzi's conception of the *dao* as the beginning of all things there is no connection to a divine being creating the universe. Zhuangzi's view that there is "no indication of the existence" of a deity has exerted a profound influence and fortified the long tradition of agnosticism in the philosophical thought of China.[23] Regarding the point of original existence Zhuangzi observes that we do not yet know the first or the final cause or the ultimate nature of reality (Legge II. 129-130).

> "Some one caused it." "No one did it." We are thus debating about things and the end is that we shall find we are in error.

> When I look for their origin, it goes back into infinity. When I look for their end, it proceeds without termination.

Looking at all things from the standpoint of an original non-existence

Zhuangzi states the possible alternatives.

> Some held that at first there was not anything. Others held that there was something but without any boundary (Legge I. 185).

> There was a beginning. There was a beginning before that beginning. There was a beginning previous to that beginning before there was the beginning (Legge II. 187).

Whether we assume that there was something in the beginning or nothing, we are equally landed in contradiction and absurdity.

> There was existence; there had been no existence. There was no existence before the beginning of that no existence. There was no existence previous to the no existence before there was the beginning of the no existence. If suddenly there was non-existence, we do not know whether it was really anything existing, or really not existing. Now I have said what I have said, but I do not know whether what I have said be really anything to the point or not (Legge I. 187).

From this maze of words Zhuangzi concludes "Let us abjure such a procedure." To go beyond the evidence and to maintain that we have arrived at truth by sheer argumentation is to claim to have knowledge without justification. But how is the truth to be determined between two opposing views? "If we would decide on their several affirmation and denials, no plan is like bringing the proper light of the mind to bear on them." Any thesis can be affirmed or denied. "The disputants now affirm and now deny; now deny and now affirm." The usual method of discrediting the view which is criticized is to show that it leads to contradiction. But the point of view that I take to examine the opposing view is necessarily limited as I can only look at the subject from my perspective. Zhuangzi stresses the impossibility of arriving at truth through disputation (Legge I. 182).

> All subjects may be looked at from two points of view – from this and from that. If I look at a thing from another's point of view, I do not see it; only as I know it myself, I do know it.

"Hence we have the saying, 'Disputation is a proof of not seeing clearly' " (Legge I. 189). We frequently fail to recognize that the individual perspective is at best only a partial perspective. To insist on the exclusive truth of one individual perspective, in Zhuangzi's view, is to be like the frog in the confines of the well who judges the sky to be as it is seen from the opening of the well. The sage does not argue in vindication of his judgements: he "argues without the form of arguments ... while men generally state theirs argumentatively, to show them to others" (Legge I. 189). Disputation and argumentation hinder active search of the *dao* which calls for a direct engagement of the individual in action. If we do not affirm or deny how do we ascertain the correctness of our beliefs and prove the falsehood of the contrary view?

> Let us give up our devotion to our own views, and occupy ourselves with the ordinary view. These ordinary views are grounded on the use of things. The study of that use leads to the comprehensive judgment, and that judgment secures the success of the inquiry. That success gained we are near to the object of our search, and there we stop. When we stop, and yet we do not know how it is so, we have what is called the *dao* (Legge I. 184).

Zhuangzi emphasizes that knowledge is not acquired by producing concurrence through conjectures and refutations but consists in adopting a common point of view. Setting aside subjective impressions and beliefs we begin with the commonly shared starting point which is based on the actual use of things. Truth is not established by winning an argument or reaching a consensus among the disputants but by considering things from their actual use and regarding them from the point of view of how things correspond to states of affairs and their correlation to other things.

How do we go beyond the perspectival limitations of our judgments?

> The sagely man brings together a dispute in its affirmations and denials, and rests in the equal fashion of Heaven. Both sides of the question are admissible (Legge I. 185).

Zhuangzi's proposal is that we find a broader perspective which incorporates both the thesis and its antithesis (Legge I. 184). The moral implication of elimination of distinctions is the elimination of partiality. But what is gained by forgetting all distinctions? The readiness to embrace the *dao* of love.

The Great Dao of Highest Love

> Tang, the ruler of Shang, asked Zhuangzi about love. Zhuangzi replied, "Tigers and wolves have love. ... The old and the young among them are attached to one another and that definitely can be described as love" (*Zhuangzi* 14, Legge I. 346)

It may be that the way of love is not a unique human virtue but found even among tigers and wolves. But surely there is *some* difference in the love between the animals of the wild and human beings? Is there no higher form of love than being attached to one another?

> Tang: May I ask what the highest love is?
> Zhuangzi: The highest love is without attachment.
> Tang: I have heard that without attachment there is no affection and without affection there is no filial piety. Is it then admissible to claim that the highest love knows no filial piety?
> Zhuangzi: Not so! Highest love is something that is incomparably high. The concept of filial piety is insufficient to describe it. What I mean is not that filial piety is too broad but that it does not go far enough.[24]

The objection against Confucian love has always been that it is too demanding: Confucius expounds filial piety as requiring unconditional love. Zhuangzi's conception of love is even more demanding than this. Zhuangzi argues that filial piety does not go far enough. Loving one's family, relations, and friends is only partial love – loving persons who stand in certain contingent relations to us. Challenging the lofty ideals of benevolence and righteousness, Zhuangzi is searching for a more enduring basis of values applicable to all without distinctions. The highest love is love without attachment. Are we ready for the great *dao* of comprehensive love?

> Great *Dao* has no name. Great speech does not say anything. Great love is not humane. Great modesty is not yielding. Great courage does not injure. *Dao* that is displayed is not the *Dao*. Speech that argues is futile. Love that is specially attached to someone or something will not be comprehensive. Modesty that is too apparent is not real. Courage that injures the nature of things will not succeed (*Zhuangzi* 2).

True modesty does not call attention to itself and real courage does not consist in inflicting injury. Wide and deep love is not attachment to an individual person or an object. It is in the *dao* of love that the most significant difference between Confucius and Zhuangzi emerges. Confucius extended *ren* as a virtue of all human beings. In Zhuangzi *ren* is extended beyond the human realm. What Zhuangzi seeks is knowledge beyond the confines of language, and modesty, courage, and love that are not exhaustible in temporal manifestations.

Where then is the highest love to be found? It is found in the activity of the man of the *dao* who comprehends that he is connected to all beings (Legge II. 115).

> The sage comprehends the connection between himself and others, and how they all go to constitute him of one body with them, and he does not know how it is so; – he naturally does so.

A true man of love loves naturally and not because he is consciously fulfilling any specific duty of filial piety or benevolence. Of what use is sage's love? (Legge I. 293-4)

> He who will administer the government of the world honouring it as he honours his own person, may have that government committed to him, and he who will administer it loving it as he loves his own person may have it entrusted him.

In Confucian ethics the rulers are to love the people as parents love their children. Zhuangzi goes further. Going beyond the politics of love only those who are committed to honouring and loving the people as they honour and love their own persons can be entrusted with the government of the world. But would such love be desirable? Consider what rival accounts of love are available. Insofar as all love aspires to expand the range of love, the full development of our loves can be seen as straining toward Zhuangzi's love without limitations. Zhuangzi's highest love is desirable if we value being freed of self-love and attachment. Would such love be possible? (Legge I. 183-4)

> A path is formed by constant treading on the ground. A thing is called by its name through constant application of the name.

Zhuangzi would reply that just as a road becomes a road because we walk on it, things become what they are to us because of our actions.

With all men he rejoices in the fellowship of the *dao* and preserves it in himself (Legge II. 115).

His source of joy has no end. His love of others never has an end (Legge II. 116).

The man of the *dao* is a universal lover of all beings. Loving all beings equally, freely and spontaneously, how can his happiness not be but deep and wide? In the *Phaedrus*, Socrates speaks of love as "a divine release of the soul from the yoke of custom and convention." But how is it possible not to be capricious in our love? Zhuangzi describes how having equal regard for all things allows us to be capacious and impartial in our love. Equal regard from the moral point of view is not based on the possession of identical properties. Indeed to regard all equally by looking beyond the differences is to adopt the point of view of love. The moral significance of Zhuangzi's highest love consists in paving the way to completely impartial love and the recognition of equality and freedom of all.

Equality

If we take a stalk of grain and a large pillar, a loathsome man and a beauty, things large and things insecure, things crafty and things strange, they may in the light of the *dao* all be reduced to the same category (Legge I. 184).

Equality of all things is the basis of Zhuangzi's ethics. In what sense are different things equal? Looking at the *dao* present in each object, the *dao* of the individual is its essence and its function. All things unfold and develop according to their individual essence. Each is activated by its own way. Individual objects considered in isolation have their distinct characteristics but from the point of the view of the *dao* of Heaven all belong to the same category. We are accustomed to distinguishing between what is different not only in our morals but also in our knowledge which begins with the individuation of distinct objects and their properties. The identity of indiscernibles – that two things which are indistinguishable with respect to all properties are to be considered identical – is a law of identity in logic but not a basis for a principle of morality. Zhuangzi discovers the *dao* which is present in all things, from the most simple to the most complex, from the highest to

the lowest and from the sublime to the mundane. To illustrate the *dao*
Zhuangzi draws our attention to the world of experience and not that of
abstract thought.

> The *dao* does not exhaust itself in what is greatest, nor is it ever
> absent from what is least; and therefore it is to be found com-
> plete and diffused in all things (Legge I. 342).

Zhuangzi gives a concrete meaning to the *dao* as the underlying principle of reality or being present in all things.

When we conceive of the *dao* in the world of action, it is how an
individual is connected or situated in relation to everything else. When
we do away with distinctions the conclusion is not that everything is
relative. Zhuangzi is frequently regarded as an adherent of relativism –
that all knowledge and values are relative to circumstances and there
are no universally applicable standards. But this is to overlook the
overarching concept of the *dao* as the unifying perspective of all divergent paths. Actions are determined not by subjective standards but
"objective situations to which we should adjust ourselves with the immediacy of the shadow adjusting itself to the moving body", "or as
water to the shape of a container."[25] For Zhuangzi what is appropriate
in action is not determined by pre-established patterns of relations or by
common aims and methods but understanding that while varying circumstances call for different courses of action, only by seeking to discern the interrelation among all things can we know the totality, the
dao. The point of eliminating distinctions is to establish the unity of all
things. There is one unified view: everything is endowed with the *dao*.

In the eyes of the true man of the *dao*, the concepts and practices of
propriety fabricate distinctions where there should be none. Zhuangzi's
objection to "the practice of ceremonies" is that "men began to be separated from one another" (Legge I. 278). From the point of view of the
dao of man – the way in which human beings are to live – there can be
no distinction between, as Zhuangzi forcefully puts it, the robber and
the ruler.

> Here is one who steals a hook (for his girdle) and he is put to
> death for it. Here is another who steals a state and he becomes a
> prince. But it is at the gates of the princes that we find benevo-
> lence and righteousness professed (Legge I. 285).

Whether in ancient China or in ancient Rome empires were built by the same means. "What are empires but great robberies?"(Augustine)

> Thieves who steal from private citizens spend their lives in bonds and chains; thieves who steal form public funds spend theirs in gold and purple (Cato).

> Many commit the same crime and face a different fate: that man gets the cross, this one the crown (Juvenal).

Zhuangzi criticizes the use to which the doctrines of the scholars are put to sanctify the conduct of unjust rulers. "When sages are born great robbers arise" (Legge I. 284). "When learned men appeared, the good ones went missing" (Seneca). Zhuangzi criticizes the "versatility shown in artful deceptions" and the ingenious discussions of the sophists which leave the people perplexed and lead to "great confusion and disorder" (Legge I. 289). He is unsparing in his criticism of "the error of sagely men."

> If an end were put to sageness and wisdom put away, the great robbers would cease to arise (Legge I. 286).

Granted that Zhuangzi's criticism is aimed at the apologists who justify aggression and plunder which were at the basis of political power, isn't it going too far to disparage all learning and claim that scholars are no better than robbers? The robbers who cause harm to material goods are acting from greed but those who affect learning are afflicted by deeper corruption of the good of the intellect.[26] What we praise in the scholar – intelligence, perseverance and determination – are also the virtues possessed by the robber. If we see that even the robbers have commendable qualities we are more likely to succeed in transforming them to become men of *dao* rather than branding them as manifestations of evil or annihilating their humanity. Zhuangzi frequently commends those who are deemed to be outcasts and ignoble as aspirants of the *dao*.

In equating the scholar and the prince with the robber Zhuangzi is questioning the standard by which actions are evaluated. Zhuangzi's point is not that there are no distinctions between right and wrong conduct but that we must discard the inequality of prevailing standards to recognize that what is moral for one is moral for all. Zhuangzi traces the causes of theft to the institution of rank and property.[27] "If jade were put away and pearls broken to bits, the small thieves would not appear" (Legge I. 286). If all were to cultivate the land side by side

79

there would be no alienated labour and class distinctions between princes and paupers. Zhuangzi urges that we do away with the hierarchy of moral standards established by social conventions. But is it possible or desirable to do away with all distinctions? What would happen to personal and social relations which are based on distinctions? Zhuangzi challenges us to examine the basis of our claims regarding the distinctions among things and inquires, "How have they become so?" He argues that conventional distinctions are based on custom and habitual usage which may be arbitrary: "They have become so because people say they are so" (*Zhuangzi* 2). Zhuangzi searches for foundations of morality beyond events of history or social institutions circumscribed by particular individual human relations.

Zhuangzi affirms the unity of all life in the universe in the chapter titled, "The Equality of Things." (Thirteen hundred years later these very same ideas and words became the foundation of Neo-Confucian ethics.[28]) From the point of view of Dao of Heaven all things are the same. The point of view of the *dao* is to arrive at unity and not separation.

> All things may be comprehended in their unity. It is only the far reaching in thought that know how to comprehend them in this unity (Legge I. 184).

The beginning of ethics is an awareness that there is a point of view from which the well-being and interests of others are taken into consideration in all our actions.

Freedom

> Once Zhuangzi was fishing by the river when the king sent two great officers with the invitation, "I wish to trouble you with the charge of all within my territories." Zhuangzi without turning round said, "I have heard that there is a three thousand year old tortoise shell the king keeps in his ancestral temple. Was it better for the tortoise to die, and to leave its shell to be venerated? Or would it have been better for it to live and keep on dragging its tail through the mud?" The two officers said, "It would have been better for it to live and draw its tail after it over the mud." Zhuangzi replied, "Go your ways. I will keep on drawing my tail after me through the mud" (Legge I. 390).

As a defender of individual freedom against the imposition of authority and tradition, Zhuangzi is unparalleled. On another occasion in response to an offer from a ruler, Zhuangzi responds: "Go away quickly, and do not soil me with your presence. I prefer the enjoyment of my own free will." Zhuangzi values freedom, "abiding alone" and "enjoying oneself in the illimitable" more highly than honour, political power or wealth (Legge I. 300). What does this enjoyment consist in? The variety of freedom Zhuangzi defends can be initially characterized as a negative conception of liberty – the absence of external obstacles or impediments, a subject of significant debate in contemporary political thought.[29]

The Confucian criticism of Zhuangzi's endorsement of freedom might take the following line. Poverty may be preferable to prosperity from the point of freedom if we agree that to receive a favour is to sell your liberty and "a traveler with empty pockets can whistle in a robber's face" (Juvenal). But we also need to recognize that we ought to take responsibility for the consequences of exercising freedom. Freedom for human beings as ethical beings may be different from freedom for natural beings. The tortoise is free to drag its tail in the mud but the angler when called to rescue the drowning empire or a sister-in-law (as in Mencius' illustration) ought to weigh the benefits of the exercise of freedom with moral obligation to others and to society. Only when people are committed to preserve the order within the society can there be freedom for individuals.

Even if we were to regard any constraint as an evil to be avoided from the standpoint of upholding individual freedom as an absolute value, freedom consists in more than following wherever our nature takes us. When we are following our inclinations without rational reflection and real knowledge of genuine alternatives for actions we cannot be said to be free. We do not make people free by leaving them alone. We need to provide moral guidelines by which people can make rational choices. Freedom in the active sense consists in more than the absence of external constraints or following one's inclinations. Personal and political freedom consist in being able to make decisions based on the knowledge of real alternatives for which our choices can have an effect in bringing about the desired consequences. To be free is to possess the ability to choose among alternative courses of actions. In this sense negative freedom is freedom only in a restricted sense. Is this really an adequate conception of freedom to establish what Zhuangzi seeks to establish – moral autonomy, authentic existence for the individual, and harmony with the whole of life under heaven?

Zhuangzi's reply would be that what he values is not simply freedom from constraints of conventions and rules but freedom of thought and action vital for authentic existence and self-development. Beginning with the *dao* of the individual, in every being there is the determining principle of how to activate its characteristics for the full development of the individual. Zhuangzi refers to this principle as its "true ruler" which is within the individual.

> Everything has its inherent character and its proper capability. There is nothing which has not these.

It is not only superfluous but harmful if we try to make all things conform to a fixed pattern. Zhuangzi establishes the ideal of authentic existence. Leaping into the boundless is the beginning of authentic existence for the individual. Zhuangzi's ideas surface two thousand years later in the West as the ideals of authentic existence and self-development embraced by Rousseau and the Romantic movement and in the defense of individual liberty by John Stewart Mill – "The individual is sovereign over his mind and body."

Zhuangzi's discussion of letting nature take its own course may appear simply as "being at ease with oneself."

> When one is at ease with oneself, one is near the *dao*. This is to let nature take its own course. This is because he relies on the *dao* and stops at this. This is the *dao* (*Zhuangzi* 2).

But inquiring how we may come to be at ease with ourselves we realize that it requires an energetic exertion. It will not suffice to investigate the needs of the self (*Zhuangzi* 2).

> If we are to follow what is formed in our mind as a guide, who will not have such a guide? Not only those who know the succession of night and day and choose them by exercising their own minds have them. Ignorant people have theirs too. To have opinions as to right or wrong ... is as mistaken as to say that "one goes to the state of Yue today and arrives yesterday."

Relying on one's own opinion is hazardous at best since all have opinions regardless of whether one possesses knowledge or not. What does Zhuangzi propose in place of justification of beliefs based on a sharp delineation of things? Zhuangzi describes the way of the sage which looks for the commonality among things. Instead of putting forth novel doctrines, he sees things as they are without imposing a narrow individual interpretation.

> The sage aims at removing the confusions and doubts that dazzle people. Because of this he does not use his own judgement but abides in the common principle. This is what is meant by using the light of nature (*Zhuangzi* 2).

To stand forth in our natural attributes means not forming isolated judgements but seeking out "the common principle."

> Only the wise person knows how to identify all things as one. Therefore he does not use his own judgement but abides in the common principles. The common means the useful and the useful means identification. Identification means being at ease with oneself (*Zhuangzi* 2).

We discover that the moral significance of being at ease with oneself and letting nature take its course consists in expanding the conception of the self until one can identify oneself with the whole of existence, even to the point of becoming one with a butterfly.

A Dream of a Butterfly

> Once, I, Chuang Chou, dreamed that I was a butterfly, flying about happily. I did not know that I was Chou. Suddenly I awoke, and there I was, visibly Chou. I do not know whether it was Chou dreaming that he was a butterfly or it was the butterfly dreaming that it was Chou. Between Chou and the butterfly, there must be some distinction. This is called the transformation of things (*Zhuangzi* 2, Legge I. 197).

In this celebrated passage Zhuangzi invites us to ponder this bewildering possibility: the whole of reality may be a dream – there is no certainty of knowledge regarding what we really are and consequently there is no certainty about what reality might be. What is meant by the transformation of things? Surely a man does not become a butterfly or a butterfly a man? Relying on nothing other than robust common sense as the basis of belief in physical reality, and the continuity of consciousness and memory surely Zhuangzi must *know* that he is a man dreaming that he is a butterfly and *not* a butterfly dreaming that he is a man. Zhuangzi raises questions regarding the criteria of personal identity. Personal identity is explained not in terms of a substance or a natural kind but as a continuous process of transformation. With this concept of the self as consisting of stages of change, we can determine what we are at a particular stage of transformation. There is an objectively verifiable set of criteria of identification for personal identity which is not determined solely by subjective means of introspection. Both we and Zhuangzi perceive directly what he is: that he is visibly Zhuangzi. He does not need to introspect to discover an enduring self throughout all changes. When he remembers dreaming that he was a butterfly we can say that there is a continuity of consciousness and that memory is a criterion of identity – even when the form of life is distinct. Dreaming and waking are different states of the same thing and not a transformation of one thing to another thing. In what sense can things be seen as undergoing transformation? Things are not transformed by my dreaming about them. My perception undergoes transformation. The change is in the mental state or the inner life not in the physical identity.

> How do I know that love of life is not a delusion? ...
> Those who dream of the pleasures of drinking may in the morning weep, those who dream of weeping may in the morning be going out to hunt. When they were dreaming they did not know it was a dream; in their dream they may even have tried to interpret it; but when they awoke they knew that it was a dream. And there is the great awaking after which we shall know that life was a great dream. All the while the unwise think they are awake, and with nice discrimination insist on their knowledge; now playing the part of rulers and now part of grooms. ... I who say that you are dreaming am dreaming myself. These words seem very strange; but if after ten thousand ages we once meet with a great sage who knows how to explain them it will be as if we met him unexpectedly some morning or evening (*Zhuangzi* 2, Legge I. 194-5).

Not only a poetic leap of imagination but logic also renders support for Zhuangzi's perspective. If it is logically possible that the world is being created every instant with all its memory intact, how can I rely on memory as the criterion of personal identity?[30] How do we know what we are? (*Zhuangzi* 6, Legge I. 254-5).

And we all have our individuality which makes us what we are as compared together; but how do we know that we determine in any case correctly that individuality? Moreover you dream that you are a bird, and seem to be soaring to the sky; or that you are a fish and seem to be diving in the deep.

Dreaming and waking are linked by Zhuangzi not only as stages of transformation but also as an illustration of the seamlessness between reality and illusion. Can we come to know what we are by closely observing our transformation? (*Zhuangzi* 6, Legge I. 254).

And moreover, when one is about to undergo his change, how does he know that it has not taken place? And when he is not about to under go his change, how does he know that it has taken place? Take the case of me and you: – are we in a dream from which we have not begun to awake?

If everything including the self is constantly undergoing change and there is no enduring self, we cannot know whether change has taken place. If we shift our gaze from the self to our encounters which bring about the change would we come to know what we are?

It is not the meeting with what is pleasurable that produces the smile; it is not the smile suddenly produced that produces the arrangement of the person (*Zhuangzi* 6, Legge I. 255).

How do we know what causes us to smile when we feel pleasure? Since we respond differently to the same objects we cannot determine whether the causes of our smile are qualities in the object or in us.

Zhuangzi's aim is not to dissolve all certainty; nor does he seek to agitate us into radical scepticism in which we are compelled to renounce all possibility of knowing anything for certain. To wonder whether he is a butterfly dreaming that he is Zhuangzi or Zhuangzi dreaming that he is a butterfly is not a postulation of a possible world in which there is a reversal of dream and reality. When I dream that I am a butterfly in a sense I have become a butterfly but not as an acorn becoming an oak tree or a caterpillar becoming a butterfly, which is simply what takes place following the course of nature. The transformation Zhuangzi speaks of is a leap of imagination which enables us to eliminate distinctions among things and develop an empathy for the inner nature of all things. This transformation is not a change of identity. I do not experience or perceive the world as a butterfly might but I *imagine* what it might be like to be one. But what is the ethical purport of this? Shelley pointed out the importance of imagination for ethics. If we are less than good it is not for the lack of edifying moral theories but because we are deficient in moral imagination which enables us to regard things from a perspective broader than our own.

In exhorting us to forgo our firm grip on the distinction between dreaming and waking, Zhuangzi invites us to enter the innermost nature of things. If we regard all reality as a constant process of transformation there is a significant shift in perspective regarding the nature of reality and the nature of knowledge. From the point of view of all that exists, from the point of view of the *dao* of heaven, there is no distinction between a man and a butterfly. All things develop in accordance with their inner nature and are part of the continuum of all that exists. As we dream with Zhuangzi's butterfly an entirely new way of seeing, thinking and knowing opens for us: the way of freedom, spontaneity, and equality.

> When one rests in what has been arranged, and puts away all thought of the transformation, he is in unity with the mysterious Heaven (*Zhuangzi* 6, Legge I. 255).

The Dao of Heaven, the Dao of Nature and the Dao of Man

> The True man is true to Heaven and to himself – he possesses true knowledge (Legge I. 135).

Rising up to the *dao* of Heaven and delving into the *dao* of nature and *dao* of man, Zhuangzi inquires, "What then is there that is so valuable in the *dao*?" (*Zhuangzi* 17, Legge I. 383).

> He who knows the *dao* is sure to be well acquainted with the principles that appear in the procedures of things. Acquainted with those principles he is sure to understand how to regulate his conduct in all varying circumstances.

To know the *dao* means knowing the way in which nature and all things operate. The practical value of such knowledge is ethical: understanding the way of nature, we can know how to act in changing circumstances. How is the standard of virtue to be determined? It is not set by individuals in isolation but is the same for all.

Hence it is said, "What is Heavenly is internal. What is human is external. The virtue of man is what is Heavenly. If you know the operation of what is Heavenly and what is human, you will have your root in what is Heavenly and your position in virtue. ... You will have returned to the essential, and may be pronounced to have reached perfection (*Zhuangzi* 17).

Zhuangzi elaborates on what is meant by the Heavenly and by the human (*Zhuangzi* 17, Legge I. 384).

Oxen and horses have four feet; – that is what I call their Heavenly constitution. When horses' heads are haltered, and the noses of oxen are pierced, that is what I call the doing of man. Hence it is said, "Do not by the human doing extinguish the Heavenly constitution; do not for your human purpose extinguish the appointment of Heaven; do not bury your proper fame in such a pursuit of it; carefully guard the Way and do not lose it;" – this is what I call reverting to your true nature.

Zhuangzi is critical of man's treatment of animals which causes them to suffer. Zhuangzi is not calling for equal treatment of all sentient beings. On the contrary, he points out that to regulate all relations by uniform standards is to fail to understand the differences among individuals. For each activity and each form of life there is a way appropriate to it. But this is not subjectivism or relativism in applying the standards of shifting sands of time. Remarking that "Water, which is life to fish, is death to man" and that since they are "differently constituted, their likes and dislikes must necessarily differ," Zhuangzi argues that "having a due relation with others coupled with benefit to oneself" consists in treating each according to its nature.

Though the duck's legs are short, if you added more on he would worry. Though the crane's legs are long if you lopped some off, he would pine (*Zhuangzi* 6).

Zhuangzi alerts us to take account of the differences of individual natures with a parable about a seabird which dies when it is given wine in the temple, music played to amuse it, and an ox slaughtered to feed it. If we were to treat the bird not "as one would treat oneself" but "as a bird would treat another bird" we would let "it float in a river or a lake, leave it to feed upon fish, to fly in formation with others, and be free and at its ease in its resting place" (*Zhuangzi* 18).

Guarding the way of Heaven and keeping man's true essence are not separate from preserving the true nature of animals. The *dao* of man, the *dao* of nature and the *dao* of Heaven are in a continuum. From the point of the *dao* of Heaven man is not the centre of the universe but a part of the continuum of all that exists. If we inflict pain on animals we fail to preserve the way of Heaven which is our true nature. Zhuangzi's view of following the *dao* of Heaven does not rely on the natural law theory – that there is a fixed standard of what is right in nature. The usual criticism against the natural law thesis is that it operates with a biased view of what is natural to bolster the claim that what is natural is good. Zhuangzi does not attribute teleology to nature. Zhuangzi does not invoke the *dao* of Heaven to lean on a pre-established pattern of what is right. Nor is he insisting that what is natural is what is good. Zhuangzi believes that we need to discern what is ethical by understanding the dynamics of particular relations as well as by considering that different circumstances call for distinct courses of action. But above all, the perspective of the *dao* of Heaven seeks to know the totality, the *dao*, of all implications and consequences. There is the *dao* of man which is aligned with the *dao* of nature and ultimately with the *dao* of heaven as the point of view of the universe.[31]

The Meeting of the Sages in the Apricot Grove

> Confucius, rambling in the forest of Tse Wei, stopped and sat down by the Apricot altar. The disciples began to read their books, while he proceeded to play his lute singing as he did so. He had not half finished his song when an old fisherman stepped down from his boat, and came towards them (*Zhuangzi* 31).

Amidst this idyllic scene, Zhuangzi's old fisherman admonishes Confucius that in his attempt to regulate ceremonies and music and to arrange "the relationships of society" he produces disorder among the people and injury to himself. When Confucius humbly seeks to be instructed – as he unfailing does in the several imagined encounters with the Daoist sages Zhuangzi presents – the old fisherman compares Confucius' efforts at rectifying the world to a man who runs away from his own shadow (*Zhuangzi* 31, Legge II. 197).

> There was a man who was frightened at his shadow and disliked

to see his footsteps so that he ran to escape from them. But the more frequently he lifted his feet, the more numerous his foot prints were; and however fast he ran, his shadow did not leave him. He thought that he was going too slow, and ran on with all his speed and he died. He did not know that if he had stayed in a shady place, his shadow would have disappeared and that if he had remained still he would have lost his footprints.

The fisherman declares that occupying oneself with what is external brings only entanglements. Rites which are prescribed by people's opinions "change according to custom" and are "always, consequently, incomplete." "Man's proper truth is what he has received from Heaven, operating spontaneously, and unchangeable."

> True grief, without a sound, is yet sorrowful. True anger, without any demonstration, yet awakens awe. True affection, without a smile, yet produces a harmonious reciprocation. Given this truth within, it exercises a spiritual efficacy without and this is why we count it so valuable (*Zhuangzi* 31, Legge II. 198).

Confucius recognizes that this constant and universal ethical foundation is what he aspires to achieve. Once more, Confucius bowed twice, then said, "That I have met you today is as if I had the happiness of getting to heaven."

Confucianism and Daoism are generally considered diametrically opposed in regard to what constitutes the best life. Confucianism advocates the cultivation of the virtues of benevolence and righteousness whereas Daoism urges us to follow the way of nature. In personal life and in politics, the Confucians stress cultivation of virtues in accordance with clearly delineated rules and sharply defined human relations within the social institutions of state and family. What Laozi and Zhuangzi advocate, casting aside learning for the sake of innocence and direct action, is not what Confucius seeks as the goal of the cultivation of personal life.

Zhuangzi's criticism of Confucius and those who seek to reform the world in accordance with established doctrines are distinct from the stock objections of the recluses. They accuse those who seek to reform the world as being misguided by excessive confidence, and a misunderstanding of human nature and the nature of reality, accompanied by the vice of flattery, subservience, and the lack of principle. The recluses argue that the only alternative is to renounce the world altogether in order to preserve one's integrity and avoid being contaminated and swept away by corruption (*Analects* 18.6). Zhuangzi's criticisms are not *ad hominem*: he does not question the motive or character of Confucius as seeking gain, fame or honour. His objections have a deeper philosophical implication as they question not only the foundation of Confucian ethics but also the nature of virtue itself and the validity and efficacy of moral principles in shaping our ethical life.

Zhuangzi illustrates the limitation of the pursuit of learning with a conversation between a wheelwright and a ruler who explains that he is studying "the words of the sages". The wheelwright announces: "What you, my Ruler, are reading are only the dregs and sediments of those old men" (*Zhuangzi* 13, Legge I. 344). The ruler demands, "How should you, a wheelwright, have anything to say about the book which I am reading? If you can explain yourself, very well; if you cannot, you shall die!" The wheelwright replies that what he knows is incommunicable by words and can only be achieved directly. There is knowledge which cannot be fully captured in a discursive analysis. True art cannot be a product of following rules. If we recognize that there is no logic of discovery in scientific theories insofar as there are no prescribed rules which regulate the formulation and verification of hypotheses we realize that creative imagination is central in science as well as in art. Virtue is not adhering to rules and knowledge is not arrived at by the perusal of books of the ancients but achieved anew in direct action. There are no precise rules that can teach us to become virtuous – following rules and the conduct of the sages are not adequate to make us wise and good.

Zhuangzi concludes that virtue cannot be taught because it is not transmittable. In the *Meno* Socrates also asks whether virtue can be taught and suggests that it comes "neither by nature nor by teaching but by divine allotment incomprehensibly to those to whom it comes."[32] Socrates' conclusion that we need first to inquire what virtue itself is before we can understand how virtue comes as a "divine dispensation" differs from Zhuangzi's more rational approach. But insofar as both Socrates and Zhuangzi set out not to instruct but to seek to stimulate us to think, their methods aim at the same goal. Zhuangzi is critical of ethics based on compliance with rules derived from convention. What he puts in place of systematic study of the classics and the conscientious observation of rites is spontaneity and freedom. "Grey is all theory and green life's golden tree."[33]

Zhuangzi states his sharp criticism of the Confucian inculcation of morality and emphasis on the duty of benevolence and righteousness in an imaginary dialogue in which Laozi severely admonishes Confucius.

> If you, Sir, would cause men not to lose their natural simplicity, and if you would imitate the wind in its [unconstrained] movements, then you can stand forth in all the natural attributes belonging to you! (*Zhuangzi* 14, Legge I. 357).

What does it mean to keep our natural simplicity and stand forth in our natural attributes? Human beings as featherless bipeds can learn from the goose and the crow who maintain their feathers without controversy.

> The snow goose does not bathe every day to make itself white, nor the crow blacken itself every day to make itself black. The natural simplicity of their black and white does not afford any ground for controversy; and fame and praise which men like to contemplate do not make them greater than they naturally are! (*Zhuangzi* 14, Legge I. 357)

However, there are problems with equating what is good for human beings with what is good for the birds. It is questionable whether goodness is a natural quality of men like the colour of feathers of birds.[34] Is what is natural entirely good and desirable? It may be that competitive and aggressive impulses and not only poverty, inequality, and oppression are also the causes of strife and harm. What evidence do we have for maintaining that the cooperative instincts are natural and self-centered impulses are not? The Confucian question for the Daoist might be: Can harmony be achieved when people are left alone to pursue their own goals? It is not certain that when their needs are met people will live in harmony. Furthermore, if we have a view of human biology as an evolving process, we cannot be so confident that there is a fixed human nature we can call forth as a set of natural attributes. Aren't natural qualities also formed by our values which enforce or sanction what we regard as desirable characteristics? If so, Confucian inculcation of virtue can guide nature and can bring about the goal which Zhuangzi seeks to accomplish by his emphasis on restoring nature. The idea of completion or full development of the inherent moral nature of man forms the common core of Laozi, Confucius, Zhuangzi, and Mencius.

It may be possible to defend Confucian values on Zhuangzi's own terms. Whether the Confucian qualities of benevolence and righteousness are also part of human nature remains an unsettled issue. But Zhuangzi, in urging that we return to our natural attributes is committed to a view of human nature as having qualities which are good. Since Zhuangzi strains to discover the *right* way to let all nature flourish, he is not indiscriminately accepting everything under the blanket of nature. Then the natural way for man may very well be that they practice Confucian values. The Confucian virtues of benevolence and righteousness are not wildly inappropriate candidates.

What can Confucius, the gentleman scholar with his love of learning, the knowledge of classics, and high regard for decorum and appropriate conduct find in Daoist insistence that we lead the low and humble life? When Zhuangzi disparages the excessive zeal of the professed disseminators of virtue, Confucius often fares badly. After an encounter with Laozi, Zhuangzi describes Confucius as being so stunned that he "could not close his mouth" and stayed indoors for three months. But in the end, Zhuangzi portrays Confucius as a person of deep sympathy and fortitude whose humility and persistent effort in bringing about a better world leads him to Laozi to seek wisdom wherever it may be found.

Zhuangzi presents an imaginary conversation between Confucius and a disciple in which Confucius acknowledges the validity of the view that the moral perfection he seeks is not the cultivation of virtue or ceremony but becoming one with the universe. Zhuangzi describes Confucius as recognizing that the knowledge of the *dao* consists not in remembrance of things past but with forgetting himself and all things so that he becomes one with Heaven (*Zhuangzi* 12, Legge I. 318).

> The man who has forgotten himself is he of whom it is said that he has become identified with Heaven.

Confucius urges the disciple who explains that he has "made some progress" and "forgot benevolence (*ren*) and righteousness (*yi*)" to go still further. He persists in his progress and forgets ceremonies (*li*) and music until at last he announces that:

> I have abandoned my body and discarded my knowledge, and so have become one with the Infinite. This is what I mean by Sitting in Forgetfulness" (*Zhuangzi* 6).

Becoming one with the infinite – this is possible if we abandon the body which means simply that we discard first the evidences of sense

92

perception and then the mind as the source of our knowledge to receive all things.

> Maintain the unity of your will. Do not listen with ears, but with the mind. Do not listen with the mind, but with the spirit. The function of the ear ends with hearing; that of the mind, with symbols or ideas. But the sprit is an emptiness ready to receive all things. *Dao* abides in the emptiness; the emptiness is the Fast of the Mind (*Zhuangzi* 4).

Sitting in forgetfulness one realizes that living in accordance with the *dao* means not peripatetic activity of dissemination of knowledge but the readiness to receive all things in *wu wei*.[35]

Inaction, Stillness and Silence

> Acting without action, this is what is called Heaven.
> To a mind that is still, the whole universe surrenders.

Man can be a mirror of Heaven in his stillness (*Zhuangzi* 12). The way of Heaven is *wu wei* - non-action or inaction, in the sense of not doing anything which is not necessary. It is silently effective without motive from within or without and consists in simply following the course of nature. The way of man, to be like the way of Heaven, must be effortless, without artifice, unconstrained, and not enforced by strenuous discipline. Above all, it must be desireless. Regarding the subject of desire (*yu*) there is a considerable animated debate throughout the philosophical writings of the classical era. The topic of desire is prominent in the *Dao De Jing* in which *wu yu*, desirelessness, and *gua yu*, reduction of desire, are equated. The first preparation for *wu wei* is *wu yu*. Zhuangzi believes that by *wu yu* the ruler would be able to acquire virtue, *de* to guide the people (*Zhuangzi* 12). If rapacious princes would not rob people of their land and possessions, the causes of suffering and poverty would be eliminated. Similar views are expressed by Confucius in the *Analects*. When asked what should be done with robbers, Confucius replies, "If you yourself were desireless they would not steal even if you paid them to." Confucius, Laozi, Zhuangzi, and Mencius agree that to be without desires which overwhelm us is a great advantage for all. As there is seldom satiety to human longing it is desirable to be without uncertain and fluctuating desires which vex the mind and keep the heart in a state of uneasy excitement. Who can live this

life of desirelessness and inaction? The life according to *dao* is not re-
served for the sage, but intended for all. Laozi and Zhuangzi find the
dao amidst those who live humble and unpraised lives. In their egalitarian view of the moral ability of all, the Daoist and the Confucian
philosophers are in agreement. Xunzi, on the other hand argues that
those who assert that they are without desires or have few desires are
not expressing themselves correctly. "There does not exist a state of
affairs in which desire is absent. This state is death."[36]

Wu wei as the central value of Zhuangzi's ethics and aesthetics consists in acting in accordance with nature. The true craftsman's work appears uncontrived and natural.

> Woodworker Ching cut a piece of wood and made a bell stand.
> When it was finished, everyone who saw it marveled, for it
> seemed to be the work of the gods. When the Marquis of Lu saw
> it, he asked, "What art is it that you have?" Ching replied, "I am
> only a craftsman, how would I have any art? But there is one
> thing: when I am going to make a bell stand, I never let it wear
> out my energy. I fast to still my mind. When I have fasted for
> three days, I have no thought of congratulation or reward or ti-
> tles. After five days I have no thought of praise or blame, skill
> or clumsiness. After seven days, I am so still within that I forget
> I have four limbs and a form and a body. By then, the ruler and
> his court no longer exist for me. My skill is concentrated and all
> falls away. After that, I go to the mountain and examine the
> heavenly nature of the trees. If I find one superlative form, and
> can see a bell stand, I put my hand to the job of carving, if not, I
> let it go. This way I am simply matching up heaven with
> heaven. That may be the reason why people wonder if the stands
> were made by spirits" (*Zhuangzi* 19)

The true man of the *dao* acts spontaneously without external constraints
or incentives for rewards from heaven. The moral person acts without
conscious application of rules and the artifice of socially determined
conventional morality. While for the Confucian thinkers the *dao* en-
sures a moral social order, for the Daoists, the *dao* frees human actions
from being bound by particular schemes imposed by the conventions of
society.[37] Propriety (*li*) is replaced by spontaneity. Confucius' exhortation is to "Spare no effort in learning" and Zhuangzi's *wu wei* consists
in "doing nothing, and yet thereby doing everything."

Wu Wei in the political domain is letting things take their own course.

> The superior man, who feels himself constrained to engage in the administration of the world will find it his best way to do nothing. In doing nothing, he can rest in the instincts of the nature with which he is endowed (*Zhuangzi* 11, Legge I. 293).

Zhuangzi is convinced that if we do not hinder the natural development of things by an imposition of artificial constraints we will eliminate much of what causes strife. Zhuangzi is critical of rule-governed morality which has proved inefficacious in eliminating suffering. The best government is the one which does not depend on the enforcement of laws. "The more law, the less justice."[38] In responding to the concern "If you do not govern the world, how can you make men's minds good?" Zhuangzi describes the complex nature of man and the extreme ranges of the human mind: it cannot be easily governed or made compliant (*Zhuangzi* 11).

> It is so swift that while one is bending down and lifting up his head, it shall twice have put forth a soothing hand beyond the four seas. Resting, it is still as a deep abyss; moving, it is like one of the bodies in the sky; in its resolute haughtiness, it refuses to be bound; – such is the mind of man (Legge I. 294-5).

In contrast to the optimistic expectation that morality is achieved through vigorous inculcation of virtues and the conviction in the inherent goodness of human nature, Zhuangzi urges that we allow the mind to become a mirror of reality (*Zhuangzi* 7, Legge I. 266).

> When the perfect man employs his mind, it is like a mirror. It conducts nothing and anticipates nothing; it responds to what is before it, but does not retain it. Thus he is able to deal successfully with all things and injures none.

Zhuangzi values the preservation of life of the people above the protection of territory even to the point of advocating peaceful relinquishing of power against aggression without resistance. It is possible to derive a political philosophy of peace and non-violence from Zhuangzi's conception of the good as that which yields rather than that which attacks or retaliates. But we fear that *wu wei* as a political strategy would be tragically ineffectual in preventing harm and eliminating suffering in the real world of violence and aggression. The ethics of non-violence of Daoism might seem to present at best an impractical and an unattainable ideal. Surely we need to know what is realizable in terms of human nature and capacity before we formulate moral goals? But if we reflect upon human history and conclude that there has been moral progress insofar as we have come to value equality and freedom of all human beings, may we not agree that this progress was brought about by the continuous effort on the part of those who sought to realize the ethical ideals?

In the political history of China *wu wei* served an important purpose. Through their renunciation of power and wealth, in their rejection of the values upheld by the throne and in their refusal to serve the feudal lords, the advocates of *wu wei* challenged directly the authority of the throne. *Wu wei* is an art to be cultivated not only by the Daoist but also by a respectable Confucian, Mencius. When he is criticized for not going to see the princes, Mencius defends himself by citing precedents of scholars who leaped over the wall or shut the door refusing to admit the prince (*Mencius* 3. 2.7). Zhuangzi's customary blunt refusal to serve the princes would not be an option open for the Second Sage. While Mencius finds such conduct "excessively scrupulous", he also disengages himself when he is weary of "presumption": "There are many arts in teaching. I refuse, as inconsistent with my character, to teach a man, but I am only thereby still teaching him" (*Mencius* 6. 2.16). *Wu wei* can be an effective political strategy when we can achieve more by refraining from action.

Can the life of *wu wei* be a happy life? Zhuangzi observes that "The birth of man is at the same time the birth of his sorrow"(Legge II. 2).

> Now the rich embitter their lives by their incessant labours; they accumulate more wealth than they can use... those who seek for honours carry their pursuit of them from the day into the night, full of anxiety about their methods ...(*Zhuangzi* 18).

Zhuangzi asks "Under the sky is perfect enjoyment then to be found or not?" and proposes that it can only come from *wu wei*, doing nothing.

> I consider doing nothing to be the great enjoyment. ... Perfect enjoyment is to be without enjoyment; the highest praise is to be without praise (*Zhuangzi* 18, Legge II. 3).

Heaven does nothing, and thence comes its serenity; earth does

96

nothing, and thence comes its rest. By the union of these two in-activities, all things are produced. How vast and imperceptible is the process! – they seem to come from nowhere! (Legge II. 3-4)

Heaven and earth for Zhuangzi are not so much the two great material forms in the universe as the great powers whose influences extend to all below and upon them. "Silently and effectively, with entire spontaneity, their influence goes forth, and a rule and pattern is thus given to those on whom the business of the government of the world devolves" (Legge I. 143). To be like heaven and earth is to be universal without being driven by fatiguing and anxious passions within the confines of individuality.

"Vacancy, stillness, silence, and non-action" are the distinguishing marks of those who have attained the *dao*. During the fourth century BCE the philosophers were concerned about the precarious way in which language was connected to the world of physical reality and the world of ideas. The philosophers writing in the Confucian tradition were seriously concerned with the correct usage of names and insisted that the names be accurately applied to corresponding objects. The gulf between language and what it aims to express was felt sharply by Confucius, who stated, "I wish that I could do without speaking." The Daoists go further. If truth is what we want, let us dispense with words altogether. Let us kick off the ladder of language lest we mistake the pointing finger for the moon. "To know is good, to think is better but to see is best" – Goethe's words echo Zhuangzi's call to "discard all learning and forget all knowledge." With clear and direct perception and awareness of things as they are in themselves we may pursue the way beyond knowledge and thought. Once we kick off the ladder of knowledge, where do we land? The way continues when the words stop. Zhuangzi would take us further than the limits of language. But he is aware that even to express the limitations of language we depend on language as he exclaims, "I wish to meet a man who has forgotten the words so that I could have a word with him."

There are two aspects of silence in Zhuangzi. The first is regarding the origin and the nature of the *dao* itself. This is the silence of Laozi – we cannot say what the *dao* itself is or what was beyond the beginning of existence. There is also the silence as all activities reach their completion (Legge I. 316). At the completion of all actions what was potential becomes fully realized into actuality and all things manifest their "proper characteristics." The true man of the *dao* has "a velvet hand and a hawk's eye."[39] He can be so still that he might be able to "enter the cage without setting off the birds singing" (*Zhuangzi* 4).

Liezi

Riding on a Wind

Liezi (Lieh Tzu), a legendary Daoist (ca. 600-400 BCE) is said to have traveled with the wind, occasionally riding on the back of the dragon to rise above the clouds. For Liezi the *dao* consists in maintaining a perfect equilibrium. This is illustrated by a story of a philosopher who was able to land a large fish with a line consisting of a single filament of raw silk.[40]

> A line will break at the point where most strain is put upon it. If the fisherman's hand had perfect equilibrium, no such point exists; the slenderest thread can bear the greatest imaginable weight without breaking.

The *Book of Liezi*, also known as *Pure Classic of the Perfect Virtue of Simplicity and Vacuity*, is the most significant Daoist text after *Dao De Jing* and the *Book of Zhuangzi*.[41] It is an engaging introduction to Daoism and is more accessible than the other two classics of Daoism. It is considered to be not an original text by Liezi, but a compilation of related ideas which incorporates the teachings of Liezi and Yangzhu (440-360 BCE). During the period of the Hundred Schools Yangzhu's brand of ethical egotism was influential for he had as many followers as Confucius and Mozi. The version of Daoism put forward by Liezi is distinct from that of Laozi and Zhuangzi. The salient features of Liezi are scepticism and hedonism. Liezi regards morality as merely the desire to be thought well of. It is best to get all we can out of life without worrying about what happens to our reputation after our death. Liezi is not content with simply advocating the gratification of the senses and every desire. He wants to convince us all that it is the best way to live since it is the natural way, and that it is harmful not to follow natural impulses and inclinations.

As a radical reaction against *wu yu*, the desirelessness of the Daoist philosophers, the Yangzhu chapter of the *Book of Liezi* interprets following nature as giving full rein to the senses and desire. What is of chief value is preservation of one own life.

Let us hasten to enjoy our present life. Why bother about what comes after death? Let the ear hear what it longs to hear, the eyes see what they long to see ... Let the body have every comfort it craves, let the mind do as it will. ... What the eye wants to see is carnal beauty; and to deprive it is to cramp the sense of sight. What the mouth desires is to speak of what is true and what is false; and if it may not speak then knowledge is cramped."[42]

Yangzhu "valued self," rejecting that which does not serve self-interest: the welfare of the self should be the sole concern of the individual.

Now my life is my own possession, its benefit to me is also great. If we discuss what is noble and mean, even the honour of being an Emperor could not compare with it. If we discuss what is unimportant and important, even the wealth of possessing the empire could not be exchanged for it."[43]

The seriousness with which the challenge of hedonism and ethical egotism of Liezi and Yangzhu was taken by the philosophers of the classical period is indicated by the discussion of their views by Zhuangzi, Mencius, and Mozi. The criticisms of the doctrine of egotism aim at showing the inadequacy of the perspective self-interest in solving the fundamental problems of ethics: "What does happiness consist in?", "What are the reasons for acting ethically?" and "What is the extent of our moral responsibility?" In the first book of *Zhuangzi* "Rambling at Ease", Zhuangzi points out that Liezi fails to obtain what he sets out to do. The unhampered enjoyment of oneself in perfect equilibrium without relying on external factors is not to be found in following Liezi.

Liezi ... rode on the wind and pursued his way, with an admirable indifference (to external things), returning, however, after fifteen days (to his place) ... but though he had not to walk there was still something of which he had to wait.

Liezi is not completely free from external influences since he still depends on the wind to move him (*Zhuangzi* 1, Legge I. 169). The preoccupation with the self makes us dependent on the external factors for the satisfaction of our wants and does not lead to freedom, spontaneity and autonomy. Zhuangzi has a better away to achieve "the enjoyment in the illimitable." "The Perfect man has no (thought of) self, the Spirit-like man, none of merit; the Sagely-minded man, none of fame."

The Confucian criticism of egotism is put forward by Mencius who places Yangzhu among his main adversaries (*Mencius 3*. II.9). Mencius denounces the egotism of Yangzhu and the universal love of Mozi which he regards as exemplifying two extremes.

> Yangzhu's choice was "everyone for himself." Though he might benefit the entire world by plucking out a single hair, he would not do it. Mozi loves all equally. If by rubbing smooth his whole body from head to foot he could benefit the world, he would do it (*Mencius 7*. I.26).

The extent of Yangzhu's influence can be gathered from the vehemence of Mencius criticism.

> The words of Yangzhu and Mozi fill the world. If the people in their opinion do not follow Yangzhu, they follow Mozi. If the principles of Yang and Mo are not stopped, and if the principles of Confucius are not brought to light, perverse doctrines will delude the people and obstruct the path of benevolence and righteousness. I am alarmed by these things, and defend the doctrines of the ancient kings and oppose Yang and Mo.

From Mencius' standpoint Yangzhu's exclusive concern with his own well-being and disregard for benevolence and righteousness would lead to a dissolution of social relations on which the moral development depend. The most forceful rejoinder to Yangzhu comes from Mozi. Mozi presents an ethical alternative to the unmitigated hedonistic egotism. While Yangzhu asked "What is most beneficial to myself?" Mozi asks "What is most beneficial to the whole world?" and seeks to show how the two questions are answered by his thesis of universal love.

3

The Hundred Schools

Mozi

Universal Love

What is the way of universal love and mutual benefit? ... It is to regard other people's countries as one's own. Regard other people's families as one's own. Regard other people's person as one's own. Consequently, when feudal lords love one another, they will not fight in the fields. When heads of families love one another, they will not usurp one another. When individuals love one another, they will not injure one another. When ruler and minister love each other, they will be kind and loyal. When father and son love each other, they will be affectionate and filial. When brothers love each other, they will be peaceful and harmonious. When all the people in the world love one another, the strong will not overcome the weak, the many will not oppress the few, the rich will not insult the poor, the honoured will not despise the humble, and the cunning will not deceive the ignorant.[1]

We begin with the daring proposition of Mozi (fl. 479 - 438 BCE): all people are to be loved without distinctions. Universal love (*jian ai*), opposition to war, and diligence were advocated as ideals before Mozi. But it was Mozi who brought these values together in a systematic discourse and arrived at a unified philosophical perspective.[2]

The study of Mozi is central to an understanding of the formation and development of the philosophical traditions in China. Mozi's ideas are significant in themselves and essential to an adequate understanding of Confucianism and Daoism since the chief proponents of both schools tackle Mozi and formulate their ideas in opposition to his theories. Until the beginning of Han dynasty (206 BCE-220 CE), the most influential theories were Confucianism and Mohism.

The *Mozi*, originally consisting of seventy-one chapters, is a compilation of Mozi's ideas and works of his followers. In the fifty-three extant chapters the topics range over "Condemnation of Confucians," "Condemnation of War," and discussions on military defense, language, definition of terms, and on causality. There are nine chapters in the *Mozi* which address defensive warfare. The *Mozi* was neglected until the eighteenth century, when a first commentary on the text appeared.

Little is known about Mozi's life. He might have begun as a follower of the Confucian school and became critical of what he saw as shortcomings in certain aspects of the Confucian tradition. In their insistence on disciplined life and scorn for ritual in stern opposition to the ceremonies and music of Confucians, the Mohists were the Spartans of China. To further the end of promoting wealth and growth of the population, they advocated economy, simple living and rejected all forms of extravagance and luxury. For the Mohists, who were warrior philosophers, honour was of utmost importance, and to die for their principles was considered an absolute duty. The *Historical Records* says of the Mohists that "Their words are always sincere and their actions decisive. They are always true to what they have promised."[3]

Mozi emphasizes that "the purpose of those who are virtuous lies in procuring benefits for the world and eliminating its calamities." Mozi explains that "Because of want of mutual love, all the calamities, usurpation, hatred, and animosity in the world have arisen. Therefore the man of humanity condemns it."[4] Universal love carried into action leads directly to Mozi's condemnation of war. Why do governments wage war? The rulers have replied: "I covet the fame of the victor and the possessions obtainable through conquest and therefore I do it."[5] Mozi replies:

> But when we consider the victory as such, there is nothing useful about it. When we consider the possessions obtained through it, it does not even make up for what has been lost... [6]

In his forceful arguments against war, Mozi enumerates the devastation wrought by warfare on people, animals, and land.

102

The multitude are injured and oppressed and the people are scattered... Does that mean to benefit the people? The benefit to the people from killing the people of Heaven is slight indeed! And calculate its cost! This is the root of destruction of life. It exhausts the people to an immeasurable degree.[7]

We may agree with Mozi that war is not beneficial. But what of the Machiavellian view that war is unavoidable since human beings are by nature like "vultures, wolves, and foxes," and that we are amoral predators in our ruthlessness, cunning, and brutality? Machiavelli argues that the best way to rule is not with love but through fear, subjugation, and force. To depend on love is to court disaster: love is unreliable since human beings are "fickle" and love only what is profitable to them at present. But just as Machiavelli cites incidents from history to support his case, Mozi turns to history to show that benevolent rule prevailed. Mozi lists the accomplishments of past benevolent rulers to argue that the precedents prove how universal love has been put into practice. The founder of Xia dynasty, Yu (2183-2175 BCE), built dams and canals for irrigation, and Wen (1751-1739 BCE), the founder of Zhou dynasty, ruled justly and humbly. Mozi confidently concludes, "It shows that my doctrine of universal love has been practiced."

But is human nature capable of universal love? Drawing an analogy between raw silk and human nature, Mozi explains,

> When the silk is put in a different dye its colour becomes also different. Having been dipped five times, it has changed its colour five times. Therefore dyeing must be attended to with care! [8]

For Mozi human nature is neither good nor evil but neutral and malleable. Only when we are continuously dipped into love do we develop the capacity and acquire the readiness to love. Universal love is realizable and dependable not only because human nature can be formed to love but also because the will of Heaven also sets the pattern for all love.

Heavenly Love and the Problem of Evil

> How do we know that Heaven loves all the people in the world? Because it enlightens them all. How do we know that it enlightens them all? Because it possesses them all. How do we know

that it possesses them all? Because it feeds them all. ... Possessing all people, how could Heaven not love them?[9]

The relation between Heaven and man is reciprocal. The macrocosmic love of Heaven for all is the model of universal earthly love among men. Mozi attributes the success of states and rulers directly to Heaven and their failure to their defiance of the way of Heaven. When the will of Heaven and the will of the rulers are aligned there is righteousness and the world is well ordered.

When Mozi moves from his doctrine of universal love in human relations to the love of Heaven for all people, this love of Heaven for man is another matter altogether and requires a leap of faith in Heaven as emanating universal love. Mozi was criticized for his belief in spiritual beings. Once, when Mozi was ill he received this challenge.

Sir, you hold that ghosts and spirits are intelligent and control calamities and blessings. They will reward the good and punish the evil. Now you are a Sage. How can you be ill? Is it that your teaching is not entirely correct or that ghosts and spirits are after all unintelligent?

Mozi replies,

Though I am ill, in what way would the ghosts and spirits be unintelligent? There are many ways (besides that of offending the spirits) by which a man can contract diseases. Some are contracted from cold or heat, some from fatigue. If there are a hundred gates and only one be closed, where could robbers not enter?[10]

Is there an inconsistency between Mozi's belief in the power of the spirits and his belief in the effort of human will which can bring about change? Mozi's explanation that some events are caused by spirits and others by natural events does not justify his belief in spirits as being rational any more than a partial belief in ghosts would be more rational than a total belief in ghosts.

How is the heavenly love related to the problem of evil that besets the real world? What does Heaven have in store for the wrong doers? It sends down misfortune.

Moreover, I declare that for the murder of one innocent person,

104

there will surely be one misfortune. Who is it that murders the innocent person? It is man. Who is it that sends down misfortune? It is Heaven. If it is thought that Heaven does not love the people of the world, why does it send misfortune because a man murders a man? This is why I know that Heaven loves the people of the world.[11]

Heaven manifests its love in retributive justice. Mozi's belief in the will of Heaven appears to be something like faith in divine justice.

There are two immediate problems which arise in relation to Mozi's invocation of Heaven: the problem of evil and the problem of fatalism. The problem of evil for all benevolent Heaven is similar for the deity in Western religions. Why does an all-loving God not prevent suffering of the innocents? If Heaven loves all, does it lack the knowledge or the power to prevent evil but have only the power to punish transgressions? We are inclined to agree with Juvenal's remark that "The wrath of the gods may be great, but it certainly is slow." If, as Mozi believes, human nature is not inherently evil, where is the origin of evil? Heavenly love does not solve the problem of evil, nor are these questions answered conclusively.

Is his claim that the will of Heaven is the direct cause of states of affairs in the human world tantamount to fatalism? If everything happens in accordance with the will of Heaven, surely there is no need to labour with universal love to bring benefit to all. We would do best to simply follow the will of Heaven and resign ourselves to fate. However, in Mozi's conception, the will of Heaven is a moral standard which is beneficial to all and not a pre-determined course of events. Rewards and punishments are sent down by Heaven and the spirits not according to fate, *ming*, but according to the conduct of human beings. His explanation of natural phenomena in terms of natural causes and not in terms of supernatural intervention is carried over to his criticism of belief in fate. Mozi's dispute with the fatalists is not equivalent to the ongoing debate on free will and determinism in Western philosophy as he is not directly concerned with whether actions are free or determined. However, since for Mozi it is not fate but human effort which determines what happens in the world, his ethics may be said to presuppose free will. Mozi declares that "the large number of fatalists among the people" has led to political failure. Mozi's criticism of fatalism is that it leads to passive acquiescence based on falsehood. Mozi demands that a theory be tested and confirmed by actual experience. This search for a general standard of clarity following an empirically verifiable procedure is the distinguishing mark of Mozi's philosophy.

If we try to apply Mozi's demands for a practical method of testing the validity of the doctrine of fate in political and social contexts to his own beliefs regarding the Lord on High, *Shanag Di*, his invocation of the will of Heaven remains problematic. But this does not diminish the forcefulness of his reasons for advocating universal love in terms of beneficial consequences. In his claim that Heaven's love enables all people to be enlightened, Mozi's egalitarian view of moral ability is no less significant than Confucius' belief that all are capable of developing the virtue of love, *ren*. In contrast to the serene rationalism of Confucius – who observed that since he has not fully comprehended natural events he could not presume to know about supernatural beings – Mozi relates episodes of spiritual beings. However, Mozi's recourse to the will of Heaven is not an appeal to a theistic origin of ethics: there is no call to submit to the divine will. Moreover, Mozi's belief in spirits did not lead him to endow these supernatural forces with absolute dominion over the entire human sphere. His concern is not with a supernatural deity to be worshipped or a personification of the power of Heaven to be feared, but with the prevention of human suffering. What Mozi advocates is not divining the will of Heaven or placating Heaven with incantations, offerings, and sacrifices to send down blessings, but reforming humanity through active readiness for universal love.

The value of the will of Heaven as a moral metaphor in the political and social context is evident. Throughout the history of China, the idea that only those who excel in virtue can govern with the Mandate of Heaven and that Heaven withdraws its support from unjust rulers has exerted a moral force above the laws imposed by arbitrary rule and provided a possibility of a check against the hubris of an all-powerful emperor. "The Son of Heaven [emperor] should not set the standard himself. There is Heaven to give him the standard." Ultimately moral standards are not set by human intervention but by the will of Heaven operating with the necessity and regularity of natural law. In order to achieve a unified action for the common good of the people the rulers need to maintain the administration of laws. Mozi's exhortation is not to the people to submit to their rulers but to the rulers to love the people: the sole duty of the ruler is to govern for the benefit of the people.

Every school of philosophy carves for us its own image of the sage. To be a Mohist sage is to be free of passions, be upright with universal love and not to lean with excessive feeling in any direction. Universal love as complete impartiality does not arise from inclination but from an equal consideration of the needs of all concerned. The sage has a gift for friendship and a deep sympathy.

> I have heard that to be a lofty man in the world one should take care of one's friend as one does of oneself, and take care of one's friend's parents as one does one's own. Only after this can one be a lofty man in the world. Therefore when he found his friend hungry he would feed him, and when he found him cold he would clothe him. In his sickness he would minister to him, and when he was dead he would bury him. Such is the word and deed of the advocate of universality.[12]

The goal of bringing benefits to the world and eliminating harm may be disputed by those who persist in partial love. Why should we be concerned about universal love? Even from a purely self-interested point of view, universal love is useful, for when we are concerned with the welfare of our friends and our family, if we could rely not only on a partial friend but on all as universal friends who are not partial to their own circle we are more likely to succeed in our goals. Mozi argues that if people could choose a ruler, "even a fool in the world, although he himself was a person who objected to universality, would choose the universal ruler."[13]

> Those who love others will be loved by others. Those who benefit others will be benefited by others. Those who hate others will be hated by others. And those who harm others will be harmed by others.[14]

Mozi argues that love of others and conferring benefits are reciprocal: universal love benefits all, the one who receives as well as one who gives love. Against Mozi, it would be quickly pointed out that if the reason for loving is that we will receive love, this is self-love and not universal love and that too often our love does not inspire love.[15] But since Mozi is concerned not with praiseworthy character or morality for its own sake but with beneficial consequences, he would argue that even from the point of view of self-interest, it is better to love than not. Mozi is not describing how we love, but commanding how we ought to love. That we do not always succeed in receiving love in return would not be a reason for abandoning the course of universal love.

Mozi must also meet the criticism from the Confucian standpoint. With the forceful clarity of his ideas and his exemplary life, Confucius has set the standard of integrity of thought and action for all times. A critical examination of Mozi's ethics by Confucian lights is therefore unavoidable. At first sight Mozi's philosophy stands in sharp contrast to Confucius' ideas. The Mohists were drawn to the life of simplicity and spurned the refinement and elegance of ceremony and ritual upheld by Confucians. Xunzi criticizes Mozi sharply: "Mozi was blinded by utility and did not know the value of culture." Confucius' statement "The superior man is informed in what is right and the inferior man is informed in what is profitable" is cited as a criticism of Mozi by Confucian philosophers. What Confucius criticizes is pursuing profit in the sense of material gain. Insofar as what Mozi means by genuine profit to people is not material gain but the general well-being of the people, Confucius' denunciation of profiteering does not weaken Mozi's argument.

The hot disputes between the Mohists and the Confucian philosophers, most vigorously sustained by Mencius, are about universal love. What is the difference between Mozi's universal love, *jian ai*, and Confucius' love, *ren*? Mozi advocates that we love all equally and values universal love for the benefit it can bring and the harm it can eliminate. Among Confucian philosophers, the emphasis is on love for one's parents and the analogous love of the ruler for the people. This focus on love in personal and political relations gives the impression that Confucian love is at best partial love between particular people. But Mozi and Confucius are not as far apart as is generally thought. For Confucius *ren* is universal. When asked what the essence of man is, Confucius replies, "*ren*." For Confucius *ren* is inherent in human nature: it is the essence of humanity. "*Ren* has its source in oneself, and cannot be derived from others." (*Analects*, 12.1). When asked what the most important moral precept is, Confucius replies: "Love all men" (*Analects*, 12.22). Confucius advocates *ren* as the foundation of all human relations. The ruler's duty to the people is universal and impartial love, without selecting or favouring the recipients and beneficiaries. If the idea of *ren* itself is to be applied consistently throughout moral life as Confucius envisaged, it cannot differ vastly from the universal love of Mozi. In their commitment to setting the world right through the inculcation of morality in all spheres of action, Confucius and Mozi are in unison.

Consequentialism of Mozi

In his thorough and persistent pursuit of righteousness in terms of what is beneficial to all, Mozi can be characterized as the first utilitarian philosopher and a precursor of consequentialism – the view that ethical actions are actions which contribute to beneficial consequences. Mozi's philosophy of universal love emphasizes the consequences and the benefits that result from such love: the elimination of harm, strife, conflict, and war. There is a parallel between Mozi's view and the utilitarianism of Bentham – that the purpose of morality and laws is to promote the greatest happiness of the greatest number.[16] Mozi's argument for universal love is analogous to the argument for impartial obligation from a utilitarian point of view.

The Mohist imperatives can be stated as: "Always love impartially" and "Always act in a way to bring the greatest benefit to people." How are the two imperatives related? Mozi argues that universal love is the way to bring the greatest benefit to people. Surveying the world filled with calamities, Mozi declares the underlying cause of all conflicts and war to be "want of mutual love."

> When we come to think about the cause of all these calamities, how have they arisen? Have they arisen out of love of others and benefiting others? We must reply that it is not so. We should say that they have arisen out of hate of others and injuring others. If we should classify one by one all those who hate others and injure others, should we find them to be universal or partial [in their love]? We should have to say that they are partial. Now, since partiality against one another is the cause of the major calamities in the world, then partiality is wrong. Partiality is to be replaced by universality. But how is partiality to be replaced by universality? [17]

What can be done about this want of love and partial love? "It should be replaced by the way of universal love and mutual benefit," and partiality should be replaced by universality. Recognizing that universal love is generally thought to be "something distant and difficult" Mozi explains that this is so "simply because gentlemen of the world fail to recognize its benefit and understand its reason."[18]

Mozi argues that the "differences of standards" has led to factions, conflict, and war, and introduces the standards of testing the validity of theories. As he calls for objective criteria of values in ethics, he is sharply critical of subjectivism and relativism.

> Some standard of judgment must be established. To expound without regard for the standard is similar to determining the di-

rections of sunrise and sunset on a revolving potter's wheel. By this means the distinction of right and wrong, benefit and harm, cannot be known. Therefore any statement must have three tests. What are the three tests? Mozi said: "Its basis, its verifiability and its applicability. On what is it to be based? It should be based on the deeds of the ancient Sage-kings. By what is it to be verified? It is to be verified by the senses of hearing and sight of the common people. How is it to be applied? It is to be applied by adopting it in government and observing its benefit to the country and the people. This is what is meant by the three tests of every doctrine."[19]

Mozi is the first philosopher to specify the criterion of verification of all ethical theories as "the senses of hearing and sight of the common people." While he retains the veneration of the sage kings, he stresses common sense and an empirical approach to ethics. Of the three tests, the most important is the third. The "benefit to the country and the people" was the standard by which Mozi determined all values. Everything must have its usefulness, and all doctrines must have their applicability, before they can have any value. This amounts to a radical rejection of intrinsic values. From an ethical point of view, what value could any idea or moral theory have independently of its applicability and possibility of beneficial consequences? What then is of the greatest benefit for the people? This is the central ethical question for the Mohists. Mozi did not conceive of benefit in terms of moral virtues possessed by people or rulers and ministers but in terms of general welfare and alleviating the suffering of the people.

Mozi's theory of universal love meets the test of applicability and utility he has set for all theories. Since Mozi does not believe in intrinsic values we cannot argue for universal love as a good in itself. To the objection, "It may be morally good, but can it be of any use?" Mozi replies: "If it were not useful then even I would disapprove of it. Moreover, how can there be anything good which cannot be of use?"[20] Mozi argues that if most people do not practice universal love it is even more necessary for us to cultivate it actively.

On his way from Lu to Ch'i, Mozi met an old friend who said to him: "Nowadays no one in the world practices any righteousness. You are merely inflicting pain on yourself by trying to practice righteousness. You had better give it up." Mozi replied: "Suppose a man has ten sons. Only one cultivates the ground, while the other nine stay at home. Then the one who cultivates must work all the more vigorously. Why? Because many eat and few cultivate. Today, if no one in the world practices righteousness, you should all the more encourage me. Why do you stop me?"[21]

Mozi urges active commitment to bring about a change for the better and to eliminate the oppression and exploitation of the poor. Mozi deplores the unjust rule of his time: the heavy burden levied by taxes, the suffering of the people who die of hunger and cold when their resources become insufficient, and the separation of families during long invasions. Mozi urges the rulers to feel towards all people under heaven exactly as one feel towards one's own people and to regard other states exactly as one regards one's own state.

> I say that when everyone regards the states of others as he regards his own who would attack the others' states? Others would be regarded like self. Universality is really the cause of the major benefits in the world; therefore Mozi proclaims universality to be right.[22]

He argues that to love others and to extend the regard we have for our own persons and property to others is to act from universality of ethical considerations. The doctrine of "universal love," is linked to the "share and share alike" practice of the professional warrior class, *xie*. Mozi's ideas have been criticized as being too idealistic for China, lacking in "metaphysical presuppositions" in comparison with Daoism and Confucianism.[23] Zhuangzi and Mencius also criticized Mozi. Were these criticisms so effective that they demolished his ideas completely? If we judge the success of ideas mainly by being associated with the originators, it may seem that Mozi's philosophy disappeared with the Mohists. But what of the ideas of universal love and opposition to war? When we look closely at the subsequent development of moral values in later philosophers, Mozi's idea of universal love has entered deeply into the Confucian tradition. In the Confucian classics we read:

> Deep love is that with which one treats the multitude (*Great Learning*).
> Love is the essence of man (*Doctrine of the Mean* 20).

Neo-Confucian philosophers have actively embraced the idea of uni-

111

versal love. Zhang Zai's declaration of the unity of all beings in *The Western Inscription* and the Cheng brothers' development of Zhang Zai's views led to the expansion of *ren* to universal love. In Kang Youwei's idea of the Age of Great Peace, there is a resounding affirmation of the universal love first vividly conceived by Mozi.[24]

This synthesis of Mohism and Confucianism is not as startling as it might seem. The Mohist ideals of universal love and opposition to war are aligned with the Confucian ideals of *ren* and world peace. Even if the ideas of Mozi have not yet been put actively into practice, they are nevertheless among the goals that human societies have aspired to achieve. In defense of Mozi's moral idealism, we might ask what values ethical theories would have if they did not set goals that are worthy of our effort. Are there more worthwhile goals than those of universal love and the benefit of the people envisioned by Mozi? By directly being assimilated into the Confucian tradition the ideas of Mozi helped to forge the political and moral philosophy that shaped the history of China.

What is the relevance of Mozi to the ethics of the present and to global concerns? An urgent task of contemporary moral philosophy is to discern a set of values and ways of putting them into action by people of divergent cultures. Mozi's philosophy can guide us in the search for a universal ethics. Altruism, good will, equal consideration of the needs of all people, and sympathy for the suffering of others are direct expressions of universality. Mozi's concern for all is what led, in spite of his substantial disagreement, Zhuangzi to exclaim, "Mozi was the best of men." As Confucius, Laozi, Zhuangzi, and Mencius advocated, Mozi also urges the ruler to inspire and lead the people by setting an example of virtuous conduct.

Is grand unification of all partial love into universal love too lofty an ideal? We turn to the Legalists who criticized Mozi sharply and dispensed with moral values and feelings of compassion and love in favour of submission to law. "Fear, not kindness, restrains the wicked."[25]

The Legalists

No lake so still but that it has its wave. No circle so perfect but that it has its flaws. I would change things for you if I could. As I cannot, you must take them as they are.[26]

In the era of the sword, during the Qin rule (221-206 BCE) the Legalists set up a strategy of government advocating laws based not on moral values but on their efficacy in maintaining order and stability. In stark contrast to the moral idealism of the philosophers in ancient China, "the Legalist School" (a term adopted in 90 BCE), stressed the primacy of law in political dominance. The Legalists advocated that the law must be applicable to all equally. In a society governed by aristocracy of blood, the Legalists insisted on ability and merit, setting aside the rule of privilege of rank and hierarchy.

Hanfeizi (d. 233 BCE), prince of Han, provided the most systematically rigourous version of the Legalist School. The *Han Fei Tzu*, which consists of fifty-five chapters in twenty books, puts forward a system of ethics for private life and political action which builds on the authority of law to enforce compliance through sanctions. In the Legalist conception law and statecraft are political artifacts and measures of expediency. The rightness of political measures is not determined by matching them with the precedents established by the sage emperors of antiquity or the principles of humanity and benevolence or the rites, but solely by their effectiveness. Laws do not correspond to the natural order of justice or the will of Heaven but are to be adapted to suit the purpose at hand. The Legalists maintained that the objective validity of law was to be tested in its application to the present as well as to changing circumstances. They advocated setting aside the ideals of benevolent rule through inculcation of virtue and propagated a political doctrine from the vantage point of the ruler and the state.[27]

The Legalists argued that the individual must submit to the state and justified the use of force in order to maintain the uniformity of thought and action. The doctrines and the practices of the Legalists led to the burning of books in 213 BCE. There has not been a Legalist School since the violent rule of the Qin era came to an abrupt end. The Legalists held sway over the Qin rulers with their "two handles" doctrine of statecraft. Hanfeizi requires "the application of the methods of straightening and bending," which consisted of strict obedience to law and the incentives given through reward and punishment. Hanfeizi stresses that "customs differ between the past and the present," and therefore "to try to govern the people of a chaotic age with benevolent and lenient measures is like to drive wild horses without reins or whips." He emphasizes that the laws must be backed by force: "It is by their claws and their fangs that tigers can triumph over dogs."[28] Nature, red in tooth and claw, teaches men how to rule. Hanfeizi stresses that "people are submissive to power and few of them can be influenced by the doctrine of righteousness."

Hanfeizi challenges Confucius and Mozi regarding their belief in the authority of the legendary sage emperors. Hanfeizi argues that the purported achievements of the ancients are not open to examination. As relics of the past they do not provide a standard of truth for the present.

> Who is going to determine the truth of Confucianism or Mohism? ... To be sure of anything without corroborating evidence is stupidity, and to base one's argument on anything about which one cannot be sure is perjury. Therefore those who openly base their arguments on the authority of the ancient kings and who are dogmatically certain of Yao and Shun [the sage emperors upheld as the paradigms of virtue by Confucius and Mozi] are men either of stupidity or perjury. Such learning, characterized by stupidity and perjury, and such an unrefined and conflicting [doctrine] practiced [by the Confucians and Mohists] are unacceptable to an enlightened ruler.[29]

Hanfeizi's rejection of the authority of tradition and custom and his insistence on direct evidence as grounds of truth introduces a new demand for certainty and verifiability as criteria of knowledge. Hanfeizi's view of human nature and moral education is diametrically opposed to the Confucian view. Confucius and Mencius believed in the inherent goodness of human beings and affirmed the development of *ren* as the basis of moral education and political rule. Hanfeizi, who was a pupil of Xunzi, accepts Xunzi's view: human nature is more prone to evil than good. In order to achieve the good for the majority, Hanfeizi advocates that the ruler "utilize the people's inability to do wrong," and not rely on "virtue and kindness" which "are insufficient to end disorder." He goes so far as to say, "the enlightened ruler does not value people who are naturally good," as there are too few of them and the ruler cannot "follow the good that happens by chance."

> The enlightened ruler pays attention only to facts and ideas that are of practical use at the moment. He does not concern himself with benevolence and morality, or listen to the empty discourses of learned people.[30]

Hanfeizi endorses the Daoist criticism of book learning and the scholarly approach to politics to discredit the Confucians. However, there is a fundamental difference between the strategy and the goals of the Legalist thinkers and the perspectives of Laozi and Zhuangzi. The goals

The Hundred Schools

of the Legalists, the imposition of order by enforcement of law and the priority of the state over the individual are precisely what the Daoist thinkers criticize most severely as the causes of evil and injustice. Even while he takes a fundamentally different approach to ethics from the Confucian traditions, it is characteristic of Hanfeizi's pragmatic approach to incorporate aspects of the Confucian approach to learning. Hanfeizi also favours ceremonies and the rectification of names which were the basis of Confucian education.

The Legalists who attacked the Confucians and Mohists refer to the idea of following nature which is unmistakably of Daoist origin.[31]

> Like water flowing and like a boat floating, the ruler follows the course of Nature and enforces an infinite number of commands. Therefore he is called an enlightened ruler.

The pervasive influence of Daoism is felt in Hanfeizi's effort to reconcile the Legalist doctrine with Daoism. The *Han Feizi* contains two chapters on Laozi. As Hanfeizi, the most thorough and tenacious of the Legalists, reflects on the vastness of the *dao* which cannot be circumscribed by any law, the pragmatic concerns of Legalism are set aside. Hanfeizi's discussion of the *dao* is significant and original. The *dao* is presented as the unifying principle of reality underlying distinct individual essences.

> Everything has its own principle different from that of others, and *dao* is commensurate with all of them as one. Consequently, everything has to go through the process of transformation. Since everything has to go through the process of transformation, it has no fixed mode of life. As it has no fixed mode of life, its life and death depend on the endowment of material force by *dao*. Countless wisdom depends on it for consideration. And the rise and fall of all things are because of it. Heaven obtains it and therefore becomes high. The earth obtains it and therefore can hold everything.[32]

Referring to Laozi's formulation of the *dao* as that which "cannot be heard or seen," and "shape without shape and form without objects," Hanfeizi recasts the *dao* as the principle of individuation and connects the *dao* with *li*, the principle of order, to explain the origin and transformation of all things.

115

Dao is that by which all things become what they are. It is that with which all principles are commensurable. Principles are patterns according to which all things come into being, and *dao* is the cause of their being. Therefore it is said that *dao* puts things in order".[33]

The conception of the *dao* as *li* became the focal point among the Neo-Confucian philosophers, more than twelve hundred years later.

We turn now to the Logicians who dazzled the world for a brief moment with their original and irreverent logic.

The Logicians

What nobler theme is there than heaven and earth?
I depend on no tradition.

Hui Shi boldly announced the arrival of an entirely new way of investigating heaven and all that happens below in the empire. In conscious opposition to the prevailing schools of thought which he regards as adhering to "traditions of a one-sided formula", Hui Shi launches the school of Logicians – also known as the School of Names. Earlier they were referred to as "Dialecticians" or "those who argue out."[34] The works of the Logicians have been lost with the exception of parts of the book *Kung-sun Lung Tzu*. The Logicians are of interest as they represent the only group of thinkers in ancient China whose primary interest and area of investigation was logic. The philosophical problems debated by the chief proponents, Hui Shi (ca. 380- 305 BCE) and Gung Sunlung (b. 380 BCE), ranged from metaphysics, epistemology, and philosophy of mind to philosophy of language and logic. Their main concern was conceptual clarification and investigation into the nature of existence, relativity, space, time, quality, actuality, and causality. Gung Sunlung stressed universality and permanence. He declares what his accomplishments are. "I proved the impossible as possible, and affirmed what others denied. I controverted the wisdom of all the philosophies. I refuted all arguments that were brought against me. I thought that I was the most wise."[35]

The Logicians' debates and distinctions show not so much the evolution of logical systems as the use of reason in discerning certain patterns of thinking. In ordinary circumstances it does not occur to us to pry apart the qualities of objects, such as hard or white, from the objects themselves. The Logicians' puzzles begin with this initial approach of taking ideas apart and scrutinizing them individually. Their fascination with paradoxes of thought and language is immediately evident not only in their selections of counter-intuitive examples but the juxtaposition of contradictory statements resembling surrealistic poetry. Hui Shi owes his place as one of the major thinkers entirely to a single passage in the earliest history of the school in the "Below in the Empire" chapter of *Zhuangzi*.[36]

1. The greatest has nothing beyond itself; it is called the great unit. The smallest has nothing within itself; it is called the small unit.
2. That which has no thickness cannot have any volume, and yet in extent it may cover a thousand li.
3. Heaven is as low as the earth; mountains and marshes are on the same level.
4. When the sun is at noon, it is setting; when there is life, there is death.
5. A great similarity is different from a small similarity; this is called the lesser similarity-and-difference. All things are similar to one another and different from one another; this is called the great similarity-and-difference.
6. The South has no limit and yet has a limit.
7. One goes to the state of Yueh today and arrives there yesterday.
8. Joined rings can be separated.
9. I know the center of the world: it is north of the state of Yan (in the north) and south of the state of Yueh (in the south).
10. Love all things extensively. Heaven and earth form one body.

What are we to make of these paradoxes? With sufficient imagination and willingness to render them to be consistent with subsequent development of knowledge, it has been suggested that the statements 1, 2, 3, 6, 8 and 9, are to be understood as claiming that "all quantitative measurements and all partial distinctions are illusory and unreal." 4 and 7 are to be interpreted as denying the reality of time and space. 5 and 10 assert that all apparent similarities and differences between things are unreal. It has also been proposed that the first nine paradoxes are intended to prove a monistic theory of the universe, that there is one simple underlying substance.[37]

Here is a further sampling of Hui Shi's wit related by Zhuangzi: "Hui Shi considered these to be the great insights of the world and tried to enlighten the debaters. And they enjoyed it."

1. An egg has feathers.
2. A chicken has three legs.
3. The city of Ying contains the whole world.
4. A dog can be a sheep.
5. A horse has eggs.
6. The frog has a tail.
7. Fire is not hot.
8. Mountains issue from holes.
9. A wheel never touches the ground.
10. The eye does not see.
11. The pointing of the finger does not reach a thing; the reaching never ends.
12. A tortoise grows longer than the snake.
13. The carpenter's square is not square in shape and a compass cannot draw a circle.
14. The hole in the chisel does not circumscribe the handle.
15. The shadow of a flying bird never moves.
16. The arrow is flying so fast that there are moments when it is neither in motion nor at rest.
17. A whelp is not a dog.
18. A brown horse and a dark ox make three.
19. A white dog is black.
20. An orphan colt has never had a mother.
21. Take a stick one foot long and cut it in half every day and you will never exhaust it even after ten thousand generations.[38]

It has been suggested that 3, 9, 15, 16, and 21 are about the unreality of distinctions in space and time. 1, 5, 6, 12, 13, 14 and 17 can be taken as asserting the relativity of all similarities and differences. 2, 7, 10, 11 and 18 raise the problems of knowledge. ("The eye is a means to seeing, does not itself see." "The knower sees by means of the eye and the eye by means of the fire but the fire does not see ... "[39]) 4, 19 and 20 are about the use of names. The similarity between 16 and 21 and Zeno's paradoxes of the arrow and Achilles and the tortoise is evident. Hui Shi emphasized relativity of space and time and change. Do these paradoxes achieve more than showing up some holes in the web of our thinking? Boldly stated as they are as exercise in eccentric logic, they do not in themselves provide penetrating metaphysical insights.

The prominence of the school can be inferred from Zhuangzi, who states that "Hui Shi made a great show in the world, taught people to be Dialecticians" with "five cart loads full of books"(*Zhuangzi* 33). Through their sophistry they were reputed to have persuaded their opponents to accept their conclusion and "making the inadmissible admissible," In this they share certain similarities with the Sophists of Greece who deployed their skill in rhetoric to overpower their opponents with their method of argumentation. Zhuangzi heaps scorn upon Hui Shi's excessive logic-chopping and on his political ambition (Hui Shi became a chief minister of the state of Wei and was anxious that Zhuangzi might replace him in office). But at the same time Zhuangzi declares Hui Shi to be the only truly stimulating opponent which indicates the central role of rational discourse in Zhuangzi's philosophy.

> Zhuangzi and Hui Shi were strolling on the bridge above the river Hao. "Out swim the minnows so free and easy," said Zhuangzi. "That's how they are happy." "You are not a fish. Whence do you know that they are happy?" "You aren't me. Whence do you know I don't know that the fish are happy?" "We'll grant that not being you I don't know about you. Then granted you are not a fish, the case is complete that you don't know the fish are happy." "Let's go back to where we started. When you said '*Whence* do you know the fish are happy?' you asked me the question already knowing that I knew. I knew it from up above the Hao" (*Zhuangzi* 17).[40]

When a logician and a Daoist wrestle about a point of logic it is the Daoist, if the Daoist is Zhuangzi, who vanquishes the dialectician in his own sport. That the Logicians were unconcerned with the moral life was the primary criticism of their contemporaries. They were severely admonished by Zhuangzi and Xunzi for their addiction to paradox and relentless argumentation. Zhuangzi states that "They are able to subdue other people's mouths, but cannot win their hearts. This is where their narrowness lies." But in a civilization where philosophy has a long tradition of engaging the moral problems and philosophers were drawn to political reform, not even the Logicians could stay aloof from ethical reflections. Hui Shi's statements, "Love all things extensively. Heaven and earth form one body" support the view that they were adherents of the doctrine of universal love of Mozi. Having embraced an all-encompassing theory of universal love, the logicians left the field of ethics intact and wielded their considerable power and dexterity in analysis in the detection of flawed arguments. To what end? Why was the keen analysis of discourse initiated by the Logicians not taken up by other able minds to build a body of knowledge that might have led to the development of logic and philosophy of language? The preoccupation of the Logicians in conjuring up paradoxes was not enticing to the philosophers who were drawn to the practical moral problems at hand.

The function of logical analysis is not the perforation of common sense with piercing wit but arriving at a method and rules for construction of valid arguments which can take us from known premises to new conclusions. The Logicians' debates were not a systematic analysis of discourse with the aim of providing ways of testing the validity of all arguments. Neither the syntax nor semantics of language were studied with a systematic rigor to yield the logic of syllogisms or symbolic logic consisting of truth functional connectives and rules for their operation. Their analysis did not culminate in a study of the method of deductive logic.

The standard criticism against the Logicians is that they went too far in their analysis of ideas, language, and thought. But the love of truth for its own sake would be justifiable if it were carried out in full measure, not only to show faulty reasoning but to search for methods and rules for discovering new truths. Their ingenuity and entertaining examples, having lost the charm of novelty and shock of surprise, did not lead to a lasting method of testing the soundness and validity of an argument. Given that the best minds in China were enlivened by ethical concerns, logical analysis flourished only briefly without developing into a full-fledged discipline in its own right. Zhuangzi regrets that Hui Shi did not develop his considerable talent beyond the pleasures of disputation and subduing the opponents. "It was like silencing an echo by his shouting or running a race with his shadow. Alas!" (*Zhuangzi* 33., Legge II. 232). Passing by the grave of Hui Shi Zhuangzi remarks "Since the death of the Master... I have had no one with whom to talk" (*Zhuangzi* 12. 3.2).

This concludes our exploration of the classical period of philosophy in China. We now turn to Buddhism, which developed as the third most significant philosophical perspective with the Confucian and Daoist thought.

4
Buddhism

From Emptiness to Enlightenment

All that we are is the result of what we have thought: it is founded on our thoughts, it is made up of our thoughts.

As a fletcher makes straight his arrow, a wise man makes straight his trembling and unsteady thought, which is difficult to guard, difficult to hold back (*Dhammapada*).

Buddhism was introduced to China from India as early as the first century and became the third major philosophical and religious movement during the Sui and Tang dynasties (589-907 CE). Buddhist missionaries continued to flow into China, and Chinese pilgrims went to India and collected Buddhist texts. A vast work of literature from the Buddhist cannon, *Tripitaka*, was translated from Sanskrit.

Buddhism begins with a general perception about life: that there is suffering in the world and that all are born to die. Once we consent to this simple observation of common experience, the question naturally arises, what causes this suffering? Is it the way the world is or is the way we experience things? The answer is that we suffer because of our desires and because we become bound by our attachments to the world of action in which all is transitory and impermanent. The obscure objects of desire which we crave cause us suffering.

Can we ever overcome suffering? We can, by becoming free of craving. These beliefs form the core of Buddhism, "the four noble truths": life is suffering, suffering is caused by craving, suffering can be eliminated by extinguishing craving, and following the "eight noble paths." The "eight noble paths" are right view, right aspiration, right speech, right conduct, right livelihood, right effort, right mindfulness, and right concentration. This is the Middle Path between asceticism and hedonism taught by Siddhartha Guatama (560-480BCE), the Buddha (Enlightened One), who, upon realizing that no sentient being is exempt from the sorrows of life, renounced his princely life to become a wanderer, and sought ways of overcoming suffering (*dukka*). Sitting under the *Bo* tree (the tree of enlightenment) in meditation he reached an exalted state of consciousness and found the way to attain release from all suffering.

Buddhism builds on the ideas of *samsara* and *karma* in Hinduism. All sentient beings are caught up in an unending cycle of continuing birth, death, and rebirth (*samsara*). The law of *karma* (action) governs all existence and the conditions of rebirth. All deeds are followed by deserved pleasure or pain and those who perform good deeds (acts of charity and compassion) in the present life can be reassured of less suffering in their subsequent lives. The idea of rebirth in Buddhism is distinct from the transmigration of souls in popular Indian thought. In philosophical Buddhism rebirth is not in afterlife detached from this world. Rebirth takes place all the time. What is carried over into rebirth is not the individual soul, but "the character of what was the original or latest person."[1]

The immortality of the individual soul has been a topic of substantial concern in the West. Philosophical and religious texts from Mesopotamia, Egypt, Greece and the scriptures of Judaism and Christianity hold forth the possibility of eternal life as the reward for good conduct. But in Hinduism, the concern is with the universal soul: the highest knowledge consists in comprehending that the individual soul, *atman* is identical with the universal soul, *brahman*. The goal is not eternal life but liberation from the cycles of birth and rebirth. In Buddhism the goal is to be released from the needs of the burdensome individual self. This is only possible if we realize that our cravings are illusory. As we achieve the state of mind which recognizes the futility of all craving we are liberated from the cause of all suffering. The ultimate goal of Buddhism is enlightenment (*nirvana*), the attainment of insight and peace.

What is enlightenment? It is a heightened state of awareness in which we come to realize the impermanence and the illusory nature of the phenomenal world and become free of all anguish and craving. What happens after the enlightenment? We are released from *samsara* and are no longer bound by the law of *karma*. Central to attaining enlightenment is the "Doctrine of Emptiness." Everything in the phenomenal world is held to be "empty" or "void" because no being is seen as having a permanently enduring self. In Hinduism it is thought that the individual self (*atman*) is identical with the absolute (*brahman*) in the universe. Spiritual liberation (*moksha*) consists in uniting the *atman* with the *brahman*. In sharp contrast to this, Buddhist philosophy denies the existence of the self: there is nothing behind our sense of the self. The argument is that for there to be a real self it would have to possess certain characteristics, such as permanence, immutability, absence of suffering, and being unaffected by prior events.[2] But clearly the self which we experience is entirely different from this. What we experience is a series of processes. In place of the concept of the *atman* as an immortal soul in the individual, Buddhism introduces the idea that the individual is comprised of five aspects or functions (*skandhas*): the physical form (the body), perceptions, feelings, dispositions and consciousness. With this analysis of the individual in terms of specific functions Buddhism seeks to eliminate the notion of the inherent self and with it banish the suffering caused by the cravings of the self. When we are enlightened we have the awareness of the non-existence of the self.

The Buddhist thesis of the non-existence of the self (*anatman*) is analogous to Hume's view that the idea of the self as an enduring substance underlying all change is a fiction. There is a further resemblance between the characterization of the self in Buddhism as consisting of events and processes and Hume's account of the self as a series or a bundle of impressions. Entering into what is called the innermost self, Hume finds that he runs against this or that impression. He can never catch a glimpse of the pure self without a particular impression. Hume concludes that the self is like an empty stage onto which the varying impressions, perceptions, and ideas enter and exit. This is essentially the idea of emptiness or void which Buddhism projects onto the whole of the phenomenal world. Although there is a similarity in their analysis of the nature of the self, there is a significant difference between Hume's mitigated scepticism and the Buddhist perspective regarding the physical world. Hume recommends that we continue to live relying on the habitual assumptions about the world – that the sun will continue to rise and that the bread will not turn into stone. Buddhism urges that we seek to transcend the phenomenal world of illusion (*maya*) and affirms the certainty of the knowledge of the absolute reality attained in enlightenment.

We must lift the veil of *maya* to see the reality beyond the world of appearances. How do we know that there is such reality and that all else is an illusion? There are difficulties with the claim that the entire phenomenal world is an illusion and that all our judgements are deluded. It may be that there is nothing behind the curtain which is to conceal the ultimate reality unless we ourselves are to go behind it.[3] The omnipresence of *maya* raises a problem for if we insist that all our judgements are illusory, we cannot maintain the distinction between illusion and reality on which the claim about illusion itself is based. Ramanuja in the eleventh century raised this objection and argued that the perception of objects has some basis in reality. If I see a piece of rope as a snake, there is still something I am seeing which is real. Even a mistaken perception involves a real apprehension of an aspect of the world.[4] Then we are back to affirming the reality of the world.

In connection to rebirth, there is a difficulty with denying the reality of the self. If there is no permanent substance called the self, how can it be said that the same person is reborn or escapes the cycle of birth and rebirth? Surely the law of *karma* presupposes that there is a continuous existence of the individual who is the agent of his actions? The proposed solution to this objection is that rebirth does not require an actual permanent self, but only a permanent or enduring idea of the self.[5]

In the injunction of the Buddha, "Do not be a friend of the world," the purity of the individual is of the highest moral significance. There is an inconsistency here: on one hand Buddhism teaches us to disregard the individual self as illusory but to preserve oneself one disregards the world. Buddhism has been criticized by the Neo-Confucian philosophers as valuing the individual well-being above all else. Hegel's remarks on "the beautiful soul" come to mind. The person with a beautiful soul turns away from the world of being and action because it is evil, hypocritical, and corrupt. He withdraws into himself; he is righteous and pure of heart. In fleeing reality and judging it critically the beautiful soul cannot escape the criticism of others that he is also culpable of hypocrisy and willfulness.[6] The Buddhist answer to this criticism is to introduce the *boddhisattvas*. If in our compassion we choose to defer entering the state of bliss and remain in the realm of *karma* to alleviate the suffering in the world and assist others on their path to *nirvana* we join the ranks of the *boddhisattvas* who will eventually ascend to Buddhahood.

Beginning in the fourth and fifth centuries and continuing until the early part of the Song dynasty in the tenth century, Buddhism stimulated philosophically inclined scholars when the other schools of thought were languishing. Buddhism nourished the imagination of the leading philosophers, poets, and painters and led people of varying interests to think deeply and unify their experiences and thoughts centered on the possibility of attaining enlightenment through individual effort. The very idea of enlightenment, or seeing things as they really are, became for the first time a tangible reality, giving ultimate meaning to life. Buddhism, in offering enlightenment, and the elimination of suffering and compassion, brought with it new possibilities of what constitutes a moral life.

Throughout the development of Buddhist thought, there have been persistent efforts to establish the belief in the central tenets of Buddhism by philosophical argument on the nature of reality, the workings of the mind, and the right way to live. The Buddhist thinkers in China in the fourth and fifth century were well versed in the Confucian classics, as well as in the writings of Laozi and Zhuangzi. The explication of Buddhist doctrines via Daoist ideas was described as "the method of analogy" which facilitated the understanding of the new doctrine of Buddhism. ("Great oneness," a Daoist term, was taken as a synonym for the wisdom or omniscience of the Buddha.)

In later centuries, Daoism was, in turn, influenced by Buddhist ideas. During the revival of Daoism in the third century scholars assimilated the speculative aspects of Buddhism merging them with the familiar and established ideas from Daoist writings. The influence of Buddhism on Daoism has been primarily on religious Daoism more than on philosophical Daoism. The Daoist philosophers did not approach Daoism as a religion built on the teachings of a master, consisting of doctrines and beliefs preserved in a corpus of literature. The religious Daoists adopted the model of the hierarchy of teachers and disciples and a monastic community from Buddhism. The practice of making statues and images was also borrowed from the Buddhists. The Buddhist doctrines of *karma* and rebirth were adapted by the Daoists, and Laozi resurfaces as one of the incarnations of the *boddhisattvas*. However, from the views of nature and man in Daoism a different moral perspective emerges. The fundamental difference between Daoist religion and Buddhism regarding life is that whereas in Daoism preservation of life is the desired goal, in Buddhism enlightenment is achieved by letting go of attachment to life. Daoism can be seen as affirmation of life, Buddhism as renunciation.

The two main branches of Buddhism, Theravada (Doctrine of the Elders) and Mahayana (Greater Vehicle) are interpreted as offering different solutions. Theravada focuses on the individual attainment of the state of *arhat* (one who has attained enlightenment) through self-discipline. Mahayana, on the other hand, stresses becoming a *bodhisattva* (one who works to relieve the suffering of others in order to bring about the enlightenment of all). Mahayana Buddhism became the major force in China. The literature of Buddhism can be separated into devotional and philosophical. Among the main texts of Buddhism which exerted significant influence in China is the devotional text titled, *The Scripture of the Pure Land.* Of the various schools of Buddhism in China, we sketch four major developments: *Jing Du* (Pure land), *Tian Tai* (Heavenly Gate), *Hua Yen* (Flower Splendour or Hundred Flower), and *Chan* (*Zen*, derived from the Sanskrit *dhyana*, meditation).

The varieties of Buddhism provide different explanations of the nature, process, kind of enlightenment, and the possibilities of eternal life. The Pure Land Buddhists emphasize the faith in *Amitabha* who can save all beings to be reborn in the land of the Western Paradise. The Flower Splendour Buddhists teach the doctrine of interconnectedness of all beings. Nothing has its own being in the sense that everything depends for its existence on the entire realm of reality. While the Pure Land appealed to the heart, the Heavenly Terrace addressed the intellect. Adopting a rational approach to the study of the scriptures in addition to meditation as the way to reach enlightenment, the Heavenly Terrace School identifies the absolute Buddha nature with each phenomenon. The *Chan* Buddhists advocate abandonment of rational discourse and the study of scriptures in favour of an intuitive grasp of the Buddha nature in a moment of sudden enlightenment. *Chan* seeks to arrive at self-knowledge through meditation.

Pure Land

> This world ... is rich, prosperous, and comfortable, fertile, delightful ... it emits many fragrant odours, it is rich in great variety of flowers and fruits, adorned with jewel trees which are frequented by flocks of various birds with sweet voices ...[7]

This is the world of Pure Land (Happy Land, Sweet Land or the Western Paradise), the perfect world created through the sheer power of concentration by *Amitabha*, the Buddha of Light who made a vow to save all beings. The Pure Land is not only a tropical paradise but also a place of lofty debate and a deep inquiry into the nature of truth as envisioned in Buddhism.

> And everyone hears the pleasant sound he wishes to hear... he
> hears of grounds of the analytical knowledge, of emptiness...
> non-existence, of calm ... of peace, of the great friendliness, the
> great compassion, and the great sympathetic joy...

The mortals who failed to achieve *nirvana* in this life can be reborn in
Pure Land in their next lifetime if they are dedicated to *Amitabha* who
sits on a lotus throne attended by *Guan Yin*, the *bodhisattva* of mercy.
Surely not everyone but only those who are deserving should be reborn
in the Pure Land? The long version of *the Pure Land Sutra* stresses that
meritorious deeds as well as faith and devotion are required, whereas
the short version specifies that only prayer and faith are necessary.

> Moreover ... all the beings who have been reborn in the world
> of Pure Land ... will be exactly like the radiant gods; of the
> same colour, strength, vigour ... keenness of superior knowl-
> edge.

The Pure Land is the place of complete equality in which all can
achieve enlightenment.

The Pure Land Sutra became one of the most popular texts during
the Tang dynasty (610-906 CE) and continues to be popular to the present. The conception of enlightenment as consisting of wisdom and
compassion presented a significant moral perspective. The Pure Land
School harbors a moral idealism: "at the heart of ultimate reality is the
compassionate wisdom revealed in the Infinite Love and Unquenchable
light of *Amitabha*."[8] The celebration of the beauty of nature appealed to
the aesthetic sensibility of the scholar-poets. The simplicity of the devotion to one *bodhisattva* and the infinitely compassionate *Amitabha* as
the key to *nirvana* appealed to the popular imagination. In the popular
Buddhism an interesting transformation took place. In the tradition of
Mahayana a *bodhisattva* can assume any form or shape to alleviate suffering of all sentient beings. *Guan Yin*, as *bodhisattva* is referred to in
China, is sometimes portrayed with eight or eleven heads or with a
thousand eyes and heads indicating her ability and vigilance to tend to
the needs of all everywhere. *Guan Yin* was originally portrayed as a
male figure with a prominent mustache. During the Tang dynasty he
begins to be suddenly portrayed as a feminine figure dressed in white.
One explanation for this is that *Guan Yin* is based on White Tara, the
consort of a *bodhisattva* in Tibetan Buddhism, whose chief attribute is

compassion.[9]

There has been a gradual inward turning among the thinkers of China and the accompanying preoccupation with the perfection of the self. The Pure Land Sutra promised with confidence to deliver truth, happiness, and absolute joy to all devotees with the sense of finality accompanied by a feeling that "all the problems which all the schools of philosophers under heaven cannot settle this way or that have been settled."[10]

Flower Splendour

In the center of a room lighted by an enormous torch, there is a figure of the Buddha. There are ten mirrors around the figure, all facing one another: one above, one below, and eight at the points of the compass. We see not only that the image of the figure is reflected in the mirrors but also that the image in each mirror is reflected in all the other mirrors. "Not only this but the multiple images reflected in each were also reflected in every other mirror, thus doubling and redoubling the images. This was like Indra's net, with its network of jewels that not only reflected the images in every other jewel, but also the multiple images in the others."[11]

This is how Fa Zang (643-712), considered to be the real founder of the Flower Splendour School (*Hua Yen*), demonstrated the central doctrine of the school to his baffled disciples. All particular phenomena and existent things (*dharmas*) arose simultaneously: the creation of the universe by itself is the origin of all things. The main ideas of the Flower Splendour are based on the Buddhist doctrine of dependent origination (interdependent arising). In Buddhism the world is not created by a divine being. If there are gods anywhere – as it appears that the Buddha did not reject the belief in gods – they are also caught up in the cycle of *samsara* as all temporal beings are. All things come into existence in an interdependent process. This process has twelve constituent elements which are continually arising in conjunction with one another. They are "ignorance, karmic predispositions, consciousness, name and form, the five sense organs and the mind, contact, feeling-response, craving, grasping for an object, action toward life, birth, and old age and death." Each of these elements is linked to others giving rise to the others. Each *dharma* shares six metaphysical characteristics: universality, particularity, similarity, difference, integration and disintegration.[12]

When an empress was unable to follow the theory of the interpenetration and identification of all the *dharmas*, Fa Zang pointed to a golden lion and wrote down the explanations in the *Essay on the Golden Lion*. In every part of the lion the whole lion is present. Take the eyes, ears and the hairs of the lion. Are they not the eyes, ears, and the hairs *of* the lion? Does it then not follow that every part contains the whole? The point of seeing the universe as an organic whole is that we can reach enlightenment through such an understanding.

> When one sees this lion and this gold, the two characters are annihilated, the passions do not arise, and although beauty and ugliness are manifested before the eye, the mind stays calm ... this is called "entering nirvana."[13]

Whereas the Indian Buddhist thinkers tended to stress the negative aspect of dependent origination – that the particular events or *dharmas* are empty – the Flower Splendour School interprets the interdependence of things to emphasize how it may be possible for an individual to transcend emptiness through correct understanding.

The *Hua Yen Sutra* teaches that all phenomena are manifestations of the principle (*li*) and every individual phenomenon is identical with the rest. All *dharmas* are empty in the sense that they are caused by the universal principle without which they would be nothing. The principle itself has no form of its own; it assumes any form of a particular thing in which it is found. Just as the principle and its manifestations are interfused in the phenomena, all *dharmas* are interdependent. Since all phenomena are productions of the one immutable principle, they are in perfect harmony with one another. Everything in the universe is the manifestation of the same supreme mind and is capable of performing the work of an enlightened being. It is for this reason that the school was called the perfect teaching of the Buddha.[14]

Heavenly Terrace

> In every particle of dust, in every moment of thought, the whole universe is contained.

The Heavenly Terrace School (*Tian Tai*) emphasized the identification of the whole of existence with every individual object.[15] The whole universe and all the Buddhas are present in a grain of sand or the tip of a hair. The basic text of the school was the *Lotus Sutra*, which teaches that all sentient beings already possess the Buddha nature so that enlightenment is reached by returning to our original nature.

The *Tian Tai* School was established by Zhi Yi (Chih-i, 538-597) who consolidated the earlier efforts of his predecessors at the *Tian Tai* mountains. His mother is said to have conceived him when in her dream she swallowed a white mouse, which the soothsayers said was formerly an elephant. On the day of his birth a supernatural light appeared in the sky. Then, from nowhere, two monks appeared to announce that Zhi would grow up to be a monk. The prediction came true. At the age of seven he visited a temple and astonished the monks by reciting a sutra after hearing it once.[16] He persuaded the fishermen along the seashore at the foot of the *Tian Tai* mountain to adopt the practice of not killing any living thing and obtained imperial consent to a decree banning fishing in the area. He was invited by the Chen and Sui emperors to hold lectures and was bestowed the title "Man of Wisdom."

"The three thousand worlds are immanent in an instance of thought," encapsulates the ontology of the *Tian Tai*. In the phenomenal world (the realm of temporary truth) there are three thousand worlds: Buddhas, *bodhisattvas*, the disciples, heavenly beings, spirits, human beings, and animals. All these worlds are believed to be interpenetrated so completely that they are involved in every moment of thought. If all things are interconnected then they all possess Buddha nature and all are capable of enlightenment. The Confucian view that everyone can become a sage has been acknowledged as having laid the foundation for this egalitarian approach to enlightenment.[17]

The Heavenly Terrace School is considered as one of the high achievements of philosophical Buddhism in China. It regarded all forms of Buddhism as the true teachings of the Buddha which were revealed gradually at various stages and saw no rivalry between Theravada and Mahayana. It provided a system of interpretation which incorporated the diverse doctrines and practices among the various sects and fostered a sense of coherence in the development of Buddhist thought in China. The Heavenly Terrace gave a philosophical grounding for the possibility of universal salvation in the Pure Land School and the thesis of interdependent causation of all things in the Flower Splendour School. Its theories are admired as "final and round doctrines of Buddhism": final because it brought together all doctrines of other schools, and round because it acknowledges the Buddha nature in all sentient beings and upholds universal salvation accepting all means as feasible. Concentration and insight are regarded as two wings of a bird moving in unison toward enlightenment. In its emphasis on the omnipresence of the Buddha nature and concentration and insight as the means of attaining enlightenment it is linked to *Chan*.

The central tenets of the *Tian Tai*, based on the theory of Nagarjuna (second century BCE), are expressed as the threefold truths: emptiness, temporariness, and the mean (or the middle, *zhong*). The customary perception of things as possessing definite characteristics is an illusion which must be abolished by concentration (*zhi*) and insight (*guan*). All things are impermanent and have no independent reality of their own, since they are produced by external causes; in this sense they are said to be empty. This is the truth of emptiness. But since they are produced they do have temporary and dependent existence; things have relative reality. This is the temporary truth. Then things are both empty and temporary. This is the truth of the mean. The three levels of truth are applicable to all phenomena. In advocating the harmony of the three levels of truth, the *Tian Tai* goes beyond the traditional Buddhist differentiation of the two levels of truth into "higher" and "conventional" which regarded the truth of ultimate emptiness and the common experience of plurality of things as being separate. In one of the great debates of the *Tian Tai*, the topic was whether "the focus of meditation should be on the actual empirical mind of the individual" with its ignorance and attachments or on "the true mind" – the pure mind of the Buddha. The dichotomy of the two minds are resolved by the middle truth of *Tian Tai* which teaches us that the individual mind must seek emptiness within the manifold of phenomena. This idea of the middle truth is a distinctive feature of Buddhist thought in China and became widely accepted throughout the Far East.[18]

Enlightenment consists in achieving the true mind of the Buddha. which knows itself.

> Question: "Is the Buddha termed such because, possessing wisdom, he is able thereby to be aware of his pure mind? Or is he so called because this pure mind of his has its own self-awareness?"
>
> Answer: "Both statements apply. According to the one he has an awareness of his pure mind. According to the other, the pure mind has an awareness of itself. Although these are described as two separate ideas, in their essence there is no distinction between them."[19]

If this explication of the true mind and the three levels of truth in *Tian Tai* have a familiar ring, it may be because we have encountered a similar view in Hegel's theory of the mind in the *Phenomenology of Mind*. The self-awareness of the pure mind in the *Tian Tai* can be compared to Hegel's absolute mind which knows itself. The three levels of truth of the *Tian Tai* are comparable to the development of consciousness in Hegel's *Phenomenology*. In the first stage the immediate world of physical surroundings is the object of individual consciousness and is accepted as constituting reality. In the next stage when we begin to look closely into our experience of the world of sense-certainty its apparent permanence is recognized as only momentary and we are immersed in the inner world of subjectivity. In the third stage the dichotomy between the external world of objects and the inner world of finite individuality is reconciled. We see nature and reality as the manifestation of the rational mind of which we are a part – this is what Hegel means when he declares that only the mind is real. He does not mean that material things do not exist. Similarly in the *Tian Tai* the explication of the true mind as the only reality which is infinite incorporates the temporary existence of the particular objects. Nothing that is partial or finite can be free. In *Tian Tai*, the mind becomes pure and free through meditation. For Hegel through reason the self-conscious mind comes to know itself to be infinite mind. The essence of the mind is freedom and philosophy is the activity which purifies and frees the mind. What are the objections against this view of the mind?

On his tombstone Kierkegaard wanted only the words "The Individual." The antithesis of Hegel's view of the absolute mind and the *Tian Tai* view of the pure mind is put forward by Kierkegaard who attributes to Hegel the thesis that man must overcome his individuality and become part of the universal. For Kierkegaard, man is an individual and not a part of the universal. Kierkegaard's denunciation of the "systematization" of the world and his stance that the irrational and the paradoxical are worthy of belief echoes the *Chan*'s cultivation of paradox and the radical rejection of reason. *Chan* restores intense individuality to the moment of sudden awakening. The motto of *Chan* might be "Abandon reason all those who seek enlightenment."

Chan Buddhism

The body is the tree of enlightenment
And the mind is like a bright mirror stand.

> Always cleanse them diligently, and do not
> Let dust fall on them.[20]

Here we have a poem written by a candidate deemed most worthy to receive the patriarchal robe of the master to continue the illustrious line as a spiritual successor. A few days later another poem was posted next to it.

> Enlightenment is not a tree to begin with
> Nor is the mind a mirror stand.
> Since originally there was nothing
> Whereon would the dust fall?

Which poem shows a true understanding of enlightenment? The writer of the second poem, Huineng, was initially rebuffed by the reigning patriarch, who discouraged him by saying that southerners did not possess the Buddha nature. He was promoted to the position of a rice pounder on the strength of his reply that for the Buddha nature there is no distinction between northerners and southerners. (The Northern School of *Chan* believed in enlightenment as a gradual process while the Southern School stressed instantaneous enlightenment.[21]) On another occasion he came upon two monks arguing about a pennant flapping in the breeze. The first argued that the pennant was an inanimate object, and only the wind made it flap. The second retorted that there was no flapping pennant, only the wind was moving. Huineng interjected: there is neither the pennant nor the wind that was flapping, only their minds. This launched Huineng as a *Chan* master. The key to everything in *Chan* Buddhism is the state of mind which symbolizes the position of every person who seeks truth.

Chan, which arose out of the intertwining of Daoism and Buddhism, is the most original and significant school of Buddhism to emerge from China. The Indian idea of meditation is merged with the Daoist conceptions of concentration and enlightenment. The *Chan* School focuses on enlightenment which comes as a flash of insight in a moment of awakening. A central difference between the *Chan* view of enlightenment and Zhuangzi's ideas is that the *dao* is not grasped at some heightened moment of direct awareness. The influence of Daoism on the development of *Chan* Buddhism is evident in the disregard for outward ceremony, the approach to startling the mind to jolt the sense of secure reality, and the penchant for paradoxes.

There are certain central tenets of the *Chan* school which were very likely inspired directly by Zhuangzi's writings: the emphasis on simplicity, irreverence toward reason, overcoming all distinctions, and a benign view of death. Zhuangzi's description of the "State of Established Virtue" could describe a *Chan* adept (Legge II. 30).

> The people are ignorant and simple; their object is to minimize the thought of self and make their desires few; they labour but do not lay up their gains... acting in a wild and eccentric way as if they were mad, they yet keep to grand rules of conduct.

Zhuangzi's ideas of minimizing the thought of the self and making one's desires few is carried to its logical conclusion in *Chan* Buddhism: we aim at getting rid of the idea of the self and suspending all desires.

> To know things as they are one must be beside oneself ... to him who does not dwell in himself the forms of things show themselves as they are. His movement is like that of water; his response is like that of the echo. Men all choose fullness; he alone chooses emptiness (Legge II. 226).

The man of the *dao* and an aspirant of *Chan* both seek emptiness. A Daoist says to a ruler: "Be like an empty boat in an open sea. Make your wants few. Wade through the rivers and float along the sea. If a man can empty himself of himself, who can harm him?" (Legge II. 32).

Zhuangzi stresses that when we do not rely on rational discourse and learning we can grasp truth more directly. The masters of *Chan* boldly abandon rational discussion in favour of paradoxical questions to startle and to propel the search for truth beyond common experience and reasoned explanations until they are dazzled by sudden illumination. What is prized is not a prolonged study or a learned discourse. All teachings of the Buddhas, reciting of the sutras, or performing the rituals of purification yield nothing and are to be abandoned. In place of argumentation and rational analysis which are hindrances to enlightenment, we have a *gongan* (*kung-an*, problem) to concentrate the mind. Consider what might be the answers to these *gongans*. "If all things are reducible to the One, to what is the One reduced?" "How do you get the fly out of the flybottle without breaking it?" "What was your face before your parents were born?" "From where you are stop the distant boat from moving across the water." Since the point of the whole exercise of the *gongan* is to go beyond logical analysis and to shake off the habit of rational thought, there are not always solutions to these riddles.

And even when an answer is given, we are not any wiser: "Three pounds of flax" is the answer to the question, "What is the Buddha nature?"

The *Chan* way of thought relishes startling juxtapositions of contraries to break away from the familiar interpretations of associated meanings to reach for an awareness beyond thought and language. The essence of *Chan* is in its method of bringing on the enlightenment. The *gongan* is designed to flummox the intellect through a conceptual torment in order that we may learn to go beyond concepts.[22] The sudden awakening is possible only at the moment of the annulment of reason. In the *Chan* conception, the mind is a simple and an absolutely indivisible unity. The *Chan* disciple strives to achieve a state of mind in which reality becomes transparent. Through meditation, discourse in riddles, and practice of various arts (poetry, painting, and archery), the *Chan* disciple seeks the direct awareness of the inseparable unity of mind.

Sitting in front of a wall for nine years, Bodhidharma, the acknowledged founder and the first patriarch of *Chan*, practiced what was known as wall contemplation, paying no attention to a monk, who beseeched that he might be taught the truth of *Chan*. To prove his sincerity the monk cut off his arm whereupon Bodhidharma began his instruction. The monk subsequently became the second patriarch. However the origin of *Chan* is not as extreme as this. In a sermon the Buddha once held up a flower in silence. The disciple who smiled – showing that he understood – was given the True Law which was brought to China in 520 CE. One of the main texts transmitted by Bodhidharma is the *Descent of the Island of Lanka*, which emphasizes the doctrine of inner enlightenment. Bodhidharma is reputed to have dismissed emperor Wu's (502-549 CE, the founder of Liang dynasty) study of the scriptures, building of monasteries, and pious deeds as being futile and insignificant since he believed that they do not lead to the knowledge of one's own Buddha nature.

When we reach enlightenment what do we know? One who achieves enlightenment overcomes all distinctions and the eight-fold negation of production and extinction, annihilation and permanence, unity and diversity, and coming and departing. We have a direct intuition of the Buddha nature in all things and know that the ultimate reality is empty or void (*sunya*). This reality is inexpressible and incommunicable and can only be apprehended directly in an inspired instant. Words are dispensed with and instead gazing, raising of eyebrows, frowning, smiling, and twinkling of eyes are indications of direct

135

grasping of the *Chan* insight. All conscious thought must be extinguished for it only perpetuates *karma* which keeps us bound to the endless cycle of birth and death with incessant longing and attachment to external objects which are fleeting and hold out only a glimmer of illusory happiness.

How is the mind to be freed and moved spontaneously to reach enlightenment? The specific methods vary from the master shouting at the novices and showering them with beatings to sitting in solitary meditation under the guidance of a master. However, if the essence of *Chan* is direct intuition and instantaneous enlightenment, to speak of a method appears inappropriate. There is a paradox in *Chan*. In order to be free one must deny the individual will and submit for a prolonged period to the master. But one must dare to question all authority, even to the point of annihilating the master in order that one may reach enlightenment directly. Dependence on any external source is a hindrance to discovering the Buddha nature within oneself. *Chan* aims at spontaneity and natural expression through intensive study and austere discipline. The sudden illumination can only be achieved after years of arduous labour. According to Huineng, Bodhidharma wrote,

> I originally came to China to transmit the teaching and save deluded beings.
> One flower opens five petals, and the fruit ripens itself.[23]

Huineng's rejoinder to this is indicative of the strategy of the *Chan* adept who challenges the acknowledged master.

> If evil flowers bloom in the mind...
> They will create the karma of ignorance ...
> If correct flowers bloom in the mind,
> Five blossoms flower from the stem.
> Practice wisdom –
> This will become the enlightenment of the Buddha.[24]

The fruit of enlightenment does not come from the flowers of evil nor does it ripen of its own accord but only through the cultivation of the mind and practice of wisdom.

The *Chan* movement coincided with a period of an unprecedented freedom of expression in literature and painting in the Tang dynasty (618-907). *Chan* masters expressed their ideas in the simple colloquial language of the day. This led to the development of poetry and prose distinct from the dominant Confucian literature displaying erudition and following the formal rules of composition. The celebrated poets Li Bai and Du Fu and the painter Wu Daozi created highly acclaimed individual styles. The leading poets of the day, Wang Wei (who is said to have been also a remarkable painter) and Su Dongpo were drawn to *Chan* ideas. In the poetry of Wang Wei we glimpse what might be meant by the Buddha nature in all things.

> Dear flat rock facing the stream
> Where the willows are sweeping over my cup
> If you say that the spring wind has no understanding
> Why should it come blowing me these falling flowers? [25]

The landscape paintings of the Song dynasty express the *Chan* spirit. In the paintings all elements from the drama of life are absent or incidental. All mountains, trees, rivers and lakes are creations of the mind and subject to the law of impermanence. They are intended to be seen as floating in the distance, having no real existence. The love of emptiness is portrayed. A solitary fisherman sits in a boat, rod in hand. The boat is adrift in the lake whose banks are not visible; "the water is indicated only by a few lines along the boat. All the rest is emptiness."[26] The painter listens to the songs of birds, waterfalls or the wind seeking to represent the spiritual essence of Buddha present in man, animal, mountain, stream or a flower. Meditating on nature, he seeks to convey through his paintings the inward essence underlying the outward forms. To capture the visions of the essence of all transient things, the painter works swiftly, spontaneously. To wield the brush promptly and unhesitatingly the painters undergo strenuous training. *Chan* is not a technique that can be transferred; it is an experience of clear perception. *Chan* is a process of distillation of meaning from a perceptual experience freed from all conceptual frameworks. One must close the physical eye to see with the mind's eye. To accomplish this, he seeks to identify himself with the object by intense concentration. A favourite theme among the painters was the bamboo "whose upward thrust signified rectitude and inner emptiness illustrated the Buddhist ideal of vacuity."

> But brief is the season of man's delight.
> Soon it falls to the ground; some dire decision uproots it.
> – Thing of a day! Such is man; a shadow in a dream.

We might take this verse as a *Chan* poem until we read the rest.

> Yet when god-given splendour visits him.
> A bright radiance plays over him, and how sweet is life!

The acuteness with which the brevity of all human endeavours is felt is expressed by the Greek poet Pindar in the sixth century BCE.[27] While the *Chan* poets hit upon the moment of instantaneous enlightenment which frees them from all yearning for earthly joys for all times, Pindar rejoices in the transcendent moment of radiance in life.

When the *Chan* movement has run its full course demolishing systematic thought with riddles and paradoxes beyond the bounds of common sense and reason, the Neo-Confucian philosophers reconstruct with the labour of reason the philosophical edifice in which the real is the rational and the rational is the real. The mind and the nature of the universe are not lawless. Turning to the Neo-Confucian philosophers, we discover affirmation of life. In their reflection on the ultimate structure of reality leading to an ethical commitment they present a comprehensive synthesis of the insights of Confucian, Daoist, and Buddhist thought.

5

Neo-Confucian
Philosophy

The Renaissance of Philosophy

There are two great periods of philosophy in China. The first is the classical age (500-200 BCE) marked by political turbulence when amidst continuous warfare and devastation of the Warring States, Laozi, Confucius, Mozi, Zhuangzi, and Mencius put forward moral philosophy as solutions to the search for meaning in the cultivation of individual life and harmony in the world. The second is that of the Neo-Confucian philosophy during the Song (960-1279) and Ming (1368-1644) dynasties. After the classical age of philosophy, there was a lull in the philosophical world as Confucian tradition became the state orthodoxy and religious Daoism and Buddhism gained ground. The ideas of Confucius, shrouded in the cult of sanctimonious veneration, had a stultifying effect on philosophical thinking. During the long interval between the classical period and the arrival of Neo-Confucian philosophy, various schools of thought contended for official position and popular appeal.

The arrival of Neo-Confucian thinkers brought about a vibrant renewal of philosophy, awakening the philosophers from a long dogmatic slumber. There is great originality of ideas expressed in forceful and energetic terms. The passion for ideas, the intensity of the language, and the considerable heated exchange are invigorating. "The Five Masters of the early Song period" – Zhou Dunyi (1017-1073), Shao Yong (1010-1077), Zhang Zai (1020-1077), Cheng Hao (1032-1085)

139

and Cheng Yi (1033-1107) – were the key figures in the revitalization of the Confucian tradition as a philosophical movement. One thinker is credited with having carried out the formidable task of synthesizing the ideas of the entire Confucian tradition into a coherent and unified system, shaping the continuous transmission of Confucian thought. This is Zhu Xi (1130-1200), who fully developed Neo-Confucianism in its final form and through his prolific writing and commentaries on the classics exerted a vast influence. There was a close relation among the Neo-Confucian philosophers. The Cheng brothers had Zhou Dunyi as their teacher, Zhang Zai was their uncle, and Shao Yong was their friend. The differences among these thinkers led to two major schools. Rationalism, or the Reason School (*Li Xue,* Study of Principle), developed from the theories of Cheng Yi and its major exponent was Zhu Xi (1130-1200). Idealism or the Mind School (*Xin Xue,* Study of Mind) was based on the theories of Cheng Hao.

The major thinkers of the Song period were steeped in the study of Daoism and Buddhism and even when they returned to the ideas of the Confucian classics, they interpreted them against the background of the dominant Buddhist learning. This explains what at first seems paradoxical: the extent of the considerable influence of both Daoism and Buddhism in the Neo-Confucian thinkers and their forceful criticism of what they regarded as the shortcomings of both Daoism and Buddhism. They argued that both Daoism and Buddhism are inadequate in their understanding of reality, inaccurate in their view of what constitutes knowledge, and misguided as a moral philosophy for the individual and for society as a whole. But Neo-Confucian philosophy is syncretic: it brings together the philosophical ideas of divergent schools to develop a coherent systematic whole. In returning to the classical texts of the *Yijing* and the *Great Learning* the Neo-Confucian philosophers created an original and penetrating interpretation and clarity of philosophical analysis reached for the first time. This is the high achievement of Neo-Confucian philosophy: the revival of the classical learning and the amalgamation of Mohism, Daoism, and Buddhism within the all-comprehensive Confucian framework.

There is a continuity and a development of fundamental ideas from Confucius and Mencius to the Neo-Confucian thinkers. The Neo-Confucian philosophers present sustained philosophical treatises on the subject of the nature of ultimate reality, the nature of man, and the possibility and the goal of moral life. Their writings on metaphysics and cosmology are intriguing and not always impenetrable. The main contributions of the Neo-Confucian philosophers are their social and political thought which are as relevant and timeless as they were in their time. We turn to the first seminal thinker of the Neo-Confucian movement, Zhou Dunyi.

> Since the time of Confucius and Mencius, Confucians of the Han era (206 BCE- 220 CE) merely had textual studies of the Classics. The subtle doctrines of the Way and the nature of man and things have disappeared for a long time. Master Zhou rose like a giant ... Although other Neo-Confucian philosophers had opened the way, it was Master Zhou who brought light to the exposition of the subtlety and refinement of the mind, nature, and moral principles.[1]

This praise of Zhou Dunyi six hundred years after his death is a fair assessment of his achievement as a philosopher.

Zhou Dunyi

> The Ultimateless (or the Ultimate Non-being, *wu ji*)! And yet also the Supreme Ultimate (*tai ji*)! The Supreme Ultimate through movement produces the *yang*. This movement, having reached its limit, is followed by stillness. Thus movement and stillness, in alternation, become each the source of the other. The distinction between the *yin* and *yang* is determined and their two forms stand revealed.[2]

Zhou Dunyi was a metaphysical genius in formulating the doctrine of the inconceivable. Drawing directly from the *Book of Changes*, Zhou Dunyi sets the direction of Neo-Confucian cosmology on the high road of metaphysics. Zhou Dunyi's most significant work is *Diagram of the Supreme Ultimate* in which "he elucidated the origin of Heavenly Principle and probed into the beginning and end of all things." In the actual diagram of the Supreme Ultimate accompanying the text, it is represented as an empty circle. Zhou Dunyi is thought to have drawn his inspiration for the diagram from a Daoist classic from the Tang dynasty in the eighth century, *Diagrams of the Truly First and Mysterious Classic of the Transcendent Great Cave*. His study of the *Book of Changes* revived philosophical interest in it, establishing it as a central text in the Neo-Confucian school. Zhou Dunyi elaborates how the Supreme Ultimate begins by producing *yin* and *yang* and the five elements – water, fire, wood, metal, and earth – and all things come to exist through their interaction. The central tenet of his cosmology is the identity of the Supreme Ultimate and the Ultimateless.

> The Five Elements are the one *yin* and *yang*; the *yin* and *yang* are one Supreme Ultimate, and the Supreme Ultimate is fundamentally the Ultimateless.

The Supreme Ultimate is the origin and "production and evolution of all things." We may venture the following interpretation for the identification of the Supreme Ultimate and Ultimateless. If the Supreme Ultimate is actuality, Being, and Ultimateless is potentiality, Non-being, when everything is produced through the Supreme Ultimate, actuality and potentiality coincide. What is gained by this identification? It can be regarded as an answer to the problem which was seen as threatening the basis of reasoning in Plato's time. The sophists argued that we cannot say that Non-being does not exist: "No one could either think or say 'what is not' because what is not never has any sort of being." In the *Sophist* Plato's solution is to show the fallacy of the argument: when we say that A is not B, we do not say that A is not something, i.e., that it is nothing, but merely that it is "other" than something.[3] In Zhou Dunyi's thesis since Non-being is inseparable from Being, we are not caught in the difficulty of affirming that what does not exist exists.

By the "transformation" and the "union" of *yin* and *yang* all things unfold and develop without end. The full development of the Supreme Ultimate is found in man. The difference between man and other beings is the degree of intelligence. Zhou Dunyi's explanation of "spirit" is not that of a ghost in the machine; the development of consciousness is continuous with the workings of the body.

> It is man alone, however, who receives all these in their highest excellence, and hence is the most intelligent of all beings. His bodily form thereupon is produced, and his spirit develops consciousness.

Zhou Dunyi explains that as we respond to external phenomena "the five principles of man's nature" – the Confucian virtues of love (*ren*), righteousness (*yi*), propriety (*li*), wisdom (*zhi*), and faithfulness (*xin*) – as well as the distinction between good and evil appear amidst our conduct. The sage emerges setting the standard for all with his Confucian virtues. Zhou Dunyi's statement that the sage, "having no desire, is therefore in a state of stillness and tranquility" reflects the perspectives of Daoism and Buddhism. Zhou Dunyi refers to the image of the sage from the *Book of Changes*: his "virtue is one with Heaven and Earth; his brilliance is equal to the sun and the moon; his course is in harmony with the state of four seasons." This view of the sage as being in harmony with the whole of existence characterizes Zhou Dunyi. He was acclaimed "as a man of exceedingly high character whose feelings were as free and as unforced as a gentle breeze in a cloudless sky." He was also known for his deep love of nature. He admired lotus flowers intensely for they were pure and serene; he would not cut the grass outside his window. Being fond of the stream *Lien Xi* (Stream of Waterfalls), he named his study after it; he was honoured as the "Master of *Lien Xi*." The Cheng brothers who studied under him declined to take the civil service examination and refrained from hunting. Zhou Dun Yi's discussion of principle (*li*), nature (*xing*), and destiny (*ming*) led to what became the three central themes in later Neo-Confucian thought.

Zhou Dunyi was critical of the pursuit of learning for the sake of learning and urged that the way of the sage is valuable only "when it is put into practice." Regarding the pursuit of material possessions as worthless he stresses that the real value of a person resides in his moral character.

> The moral person considers a possession of moral principles to be honour, and peace in his person to be wealth. Therefore he is always at peace and never discontented. To him gold and jade are as insignificant as a speck of dust. Nothing can be added to the great value of possession of moral principle and peace in the person.[4]

The distinguishing virtue of the sage is sincerity. "Sincerity is honesty, earnestness, being true to oneself, being true to the nature of all things in the universe." Zhou Dunyi develops the concept of sincerity from the *Book of Changes*.[5]

> Sincerity is the foundation of the sage. It is the foundation of the Five Constant Virtues (love, righteousness, propriety, wisdom, and faithfulness) and the source of all activities.

But surely sincerity by itself is not sufficient to establish a moral order in the wide world? Zhou Dunyi approaches the perennial moral problem: our own immorality and the wrongdoing of others.[6] Zhou Dunyi's ambivalence regarding the source of evil generated a considerable discussion among subsequent philosophers: "Sincerity [in its origin] engages in no activity, but is the subtle, activating force giving rise to good and evil."[7] If sincerity is the original state of man's moral nature which is perfectly good, as Zhou Dunyi maintains, how can it give rise to both good and evil? Zhou Dunyi adheres to Mencius' view: human nature is inherently good but as it interacts with external things, good and evil emerge. Evil is the result of man's failure to stay true to his real nature, sincerity. In a chapter on "Love and Reverence," Zhou Dunyi explains that evil is an error which can be corrected. His solution to the problem of evil is to persevere in correcting one's mistakes and exhorting others to do the same. This is similar to Plato's view that wrong actions are the result of mistaking what is not good as the goal and that the way to correct "involuntary misdemeanors" is through instruction.[8]

In his characterization of the sincerity of the sage Zhou Dunyi incorporates the ideas of Laozi and Zhuangzi: "One who is in accord with his nature and acts with ease is a sage. One who returns to his nature and adheres to it is worthy … The state of absolute quiet and inactivity is sincerity."[9] In Zhou Dunyi's philosophy we also find echoes of Mozi's philosophy: "The way of the state is nothing other than absolute impartiality. Heaven and Earth are nothing other than absolute impartiality."[10] Zhou Dunyi's impartiality prepares the way for Zhang Zai's conception of the unity of all beings.

Zhang Zai

> Heaven is my father and Earth is my mother. We, small beings, are commingled in their midst. Therefore that which is part of the universe is my body and that which moves the universe is my nature. All people are my brothers and sisters, and all creatures are my companions.[11]

This is a celebrated passage from "the Western Inscription," a short essay of Zhang Zai (1020-1077) from the *Correct Discipline for Beginners*. "The Western Inscription" became the basis of Neo-Confucian ethics. Cheng Yi exclaimed that there has been nothing of equal magnitude since Mencius. As Cheng Yi explained, the focus of "the Western Inscription" is the development of love (*ren*). Zhang Zai, in the year before he died, had a strange dream and hastened to tell his disciples about it. He then compiled what he had said in the *Correct Discipline for Beginners*: "This writing is the product of my applied thought over many years. Its doctrines, it may be hoped, are in accord with those of the former sages."[12] The dream continues,

> Honour those who are advanced in years; to act with respect for the aged is the way it should be. Show kindness to the solitary and the weak; to show tenderness toward the young is the way it should be... All persons in the world who are exhausted, worn out, or ill or are without brothers or children, wives or husbands are all my brothers who have become desolate and have none to whom they can appeal.

The respect and kindness we ought to show to the aged and the young arise from our recognition that we are connected to all living beings under the same heaven. We are to regard the universe with the respect we have for our parents and regard all men of the world as our brothers and all creatures as our own kind. Every human relation has its specific moral requirement, but love is the common foundation for all relations. Zhang Zai's view of universal love for all had significant impact on the philosophers of his time and on the development of Neo-Confucian thought. We have a moral basis for extending concern for the well-being not only of those to whom we are linked by choice or kinship but of all persons equally. Zhang Zai's ethics is based on overcoming the distinction between the self and others to bring the individual into unison with the universe. "By expanding one's mind one is able to embody the things of the whole world."

Making an effort to comprehend the whole of the world is the beginning of ethical development. When we come to know the workings of the universe we are able to regard all beings as participating in the development of all forms of life. The senses show the differences; it is the understanding that draws connections and shows the relations among isolated incidents in the multitude of phenomena. Zhang Zai's belief that "The mind commands man's nature and feelings" encapsulates a central tenet of Neo-Confucian thought. In asserting that the mind is not limited by the senses, Zhang Zai connects his thesis to Mencius' view that "He who has completely developed his mind, knows his nature. Knowing his nature, he knows Heaven" (*Mencius* 7. I.1).

Elaborating on sincerity and enlightenment, Zhang Zai emphasizes the unity of all beings. "As he views the world, there is in it not one thing that is not his own self."

> What I call sincerity and enlightenment is a condition in which there is no perceptible distinction between the small and the great, that is, between one's own nature and the way of Heaven.

Zhang Zai's explanation of sincerity builds on the view of the *Doctrine of the Mean*. For Zhang Zai the highest extension of knowledge is an ever-expanding comprehension and action without any distinctions of particulars. The goal and the means of knowledge of the self and the world and morality are the same: to comprehend all things and act, in accordance with the knowledge of the totality of existence, for the well-being of all. Referring to the way of the sage, Zhang Zai writes of the highest knowledge:

> Nature is the one source of all things, and is not the private possession of one's own ego. Therefore his establishment must be an all-inclusive establishment, his knowledge must be an all-embracing knowledge, his love must be a universal love, and his achievement must not be a solitary achievement.

As knowledge widens to comprehend the inner workings of all beings, ethics becomes an ever-expanding concern for all. Good will, kindness, altruism, and love would then become broadened to apply to all human relations. What kind of love does the sage have? Universal love, the very same *jian ai* of Mozi. Echoing Mencius' objection to Mozi that he does not distinguish between the special affection for one's parents and the weaker affection one feels towards people in general, a disciple of the Cheng brothers criticized Zhang Zai. It was replied that in "the Western Inscription" there are distinctions in love whereas for Mozi love lacks all distinctions. But this reading of "the Western Inscription" is difficult to defend in the light of Zhang Zai's emphatic assertions regarding the knowledge of the unity of all beings generating universal love for all. If all men are my brothers and heaven and earth are my parents, how can Zhang Zai be taken as advocating partial love based on distinctions? Furthermore if universal love is rejected as a way of all human relations how do we move beyond personal attachments to ethical actions based on good will and concern for others?

Zhang Zai's interpretation of *ren* as having a central place in ethics was acknowledged by his nephews, the Cheng brothers, who later became his critics. While Zhang Zai believed that the full development of our nature includes all men and all sentient life and that all of nature followed a sequence, the Chengs affirm the simultaneous development of all. The Cheng brothers establish importance of the idea of the unity of man and the universe in Neo-Confucian thought. The development of the concept of *ren* has a long and continuous history in Confucian thought just as the concept of the *dao* has in Daoist thought. It took fifteen hundred years for an original thinker to put the two together in a single system. This thinker was Cheng Hao.

Cheng Hao and Cheng Yi

> The student must first of all understand the nature of *ren*. The man of *ren* forms one body with all things without any differentiation. Righteousness, propriety, wisdom, and faithfulness are all expressions of *ren*. Nothing can be equal to this Way (*dao*, that is, *ren*). There is no need for caution and control. Exhaustive search is necessary when one has not understood principle, but if one preserves *ren* long enough, it will naturally dawn on him. Why should he have to depend on exhaustive research?[13]

Cheng Hao's starting point is *ren*. He emphasizes sympathy and universal concern for all life: "All operations of the universe are our operations." Cheng Yi also stresses that "The man of *ren* regards Heaven and Earth and all things as one body." Cheng Hao's identification of *ren* with *dao* and his explanation of *ren* as dawning on us without strenuous search and learning answers the standing criticism of Zhuangzi against Confucius' effort at inculcating *ren*.

Zhou Dunyi and Zhang Zai paved the way for the emergence of Neo-Confucian philosophy as an original school of thought. With the Cheng brothers Neo-Confucianism is firmly established as a significant philosophical tradition. While the problems discussed by the Chengs were for the most part similar and they shared fundamental beliefs regarding the unity of man and the universe, they reached different conclusions. Cheng Hao (1032-1085) from the age of fifteen is said to have "set his mind enthusiastically on the search for truth (*dao*) ... His spiritual endowment surpassed that of other men. His character of unblemished harmony permeated his countenance to his very back."[14] Cheng Yi (1033-1108) is described as "an omnivorous reader whose learning was rooted in sincerity. He took the *Great Learning*, *Analects*, *Mencius*, and *The Doctrine of the Mean* as his guide, and delved into the Six Classics. Whether active or still, speaking or silent, he always took the Sage (Confucius) as his teacher, and refused to remain idle as long as he failed to attain to him."[15] Cheng Hao's theories led to the formation of "the School of the Study of Principle," culminating in the philosophy of Zhu Xi. Cheng Yi's views led to "the School of the Study of Mind," vigorously sustained by Wang Yangming.

Cheng Hao pays homage to Zhuangzi in his explanation of what is meant by "the calmness of human nature."

> By calmness of nature we mean that one's nature is calm whether it is in a state of activity or in a state of tranquility. One does not lean forward or backward to accommodate things, nor does he make any distinction between the internal and the external.[16]

We recognize here the characteristic method of Cheng Hao in arriving at a reconciliation of conflicting views. Without directly criticizing Mencius who maintained the distinction between what is due to the internal nature of man and what is caused by the contact with external things, Cheng Hao puts Mencius' idea neatly in the Daoist frame of forgetting the distinction.

> Mencius said, "What I dislike in your wise men is their forced reasoning." Instead of looking upon the internal as right and the external as wrong, it is better to forget the distinction.

What Cheng Hao foresees as the result of forgetting distinctions is the tranquility of mind conceived by Zhuangzi and the Buddhist contribution to philosophy: enlightenment.

> When such distinction is forgotten, the state of tranquility and peace is attained. Peace leads to calm and calm leads to enlightenment. When one is enlightened how can the response to things become an impediment?

He is critical of the Buddhist approach which denigrates the external and promotes the internal life but nevertheless he values the mental discipline of mindfulness, meditation and equanimity in the Buddhist practice in his essay, "Tranquility in Human Nature." He explains tranquility as the quietness in action which prevents the mind from becoming agitated and uncertain. Cheng Yi characterizes the sage as one who can control his emotions of joy, anger, sorrow, fear, love and "adjusts his expression to the principle of the golden mean."[17] This Confucian sage would readily qualify as a Buddhist sage. Cheng Hao's explanation of enlightenment answers the criticism of Buddhism by Neo-Confucian thinkers – that it is nihilistic in its denial of the reality of the world and is egotistic in the rejection of the world of human affairs to seek the salvation of one's soul. Cheng Hao explains that the way to achieve enlightenment is not to turn away from the external world but to extend *ren* to all of existence.

> Man is not the only perfectly intelligent creature in the universe. The human mind (in essence) is the same as that of plants and trees, birds and animals. It is only that man receives at birth the Mean of Heaven and Earth (balanced force).[18]

The ideas of the Cheng brothers launched Neo-Confucian philosophy. It was the achievement of Zhu Xi then to encapsulate the central ideas of Confucian and Neo-Confucian philosophy and build a solid philosophical tradition.

Zhu Xi

> What is there beyond Heaven?

Startling his father with this question Zhu Xi (1130-1200) revealed his philosophical bent of mind at the age of four. To ask what is beyond what was universally accepted as the ultimate origin and source of all physical reality and moral life shows the daring and inquiring mind characteristic of Zhu Xi, who became renowned as the foremost philosopher after Confucius, Mencius, Laozi, and Zhuangzi. Zhu Xi's philosophy is a summation of the Neo-Confucian philosophy up to his time. In Zhu Xi we find the characteristic strength of philosophical thought in China. Zhu Xi's philosophy links the fundamental concepts of Neo-Confucian thought and expands their interconnections as a purposeful metaphysics, theory of knowledge, and moral philosophy. Before the existence of the physical objects in the present world what was there?

> "The Ultimateless! And yet also the Supreme Ultimate!" [These words] do not mean that it [the Supreme Ultimate] is a physical

something glittering in a glorious manner somewhere. They only mean that in the beginning, when no single physical object yet existed, there was then nothing but principle. ... And because this principle is multiple, therefore physical objects [in the existing universe] are also multiple.

There are no Elysian fields of non-existent entities "glittering in a glorious manner somewhere" according to Zhu Xi. Prior to physical existence of objects in space and time, there was only the principle, in the sense of the idea or the concept of objects. Zhu Xi explains that "When a certain thing is made, there is in it a particular principle. For all things created in the universe, there is in each a particular principle." All things in the physical world stand to their principles as a drawing of a circle stands to the idea of the perfect circle. The principle itself is wholly good in itself but when it is imperfectly embodied in matter, the objects themselves lack goodness or perfection. Zhu Xi's theory of principles is in this respect similar to the Platonic theory of forms: both the principles and the forms are perfect, enduring, changeless, and permanent. For each thing that exists there is a principle for what that kind of a thing should be, which Zhu Xi calls "the ultimate." "For every object there is an ultimate, which is the normative principle [of that object] in its highest ultimate form." In Zhu Xi a metaphysical concept of the principle, *li*, becomes also an ethical concept – a remarkably seamless generation of what is from what ought to be. What exists comes to exist not haphazardly but in accordance with its principle – what a particular object is in its essence, function, and purpose. If we take the totality of all things in the universe and the principle according to which they come to exist and function – this aggregate of the principle is what Zhu Xi designates as "the Supreme Ultimate."

What is the relation of the myriad things to the Supreme Ultimate? In every individual object not only is there its own principle which make it what it is, but the Supreme Ultimate in its entirety! Zhu Xi states,

> Originally there is only one Supreme Ultimate; yet each of the myriad things partakes of it, so that each in itself contains the Supreme Ultimate in its entirety. This is like the moon, of which there is but one in the sky, and yet, by scattering [its reflection] upon rivers and lakes, it is to be seen everywhere. But one cannot say from this that the moon itself has been divided.

Zhu Xi describes the good in each individual as the reflection of the good of the Supreme Ultimate.[19] "The moon reflecting itself in the thousand streams" is Zhu Xi's metaphor for the instantiation of the universal in numerous particulars. A human being is determined not by the individual genetic structures alone, but by what all human beings have in common, or in Zhu Xi's terms, the Supreme Ultimate of all individual principles. The existence and actions of an individual object are inter-linked with the existence and actions of the entire universe. From this explanation of the Supreme Ultimate the grand summation of all that is good in the universe among all existing things is taken in one framework of valuation.

The earliest predecessor of the identification of the minute and the particular with the great and the universal is the identification of *atman*, the individual soul with the *Brahman*, the universal soul in Hinduism. But closer to home, Zhuangzi's view of the *dao* as being present in all things is the direct precursor of Zhu Xi's conception of the Supreme Ultimate. Both in Hinduism and in Daoism the identification of the individual with the particular is metaphysical and moral. As the conclusion to his sweeping synthesis, Zhu Xi identifies the Supreme Ultimate with the *dao*, achieving the final reconciliation of Daoism and Neo-Confucianism. If the universal is contained in the particular, the universal good is the individual good. For Zhu Xi, the nature of human beings encompasses the Supreme Ultimate in its entirety. The sage exemplifies the principle of a human being more completely, actively, and intensely. The moral person develops more fully the ability to embody all principles in his range and depth of understanding and action than an unthinking person acting for himself alone.

In his discussion of human nature Zhu Xi criticizes both Mencius and his opponents as having failed to take into account man's physical nature. "When Mencius says that nature is good, he speaks of it only with respect to its origin, and says nothing about it as found in the physical element. Thus he fails to make a clear distinction." Zhu Xi adheres to a dualist perspective to the extent that he regards the principle which determines what the mind of the human being is to be constant, and not physical, but views the feelings as fluctuating with the changes in the physical state. Zhu Xi considers the source of imperfection to be in man's physical nature. He distinguishes feelings which arise from "human desire" and moral values which are inherent in "heavenly principle."

Love (*ren*), righteousness (*yi*), propriety (*li*), and wisdom (*zhi*)

151

constitute the nature. This nature has no shape that can be touched; it consists solely of principle. The feelings on the other hand, are susceptible to perception. They consist of commiseration, shame or dislike, modesty and yielding, and a sense of right and wrong.

The virtues which are determined by principle are constant but the moral sentiments vary with perception. We know that the virtues are inherent in human nature because they are manifested in the corresponding feelings.

> The fact that the mind is able to do so much is ... because it has within it many normative principles. ... How may we know that it possesses these four virtues of love, righteousness, propriety, and wisdom? We know this because of its feeling of commiseration, we may know that it possesses love; because of its feeling of shame and dislike, we may know that it possesses righteousness.

This is a reinforcement of Mencius' argument for the inherent goodness of human nature. Drawing from Confucius, the *Doctrine of the Mean*, and the *Great Learning*, Zhu Xi presents the moral ideal as "the conquest of self and return to propriety," and urges that we "advance toward equilibrium and harmony" as we aspire to "the exemplification of illustrious virtue." Zhu Xi explains that "Man's nature is originally clear, but it is like a pearl immersed in impure water"; once it is removed "it becomes lustrous of itself." What causes human nature to lose its inherent virtue? "If each person could himself realize that it is human desire that causes obscuring, this would bring enlightenment (*ming*). It is on this point alone that all one's efforts must be concentrated." Zhu Xi condenses "the teachings of the sage, whether they be a thousand or ten thousand words," to one point: "that man should preserve heavenly principle (*tian li*) and extinguish desire."[20] Here, in spite of Zhu Xi's severe criticism of Buddhism, is a direct echo of the Buddhist conviction that desire causes suffering. However, Zhu Xi does not follow the Buddhist renunciation of the world. Instead, he turns to the Confucian classics and to the tradition of learning and inquiry incorporating the Cheng brothers' idea of earnestness (*jing*) – absolute seriousness of purpose and attentiveness to conduct. Citing from the *Great Learning*, Zhu Xi advocates extension of knowledge as the means of being free of desire.

... one should pursue the "investigation of things." Today investigate one thing, and tomorrow investigate another. ... then human desire will automatically be dissolved away.

Zhu Xi interprets the "investigation of all things," in the *Great Learning* primarily as a moral inquiry of self-knowledge and not as an inquiry into the objective knowledge of reality. This was severely criticized by the Idealist school of Neo-Confucian thought who argued that effort of this kind did not lead to moral development. The chief proponents of the Idealist School were Lu Xiangshan and Wang Yangming. According to the Idealist School, each individual thing in the universe is determined by its principle. The principles are independent of what happens in the physical world and are not altered by the changes when they are embodied in concrete objects. Furthermore all the principles are present in our mind.

Lu Xiangshan

The universe is my mind, and my mind is the universe.[21]

With this identification of all that exists with the mind, Lu Xiangshan (Lu Jiu Yuan, 1139-1193) establishes the Idealist school (Mind School) of Neo-Confucian thought. Lu develops the ideas of Cheng Hao, who held that self-cultivation consists in comprehending love (*ren*) and cultivating it with sincerity (*cheng*) and earnestness (*jing*); all else is of little consequence. When Lu was criticized as having "no other tricks" than the belief that "Let a man first firmly establish the nobler part of his constitution," he replied, "True indeed!" He builds on Mencius' statement, "He who has developed completely his mind knows his nature. Knowing his nature, he knows heaven" (*Mencius* 7. I.1). Rejecting Zhu Xi's method of "investigation of things" as a means of extending knowledge, Lu argues that "the words of the sages are self-evident" and that to exhaust one's energy in commentaries only makes one's burden heavier. We should, instead, return to the "original mind." Following the famous debate with Zhu Xi, Lu wrote a poem.

Work easy and simple is in the end lasting and great;
Activities involved and complicated are in the end aimless and inconclusive.

Lu's poem echoes the idea of Laozi, "As the practice of learning daily increases, the practice of the *dao* daily diminishes." (*Dao De Jing* 48). Lu criticizes Buddhism, contrasting it sharply with Confucianism.

> I use these two words, righteousness (*yi*) and profit (*li*) to distinguish between Confucianism and Buddhism. They are also referred to as unselfishness and selfishness.

Lu explains that the Confucian thinkers regard human beings as having the capacity to perceive right and wrong and to correct their shortcomings by acquiring the knowledge of how to equate "the way of man" with the "way of earth" and "the way of heaven". Buddhism, on the other hand, views man as undergoing "life and death, the wheel of transmigration, sorrow and vexation" and regards life "to be extremely painful, and so seeks to escape from it." "Being righteous and unselfish Confucianism deals with the world; being profit-seeking and selfish, Buddhism withdraws from the world." Confucianism seeks to set the world right, while Buddhism seeks to escape from the world. Lu's view of the unity of man, earth, and heaven expresses the fundamental view of Daoist thinkers shared by Confucian and Neo-Confucian philosophers: that there is an understanding and an agreement about what is right not simply from an anthropocentric point of view but from a universal perspective which encompasses the broader concerns of "heaven and earth".

The Idealist School developed a theory of the identity of all minds with the universe and seeks to derive from it a moral theory. Lu states: "My mind, my friend's mind, the mind of the sages generations ago and the mind of sages generations to come are all one." If the universe is all I can conceive of, if by universe we mean the totality of all that has been conceived and is possible to conceive of, and if by my mind we mean the capacity to conceive of all that exists, all that is, then the content of the universe and the content of the mind cover the same set of objects. The meanings of the terms "universe" and "mind" range over the same domain. But even on an idealist view, this argument does not work, because the contents of my mind are, apart from the actual concepts I have, only capacities, whereas the contents of the universe include actual concepts that some people other than myself have had. "It is like two identical colouring books, but one has had far more pages coloured in than the other."[22]

154

Wang Yangming

The Universe within the Mind

> The mind of man constitutes heaven in all its profundity, within which there is nothing not included.[23]

With the sweeping declaration that "There is nothing under heaven external to the mind," Wang Yangming (1472-1529) launches the theory of knowledge which led to the culmination of the Idealist School of Neo-Confucian philosophy. Wang recognizes the oddity of the claim that all things are inside the mind. A friend points at the flowers and trees on a cliff and asks, "You say there is nothing under heaven external to the mind, what relation do these high mountain flowers and trees, which blossom and drop of themselves, have to my mind?" Wang replies, "When you do not see these flowers, they and your mind are both in the state of calm. But when you look at them, their colour at once becomes clear. From this fact you know that these flowers are not external to your mind."[24] We can agree with Wang that we know that objects have certain qualities when we perceive them. To prove that all things are within the mind and cannot exist outside the mind, Wang regards it as sufficient to point out that only when we perceive the things their characteristics are clear.

In Wang's doctrine is there a conflation between ontology (what exists) and epistemology (what we know)? Clearly what exists is independent of what we can conceive of and can know. We may agree that the existence of objects is inferred from our perceptions. But it does not follow that all objects are mental entities or that they are part of our mind. It is possible that there are objects about which we do not have ideas since they are not known to us. Existence cannot be deduced from an idea as the mind can conceive of what does not or cannot exist, the phoenix and the round square.

If reality is in the mind, what is causality? Surely the external objects are the causes of our perceptions? Wang's conception of reality can accommodate causality by incorporating Kant's explanation that causality is not merely a constant conjunction but a necessary connection. It is a category of understanding which is not found in experience and not directly perceived. The temptation to draw parallels between Wang Yangming's ideas and the varieties of idealism in the West is almost irresistible. As in Kant's transcendental idealism, for Wang

155

Yangming the concepts and the categories are not part of the external physical world but features of the mind. The undifferentiated manifold of phenomena is clearly discernable only with the individuation of things by the active rational mind. Forms, colours, and relations are perceived distinctly only when we bring the concepts and the categories of understanding. But going further in the direction of Idealism Wang Yangming states that things "cease to exist" if I stop thinking about them. When we grasp the qualities of the objects and hold them in our mind, the mind can be said to contain the universe. The universe is in the mind in the sense that the knowledge of the universe is in the mind; the ultimate structure of reality is reflected in the mind. He identifies the mind with reason: "The mind itself is identical with reason. ... Is there any event or any reason in the universe, that exists independently of the mind?"[25] The mind is "simply spirituality or consciousness."

Wang Yangming's view of objects as ideas in the mind can be related to the empirical idealism of Berkeley and his view of the mind as reason to the rational idealism of Hegel. "We eat, drink, and clothe ourselves in ideas," as Berkeley has told us. According to Berkeley we know that the external world exists only insofar as its constituents can be either directly perceived or are potential objects of our perception. I know that my house, Berkeley persuades us, exists because I perceive it and when I am away from it I can say with confidence that it exists because I would be able to perceive it if I were there. To maintain, as the materialists do, that the external world exists independently of the perceiving mind is, Berkeley points out, is to make an unsupported claim. Hence the dictum, "To be is to be perceived." Wang Yangming's position is discernibly different from the subjective idealism of Fichte in which the individual subject constitutes the basis of reality and all certainty. For Wang Yangming the mind that contains the universe is not the individual mind of a "small man" but the universal mind of the sage.

Wang Yangming explains that moral values originate as ideas in our mind first and not from external factors.

> If I seek the reason of filial piety in my parents, is it then, really in my own mind or is it in the person of my parents? If it is in the parents is it true that after my parents pass away my mind in consequence lacks the reason of filial piety? ... The mind originates the idea, and the nature of the idea is knowledge. Wherever the idea is, we have a thing. For instance, when the idea rests on serving one's parents, then serving one's parents is a

156

"thing", ... therefore I say that there is neither reason nor thing apart from the mind.[26]

Wang Yangming's argument that values come to exist as conscious endeavours to realize them in action and that they do not exist as a part of the natural world independently of the reasons for putting them into action is more plausible than his claim regarding the flowers existing in mind. Wang Yangming does not derive all knowledge from within the mind or deny the reality or relevance of the physical world and tangible actions. He reaffirms the Confucian engagement in the world of action and is critical of the introspective turn of mind in religious Daoism and Buddhism.

> If one wishes to extend one's intuitive knowledge, does this mean that one should stupefy oneself with shadows and echoes, and suspend oneself in empty unreality? It is necessary to accept the reality of [external] affairs. Hence "extension of knowledge" necessarily consists in the "investigation of things."

Knowledge and action are simultaneous: one cannot exist without the other – both take place in the external world.

The Unity of Knowledge and Conduct

> Knowledge is the beginning of conduct; conduct is the completion of knowledge. At the moment of comprehension, though one may then speak solely of knowledge, conduct is already necessarily included therein and though one may speak solely of conduct, knowledge is already necessarily included therein.[27]

If Wang Yangming is interpreted as maintaining that just to understand an action as being good leads to the action being performed, clearly he is curiously oblivious to the absence of a necessary causal connection between recognition and motivation.[28] Ordinarily we say that we know something to be wrong but we do it nevertheless either because we cannot help ourselves or we deliberately choose what we know to be wrong because we desire it. Let's imagine that we stand with Milton's Satan and declare "Evil be thou my good." We desire evil, in this case destruction, believing that we know it to be evil. But if we keep on doing what we claim to know to be wrong it becomes questionable in what way we really know that what we do is wrong. What is the difference, aside from the claim to knowledge, between someone who chooses evil out of ignorance and someone who chooses evil claiming to know that it is evil? In their actions there is none. How can the claim to knowledge be verified or falsified apart from their actions? Wang Yangming is not introducing a technical sense of knowledge. We ordinarily judge what a person's knowledge of a subject is by considering his attempts at carrying it out into action. If we disregard actions as a way of ascertaining what a person knows then knowledge becomes a closed circuit. The claim to knowledge is not a private affair but open to public criteria of verification or falsification. If there is no objective correlative of action for my knowledge then it would seem to be a vacuous claim.

The knowledge which is inherent in the mind is not only theoretical but knowledge of how to act: it is moral knowledge. We may fail to act on our knowledge because of impulsiveness, incontinence, weakness of will, self-interest, and malice. When we admit that these are the causes of wrongdoing do we think that they arise from some knowledge or it is because we do not know how to act with benevolence, self-control, and strength of will? When we act wrongly, can we ever say that our wrongdoing is *because* we know something which causes us to act wrongly? If we fail to do the good, it is only because we do not really know the good. Here we have the view of evil as the ignorance of the good first clearly articulated by Plato coming to life again in the mind of a philosopher in China one thousand eight hundred years later. Plato believed that to know the good is to do the good and that evil is the result of ignorance of the good.

But surely we can know something to be wrong and still want to do it just as we can know something to be good and not want to do it?

> People today all know that filial piety is due the father, and respect is due the elder brother, nevertheless, they are unable to practice such filial piety and respect. This indicates that knowledge and conduct are two separate things.[29]

In response to the objection that knowing and acting are distinct Wang Yangming states,

> This is owing to the separation caused by selfish desires, and does not represent knowledge and conduct in their original state. There is no such thing as knowledge which cannot be carried into practice, for such knowledge is really no knowledge at all.

Knowledge is the guide of conduct and conduct is the work carried out by knowledge.[30]

Wang Yangming explains that knowledge, as the activity of the mind, is directed to specific goals. For instance when the thoughts of "being benevolent to people and creatures" or "serving one's parents" arise in the mind, they are directed toward concrete actions. Wang Yangming argues that if these thoughts are not carried out in action it is only because the mind is obscured by selfish desires. Once we are rid of these selfish desires, the mind's intuitive knowledge of virtue will directly lead to right conduct. "There has been no one who really has knowledge and yet fails to practice it."[31]

Wang Yangming's view of "intuitive knowledge" is similar to Plato's thesis of innate knowledge.

The nature which Heaven has conferred on us, the original state of our mind, is spontaneously intelligent and keenly conscious. Any idea which arises is without exception directly comprehended by this "intuitive knowledge" of our mind.[32]

Even before we debate whether the mind is good or evil, how do we know that there is any such original substance? The mind for all we know may be a tabula rasa until it receives the impressions from the senses. Building on the central idea of the *Great Learning* that the structure of the mind corresponds to the structure of reality – "The mind of man is formed to know the principle of things" – Wang Yangming connects the knowledge of reality with the ability to know the good and to do the good. Wang Yangming emphasizes that intuitive knowledge is not only the knowledge of the physical nature of things but also the mind's knowledge of right conduct. The mind is naturally intelligent, conscious, and possesses the ability to understand all ideas.

If the mind contains the universe, it is infinite. Its knowledge is infinite. Then how do we account for our ignorance of the ten thousand things? Wang Yangming explains how we have deviated from the original state of omniscience. "Originally the mind is nothing but this single heaven, but because of the barriers caused by selfish desire, we have lost this original state of heaven." Referring to this original state of the mind as "intuitive knowledge," Wang Yangming is confident that by concentrated effort we can become one with the knowledge of the universe. Nothing is alien to the mind: "If [the ideas] are good, the intuitive knowledge in our mind comprehends it directly, if they are evil, this too the intuitive knowledge comprehends directly." Mencius approached the existence of evil and the goodness of the original nature of the mind. For Mencius evil consists in the failure to realize the ability to do good because of incomplete knowledge. Wang Yangming's explanation of the idea of the original goodness of human nature as "intuitive knowledge" builds directly on the idea of the highest good as manifesting virtue and loving the people from *Great Learning.*

> ... the highest good is the supreme standard for manifesting illustrious virtue and loving the people. Our heavenly-confirmed nature is purely and utterly good. What cannot be obscured in it is the manifestation of the highest good, and constitutes the illustrious virtue in its original state, which is also what I call intuitive knowledge[33]

Wang Yangming takes up the question of whether good and evil are characteristics of physical objects and phenomena in themselves or whether they arise from our interests.

> While pulling out weeds from among the flowers, I asked, "Why is it so difficult to cultivate the good in the universe and get rid of evil?"

> This way of looking at good and evil entirely from the point of view of the individual is incorrect. In the plan of growth of the universe, flowers and weeds belong to a single category. How, then, can they be differentiated as good or evil? Wishing to have flowers to look at, you consider them good and the weeds evil but should you wish to use the weeds, you would on the contrary consider them good. Thus such good and evil spring from the likes and dislikes of our own mind, so that I know them to be erroneous. [34]

The natural world is neither good nor evil. Values are not qualities of the objects themselves but come to existence with human concerns and interests. Things are neither good nor bad in themselves but our preferences confer values on them.

> In the state of calmness, which is that of reason, there is neither good nor evil. In the state of agitation, which is that of passion, both good and evil are present. As long as one remains unmoved

by passion, there will be neither good nor evil, and this is the state of the highest good.[35]

The highest good is beyond good and evil. Wang Yangming is not urging complete detachment from all feelings. "Not to act according to one's likes and dislikes does not mean to be wholly lacking in likes and dislikes, for this would be the same as being wholly lacking in consciousness."[36] To feel anger at what is not right is to be in conformity with what is proper. In our likes and dislikes if we do not act from calculating self-interest, that is what is meant by not being moved by passion. Evil is explained as being caused by excessive attachment to the feelings of "joy, anger, grief, fear, love, hate, and desire," which obscure intuitive knowledge of the good. Once we become "conscious, the obscuring is dispelled, so that [the mind's] original condition is restored." As Cheng Hao stated: "the sage expresses joy at things which properly call for joy, and anger at things which properly call for anger." But he is not overcome by joy or anger in his mind which, like a clear mirror, retains its "empty impartiality, with which, when things appear reacts accordingly."[37] This is closely related to the Daoist view: in Laozi and Zhuangzi the mind of the sage was likened to a mirror reflecting all perspectives.

Wang Yangming's view that the highest good consists in being unmoved by passion and his sympathy for the suffering of all beings is related to Buddhism. Even as he criticizes Daoism and Buddhism, Wang Yangming clearly recognizes the connection between his philosophy and Daoism and Buddhism. He states that "Relying on them and then disregarding them, departing from them and then returning to them, I both believed them and mistrusted them."[38] Wang Yangming's philosophical evolution is representative of the major Neo-Confucian thinkers. He believes that both Daoism and Buddhism aspire toward virtue but are mistaken in their approach: "they fell into the error of vacuous and empty meditation, and failed to do anything for family, nation, or the world."[39] He criticizes both the Daoist search for immortality and the Buddhist desire to escape from the suffering of life and death as obstructions to true knowledge which consists simply in following intuitive knowledge and avoiding "the slightest addition or reduction."

But how are we to put this equal regard for all into action? In his reply to the question, "If the great man has a common unity with all things, why is it that the *Great Learning* refers to what is 'more important' and 'less important'?" Wang Yangming explains that "It is natural that there should be things of greater and lesser importance." He states that "animals and plants are both to be loved, we nevertheless endure the use of plants to nourish the animals." "And though men and animals are both to be loved, our minds nevertheless endure the fact that we kill animals to feed our parents..." Wang Yangming recognizes that we regard things as having degrees of varying importance.

> Love is to be shown both to our close relatives and the passerby on the road. Yet suppose there be but a single dish of food or bowl of soup, and that life or death depend upon whether they be gained or not. When it thus becomes impossible to fulfill our love in both cases, we then prefer to save our close relatives rather than the passerby. Our mind endures this, moreover, because according to natural principle, it is proper that we should act in this way.[40]

Has Wang Yangming shifted the ground on which he defended the inherent goodness of man as intuitive knowledge? It is not possible to consistently maintain that there is equality among all things and uphold gradations of love in this fashion. Wang Yangming's metaphysics and theory of knowledge call for the unity of all within the mind. Does his ethics endorse partiality? If we maintain that it is morally acceptable to put forward gradations of love have we not collapsed ethical considerations with personal loyalties and attachments and given up the idea of moral responsibility as consisting of impartial obligations independently of sentiment and inclinations? Would this not take us back to the unreflective stage of subjectivism and relativism in ethics? Wang Yangming and the philosophers who, following Mencius, defend love with gradations need still to answer Mozi's criticism that when love remains on the level of personal affections and commitment we cannot resolve the strife and conflict that arise from partisan interests. Even if Wang Yangming's explanation of the initial growth of *ren* in close family relation is accepted we still need to ask what the purpose of *ren* is if not extending it to all dimensions of human relations.

The moral impetus of Confucian love and Mozi's universal love is not to discriminate among the recipients of love as worthy or less worthy but to love all. As *ren* develops it can only approximate universal love closer and closer. We can seek to render Wang Yangming's ethics consistent by turning to his view of the highest good. *Ren* is love which is boundless, but it develops in stages gradually from the relations among the members of the family and friends. Wang Yangming is not advocating gradations of love as the final expression of *ren* but stages culminating in unity with the whole of existence.

> The great man is in all-pervading unity with heaven, earth, and all things. He regards all beneath heaven as one family, and the state as one man.

Wang Yangming conceives of virtue as the ability to encompass the entire universe in the mind with love, *ren*, and to actively cultivate extending *ren* to the whole universe. The direct predecessor of Wang Yangming's thesis of *ren* is found in Cheng Hao who drew his inspiration from Zhang Zai's unity of all beings. The idea of unity of all things, first explicitly set forth in "the Western Inscription" by Zhang Zai, forms the common core of beliefs among the Neo-Confucian philosophers, even when they diverge substantially as two schools of thought, Rationalism and Idealism. Wang Yangming states that those who "make cleavage between the self and others are small men." The subjectivism and relativism in ethics which emphasize the differences of values, principles, and practices among individuals and societies are regarded by Wang Yangming as the result of failing to see the unity among all beings. What distinguishes the great man is not any difference in purpose or ability.

> The reason that the great man is able to be one with heaven, earth, and all things, is not that he is thus for some purpose, but because the love (*ren*) of his mind is naturally so and thus makes possible this union. But why should this apply only to the great man? The mind of the small man is exactly the same, only he himself makes it small.

In what way is the mind of the great and the small man alike? Once more our attention is drawn to the child about to fall in the well, first rescued by Mencius more than a thousand years ago and then by Lu Xiangshan and now again by Wang Yangming .

> For this reason when he sees a child about to fall into a well, he too will certainly experience a feeling of alarm and distress. This is because in his love he is one with the child. The child, like him, belongs to the same species.

Drawing upon Mencius' doctrine of innate knowledge of the good and the ability to do the good Wang Yangming extends the sympathy we feel for the suffering of another human being to all sentient life.

> When he hears the pitiful cry or sees the frightened appearance of a bird or beast, he will certainly find it unbearable to himself. This is because in his love he is one with birds and beasts. The birds and beasts like him have consciousness and feelings.

The state of true knowledge consists in our identification with the entire universe.

> When he sees plants and trees being torn and broken, he will certainly experience a feeling of sympathy and compassion. This is because in his love he is one with the plants and trees. The plants and trees, like him, possess life. And when he sees tiles and stones being smashed and destroyed, he will certainly experience a feeling of concern and regret. This is because in his love he is one even with tiles and stones.

Wang Yangming opens love to embrace the whole world of nature. The central tenet of Neo-Confucian thought, extension of ren to all beings, implies that we value the preservation of all life equally. Not limiting ourselves within the confines of narrow concerns we are fully engaged in the world in our active readiness to love.

6
Changing Harmonies

Reflections on Continuity

> White as lilies, pure candles,
> Like stars, modestly bowing –
> Radiates from the centre of the heart
> Red-rimmed ardour of desire.
>
> So bloom early narcissi
> In rows in the garden.
> In their goodness they know well
> For whom they wait so neatly arranged.[1]

Drawing upon the reservoir of the poetry of China, in this poem from *The Chinese-German Book of Hours and Seasons* Goethe expresses the elective affinity he found in the literature of China. He remarked how similar he is to the people of China in the way that he thinks and feels, adding that when his ancestors "were still living in the woods" literature in China was already highly developed. The philosophers of China have sought ideas of universal validity from a vivid awareness of the concrete facts of life.

We began this study with the view that an exploration of philosophical thought in China is an important part of understanding the development of the human mind. Philosophy in China, beginning with the *Book of Changes*, spans over three thousand years. Emphasizing the continuity of ideas rather than ruptures can help us to weave our own tapestry of the history of ideas. Reflecting on the continuity of ideas between the philosophical reflections of China and the West we discover a vantage point from which the ideas can be approached with a fresh mind. We have seen that in the philosophy of China the familiar ideas and problems in Western philosophy are cast in a new light.

The thinkers of the Enlightenment who sought encyclopedic knowledge through direct and rational investigation of all fields of experience and thought held the civilization of China in high esteem. Christian Wolff, who believed that both theology and ethics could be founded entirely on natural reason, admired the philosophical thought of China. Diderot writes:

> These peoples are superior to all other people of Asia in antiquity, art, intellect, wisdom, policy, and in their taste for philosophy; in the judgment of certain authors, they dispute the palm in these matters with the most enlightened peoples of Europe.[2]

Voltaire states:

> The body of this empire has existed for four thousand years, without having undergone any major alteration in its laws, customs, language, or even in its fashions of apparel. The organization of this empire is in truth the best that the world has ever seen.[3]

It is a matter of debate whether the teachings of the philosophers produced philosopher kings in China or whether the system of government, unified and centralized by the pre-eminence of the emperor, was better for the people than the political rule in the Western world. In the West order depended on the balance of power between governing bodies within one state and separate nation states.[4] Even as they failed to live up to the ideal of the Son of Heaven, all emperors knew that if they were viewed as trampling on the virtues of the sage rulers extolled by the philosophers which were at the foundation of their society, they would forfeit the title by which they held the throne. The recourse to the Mandate of Heaven provided a tendency to check the violence of the oppression and maintain the self-respect of the people all along the course of history of China.[5]

With all the inventiveness, resourcefulness, and agility of mind, why was there no great scientific revolution in the history of China? There are distinct responses to this. Acknowledging the technological advances of China (from the compass and gunpowder to paper and printing), A. C. Graham states that

> ... there can be no longer any doubt about the immense fertility

166

of China in practical inventiveness; it may be an error of perspective even to see it as declining in recent centuries, since the unprecedented acceleration of technological progress in the West has made all other cultures seem stagnant by comparison.

The whole question of why the Chinese have never arrived at modern science seems to me a pseudo-problem. One generally asks why an event did happen, not why the same complex set of conditions did not come together at some other time and place. Thus the formation of an empire, covering a fifth of mankind and still after several thousand years, surviving even the extreme pressures of the 20th century, is an event which like the Scientific Revolution has happened only once in history. We may ask what unique conjunction of factors has stabilised China, we do not ask "Why have not Egypt and Babylon lasted to the present day?"[6]

Persuasive as this explanations is, the question why there were no great scientific thinkers in China persists. Another response could be that science, as it developed from the natural philosophers of ancient Greece, is a search for the explanation of all phenomena and has progressed through relentless and persistent search for truth for its own sake. Reason – pure reason and not reason in the service of seeking solutions to urgent moral problems or useful inventions – led to the development of scientific thinking. Throughout the history of China, philosophical minds were enlivened by the search for the good more than the search for truth.

Contemporary scholars endorse the esteem of the civilization of China by the philosophers of the Enlightenment. Arthur Waley states that philosophical discussion in ancient China present in a fully developed form the ideas which are investigated considerably later in the West.[7] Jacques Gernet explains that

> ... the modern world owes much more to China in matters of technology, science, and institutions than most people imagine – from silk, paper, and firearms to the examination system. We would not be what we are without China.[8]

When we investigate the diverse schools of thought they are not homogenous in method or aim. They engage in an ongoing investigation of certain central concerns and they share recurrent themes and goals. From *Dao De Jing*, the first complete philosophical text from the seventh century BCE, there is a continuous line of the development of ideas from Laozi to the present. The entire tradition of philosophical thought in China was carried forward by thinkers with a deep and broad knowledge. Zhuangzi and Hanfeizi, who severely criticized the scholarly tradition, were renowned for their extensive learning. Laozi and Zhuangzi recognized that "wisdom has its excesses just like folly, and they should be equally restrained."[9] To a certain extent, the sharp criticism of the excesses of scholars by the Daoist thinkers and the Legalists anticipate the kind of sobering effect the ordinary language philosophers and the logical positivists of the analytic tradition had on some of the heady metaphysics in Western philosophy. Horace's remark, "The mountain groaned loudly in great labour and bore a tiny mouse" comes to mind when we ponder upon the penchant for minutiae and for dissection of arguments which are taken as philosophical insight.

The modern mind divides, specializes, and thinks in categories, whereas the classical perspective in China was the opposite. The philosophical approach taken in China tends to see things and ideas in terms of relations or relatedness rather than in isolation. The philosophical sensibility of China is synthetic, whereas in the West it is analytic. Even as the rival schools of thought are vigorously putting forward initially contrary theses, their conclusions incorporate rather than annihilate the opposing views in a broader frame of reference. The discernment of sharp differences is seen as a part of the greater whole as the *yin* and *yang* are complementary and not opposites within the circumference of the same circle. To take the widest view and to see things as an organic whole so that even the particular details and the individual events are fixed firmly into a universal frame – this is perhaps the most characteristic feature of the way of thought in China.[10] This instinct for seeing things as a whole and the sense of the wholeness of things are at the heart of the Daoist philosophy leading to their regard for all life. This awareness of wholeness is reflected in the language of Laozi and Zhuangzi. To know what the *dao* is we need to see things as integral parts of the process of an all-encompassing reality. All schools of thought invoked the idea of the *dao*. Among the different schools of thought there is a tacit understanding regarding the centrality of the *dao* as the foundation of ethics and reality.

Philosophical writing in China, in comparison with the traditions in the West, is remarkably free of technical vocabulary comprehensible only to the scholars. Because the explanation of the nature of ultimate

168

reality and the search for the realization of the ethical life are not built on competing philosophical systems but on a foundation of shared insights, the continuity of philosophical dialogue yields perspectives which are successive refinements of earlier formulations rather than a series of conjectures and refutations. But at the same time, in place of clarity and distinctness we find the inherited vocabulary which has taken on an accretion of meaning, and we need to work through the complexity of accumulated layers of interpretations that can stand in the way of our grasping the meanings.

The dynamism of philosophical thought throughout the history of China was generated by multiple opposing strands. In the classical period it was the battle of ideas within the Hundred Schools of philosophy. However, the Hundred Schools which included men of agriculture, diplomats, and military strategists had one common primary concern, which dominated all philosophical thought throughout the long history in China: the development of man's moral nature as an individual and as a member of society. During the Neo-Confucian era, it was Confucianism, Daoism, and Buddhism that stimulated the philosophical debate.

The most influential person in the entire civilization of China was not a conqueror of territories or men but a philosopher, the first teacher of the people and the rulers, Confucius. When Confucius' ideas became ossified as icons of state religion, the inward momentum of cultivation of virtue and initiative of changing the world for the better were lost. But the insight expressed in the two Confucian ideas, benevolence and the right life – in Confucius' words, "Love all men" and "Do not do to others what you do not wish for yourself" – are as timeless as the injunctions of Delphi in ancient Greece – "Know thyself" and "Nothing in excess" – and have persisted throughout all political upheavals and natural calamities. Again and again, the moral insight of Confucius, the ideals of love of humanity, moral development, and just society have resonated across vast stretches of time and space.

The Principle of Reciprocity – "Do not do to others what you do not like yourself" as first formulated by Confucius, captures the common starting point in ethics. In the ethical traditions of Hinduism, Judaism, and Christianity we find analogous formulations of the Principle of Reciprocity, also known as the Golden Rule.[11] From the Indian epic *Mahabharata*, we have "Let no man do to another that which would be repugnant to himself." "What is hateful to you do not do to your neighbour," said Rabbi Hillel. Christianity advocates "Love your neighbour as yourself."

We have seen that in his discussion of *li* (propriety, right actions or rules for appropriateness of actions) Confucius transforms the concept from an external rule to an internal moral sense. For Confucius ethical actions are not determined by compliance with tradition and custom but by our continuous effort in realizing *ren*. There is a parallel between Confucius' and Jesus' teachings. In his rejection of the rule-based morality of the Pharisees and calling for an interior conversion in the tradition of the great Hebrew prophets, Jesus can be compared to Confucius. While there is a fundamental difference between Jesus as an advocate of religious faith and Confucius as a teacher of human values, they both affirm going beyond the observation of law to act with an inner conviction of the necessity of love of humanity.

When Confucius is asked "What do you think about the principle of rewarding enmity with kindness?" he replies, "Reward enmity with just treatment and kindness with kindness (*Analects* 14.36). By just treatment or uprightness Confucius does not mean justice as severity which would imply repaying evil with evil. By uprightness Confucius means absolute impartiality, taking guidance from what is right instead of one's own subjective preferences. Five hundred years later in the Christian tradition we have the reply "Turn the other cheek" and "Love your enemies." Confucian *ren* does not go as far as the love of one's enemy but calls for just treatment. There is a debate in the *Analects* among the disciples.

> Tzu Lu said, "When men are good to me, I will also be good to them; when they are not good to me, I will not be good to them." Tzu Kung said, "When men are good to me, I will also be good to them; when they are not good to me, I will simply lead them on, forwards it may be or backwards." Yen Hui said, "When men are good to me, I will also be good to them; when they are not good to me, I will still be good to them."

When they turn to Confucius for his verdict, the Master says,

> The words of Tzu Lu [the soldier disciple] are such as might be expected among the wild tribes; those of Tzu Kung are such as might be expected among friends; those of Yen Hui [Confucius' favourite disciple] such as might be expected among relatives and family.

While Confucius determines right conduct based on what is moral in

170

personal relations, Laozi is guided by the general moral principle of unconditional goodness. Laozi advocates returning good in all circumstances.

> To the good I am good; to the non-good I am also good, for life is goodness. To the faithful I am faithful; to the unfaithful I am also faithful, for life is faithful (*Dao De Jing* 49).

Is Laozi putting forward an ideal too lofty to be realized? The sage remains constant in his conduct and does not deviate from goodness and fidelity.

> The sage adheres to his duty and demands nothing of others. Whosoever has life adheres to his duty, whosoever does not have life adheres to right (*Dao De Jing* 79).

Dao De Jing sets forth an ethics of duty rather than one of rights. In the *Dao De Jing* there is an implicit belief in the inherent goodness of human nature. Daoist philosophers turn to the receptivity of the human mind to the good as the best and most reliable incentive instead of inculcation of virtues by following the rules of morality.

What are the movements of ideas and schools of thought that enliven the philosophical debate at present? In the late nineteenth century the philosophers in China turned to the West to seek fresh solutions beyond the philosophical tradition of three thousand years. They have amalgamated and grafted the branches of philosophy from the West onto the inherited philosophical theories. Foremost in shaping the political life of China has been the philosophy of Marx.[12] More recent developments of Western philosophy, such as phenomenology and postmodernism, are also drawing interest. Applied ethics is becoming established as a significant field of philosophical investigation.

Daoism offers a viable ethical perspective for the future as it can be interpreted as advocating setting the boundaries to prevent accelerated encroachment on the natural environment. Zhuangzi is critical of the shortsightedness of human contrivances which "disrupt the quietness in the mountains and the rivers" and interrupt the round of the four seasons. Zhuangzi objects to stringed arrows, basket nets, and pitfalls as disordering the birds, fish, and animals and causing ecological damage (*Zhuangzi* 9, Legge I. 288).

> The knowledge shown in the making of bows, cross-bows,

171

hand-nets, stringed arrows, and contrivances with springs is great, but the birds are troubled by them above. The knowledge shown in the hooks, baits, various kinds of nets, and bamboo traps is great, but the fishes are disturbed by them in the waters. The knowledge shown in the arrangements for setting nets, and the nets and snares themselves, is great but the animals are disturbed by them in the marsh grounds.

Zhuangzi criticizes actions which inflict suffering on animals.

Horses can with their hooves tread on the hoarfrost and snow, and withstand wind and cold... they prance with their legs and leap: this is their nature. Saying, "I know how to manage horses," men proceeded to singe and mark them, to pare their hooves, to halter their heads, to bridle and hobble them, and to confine them in stables and corrals. When subjected to this treatment, two or three in every ten of them died... In front there were the evils of the bit and ornamented breast-bands, and behind were the terrors of the whip and switch. (When so treated) more than half of them died (*Zhuangzi* 9, Legge I. 276-7) .

Zhuangzi refers to the state of nature in which harmony prevailed.

At that time, in the hills there were no footpaths, nor excavated passages, nor dams. Birds and beasts multiplied. Yes, in the age of perfect virtue, men lived in common with birds and beasts, and were on terms of equality with all creatures, as forming one family (*Zhuangzi* 10, Legge I. 278).

Zhuangzi's regard for the natural environment and all life is directly linked to the contemporary moral issues of the protection of the environment as the habitat of sentient life.

When asked in governing what it is that the state cannot do without, Confucius indicated that it is virtue and then the means of livelihood. Mencius emphasizes the importance of improving the material well-being of the people. Addressing a ruler Mencius states,

There are people dying from famine on the roads, and you do not issue the stores of your granaries for them. When people die you say, "It is not my fault; it is because of the poor year." In what does this differ from stabbing a man and killing him, and then saying – "It was not I, it was the weapon"? (*Mencius* 1. I.3)

Mencius is emphatic in his exhortations to the rulers that poverty should be eliminated by reforming the economic measures of distribution of wealth and instructing people in securing the means of livelihood. Mencius argues that to regard death from famine and poverty as a natural disaster and to maintain that it was not intended is to fail in fulfilling the responsibility of humane government. Mencius' argument lays the groundwork for a subject of central importance in contemporary ethics: the moral responsibility of affluent nations and individuals to assist in alleviating the suffering of the people in the impoverished countries. When there are readily available resources to prevent death, not to use them because of indifference or preoccupation with one's own prosperity is as reprehensible as killing people. Peter Singer has argued forcefully that we have a moral obligation to contribute to prevent death and relieve suffering caused by famine and poverty. Mencius rejects the claim that there is a moral difference between acts and omissions. This view has also been supported by contemporary philosophers. If actions are judged according to whether they violate certain rules, or by intentions, it is thought that there is a moral difference between acts and omissions – whereas if actions are judged by their consequences there is no difference between the two.[13]

The tradition of moral philosophy is the great legacy of philosophical thought in China. In reading the ancient texts, the precise terms of the explanations may appear remote from the present, but the essential ideas are timeless and ever present at the centre of all philosophical activity. We join Confucius in his persistent effort at living ethically and learning how we might put *ren* into practice. The Principle of Reciprocity calls for treating others as one would treat oneself. Both the Daoist view of regarding all equally and the Principle of Reciprocity call for setting aside the distinction between the self and others. With Zhuangzi we strive to establish moral autonomy, freedom, and equality of all. The right way to live is not laid out for all eternity by the ancient sages nor does it consist in pursuing the straight path of virtue but is to be discovered by those who question everything and dare to go beyond the traditions of ceremony, ritual, and piety (*Zhuangzi* 24, Legge II. 112).

The feet of man on the earth is but on a small space, but going on to where he has not trod before, he traverses a great distance easily; so his knowledge is but small, but going on to what he does not already know, he comes to know what is meant by Heaven.

Harmony and Change

The ideal of being in harmony with nature permeates all of philosophical thought in China. The life of the people of the land was directly linked with the cycles of nature. At the first clap of thunder signifying the beginning of the summer planting season, the season of courtship opened and marriages which were prohibited in winter could take place.[14] Harmony is conceived as a process of creation and the balance between two opposite states in the natural and the human world. In the *Book of Changes, Yijing*, all things are seen as coming to exist through the interaction of the two opposing principles of *yin* and *yang*. It arises from a dynamic activity in contrast to the static immobility of homogeneity. The human world of action, the intermediary world between Heaven and Earth, is the world of balance and harmony. But this is not a pre-established harmony as the harmony of the spheres but constantly changing, newly found harmony which is composed of changing constituents, circumstances, and purposes. Harmony is created from the changing relations among the individuals and is the unifying principle by which things come to exist.

Harmony is seen as the completion of all activity. The conception of harmony as originating not from uniformity but differences is directly linked to the actual historical development in China. The civilization of China was constituted by a multitude of people from widely different origins, distinct in language, character, and custom.[15] As harmony arises from equalizing the differences, the search for harmony propels us to initially seek out an understanding of that which is different until reconciliation is reached. Of the variety of harmonious relations, the ultimate harmony is seen as happiness and unity among all people. Philosophy sought to unify the people with immensely varied beliefs, customs, habits of life and political allegiances by forming the ethical foundation.

All schools of thought have presented conceptions of harmony and ways of achieving it. From Laozi, Zhuangzi, Mozi, Confucius, and Mencius to the Neo-Confucian philosophers, every major Chinese thinker sought to chart the moral path of man in the constantly changing world. The Daoist philosophers sought to derive a pattern of life from the way of nature. The conception of a person in Confucian ethics is essentially a social being while Zhuangzi conceives the individual as an autonomous being. The ethical goals for Confucius and Zhuangzi converge on the point of concern for the well-being of the people but the means are different. For the philosophers in the Confucian tradition, harmony is achieved by realizing the love of humanity (*ren*) in action, guided by knowledge of the classics and proper conduct (*li*) and emulating the paradigms of virtue of the sage rulers of antiquity. The goal of study is a harmonious self-cultivation – striving for intellectual, moral, and aesthetic virtues simultaneously. In political life the goal of laws and institutions is justice as harmony in the state. The same virtues – benevolence, altruism, righteousness, and sincerity, and rules of propriety – apply in personal ethics and political morality. Both for the individual and society the harmonious cultivation of human relations in all spheres of action is the goal (*Mencius* 3. I.3). Politics is understood primarily as a matter of harmonious human relations based on virtue rather than an impersonal institution based on a contractual agreement or on government by law.[16]

But in a world of continual strife and conflict how can harmony be achieved? When he is asked how one can excel in virtue and eliminate ingrained evil, Confucius responds enthusiastically (*Analects* 12. 21),

> Truly a good question! If we first do what is to be done and only then be concerned about success – isn't this the way to excel in virtue? To attack evil that is within oneself and not to attack the evil of others – isn't this the way to correct evil?

Confucius emphasizes that when we see good conduct we ought to seek to learn from it and when we encounter flawed actions we should look within ourselves to correct our own shortcomings.

> The moral person seeks to perfect the good qualities of men, and does not call attention to their bad qualities. The small man does the opposite of this (*Analects* 12. 16).

Confucius' response to the problem of evil calls not for punishment of wrongdoing but self-reflection and the cultivation of virtue in those who have political authority.

There are two philosophers who were not convinced of the validity of Confucian ethics: Hegel and Kant. Hegel's remarks on Confucius reflect the divergent aims of philosophy as the construction of a coherent theory of knowledge of reality and philosophy as the analysis of

175

ethical problems and commitment to bring about a better world.

> We have conversations between Confucius and his followers in which there is nothing definite further than a commonplace moral put in the form of good, sound doctrine, which may be found as well expressed and better, in every place and amongst every people... He is hence only a man who has a certain amount of practical and worldly wisdom – one with whom there is no speculative philosophy.[17]

In the speculative philosophy of Hegel we have an antithesis of the Confucian conception of philosophy as actively engaging the ethical and political life. While Hegel finds Confucius too general, Kant finds Confucius too specific. Kant states that "a concept of virtue and morality never entered the heads of the Chinese," and that "their teacher Confucius teaches in his writings nothing outside a moral doctrine designed for the princes."[18] In his lecture on logic Kant writes that philosophy comprises four questions: "What can I know?" "What ought I to do?" "What may I hope?" and "What is man?" Had Kant, who lectured on the philosophy of China in his course on "physical geography", undertaken to study the moral philosophy of China extensively it is more than likely that he would have recognized that Confucius and the philosophers of China sought the answers to the questions which he regarded as fundamental in philosophy.

Kant's opposition to war and his recommendation that when we encounter evil we conquer the evil within ourselves is worthy of comparison with the teachings of Confucius. To counteract the subjective freedom of the individuals which leads to conflicts, Kant urges us to be vigilant against the "weakness of human nature" within ourselves. Actively seeking to establish the ethical foundation of perpetual peace Kant states that

> ... true courage does not consist in defying with strong resolve evils and sacrifices which must be undertaken along with the conflict, but rather in detecting and conquering the crafty and far more dangerously deceitful and treasonable principle of evil in ourselves, which puts forward the weakness of human nature as justification for every transgression.[19]

Kant has an important recommendation which, if it were to be adopted as an individual and a political approach to conflict, could be an effective deterrent against violent retaliation to aggression and may lead to a peaceful resolution of conflicts. Socrates also emphasized that "one ought not to return a wrong or do injury to any person, whatever the provocation." Socrates stressed that "Whatever the popular view is, and whether the alternative is pleasant or even harder to bear, the fact remains that to do wrong is in every sense bad and dishonourble for the person who does it."[20]

When Confucius is asked, "What do you say to killing the unprincipled for the good of the principled?" he replies

> On carrying on your government, why should you use killing at all? Let your evinced desires be for what is good, and the people will be good. The reaction between superiors and inferiors is like that between the wind and the grass. The grass must bend, when the wind blows over it! (*Analects* 12. 19)

Confucius stresses that the rulers need to be just for there to be justice among people. The cause of social evil is an unjust government of corrupt ministers. "How true is the saying: 'If good men ruled the country for a hundred years, they would ... abolish capital punishment' " (*Analects* 13.11). The view of justice as benevolence was not restricted to Confucius. Laozi also argues against capital punishment. The laws enforcing justice as retribution and punishment were seen as having originated in the time of decay.

The Daoist philosophers, Laozi and Zhuangzi, advocate complete non-violence for the sake of preserving the harmony and well-being of the people.[21]

> War and force of arms are ignoble and bring devastation.
>
> He who would assist a lord of men is in harmony with the *dao* and will not assert his mastery in the kingdom by force of arms. Such a course is sure to meet with its proper return. Where armies have dwelt, thistles and thorns grow, behind battles, years of hunger (*Dao De Jing* 30).

The goal of harmony is embraced also by Xunzi. Referring to the feelings of like, dislike, pleasure, anger, sorrow and joy, as "natural feelings", Xunzi does not advocate eliminating all feelings or suspending desire but urges that they be developed in harmony with all things (*Xunzi* 118). Xunzi seeks to extend the moral transformation of natural feelings to altruism to strangers. To bring all the components to "each of the ten thousand things, attain its harmony" – this is what Xunzi refers to as the world of the sage. The goal of being in harmony with the whole of existence is what leads us directly to Daoism, where it is the center of ethics.

Mozi urged all to actively put universal love into action to alleviate suffering in the world. Mozi's reply to the ethical egotist is relevant to the contemporary debate between defenders of objective morality and those who uphold the strategy of self-interest. An opponent of Mozi declares:

> I am different from you, I am incapable of concern for everyone. ... If you hit me it hurts, if you hit someone else it doesn't. Why should it be what doesn't hurt that I ward off rather than what does? Therefore, [for self-preservation], there are occasions for killing someone else on account of myself, none for killing myself on account of a benefit [to others].[22]

Mozi asks him "Are you going to hide your view? ... or tell others about it?" To the reply, "Why should I hide my view? I shall tell others about it", Mozi states:

> In that case, if one man, ten men, the whole world are persuaded by you, then one men ... the whole world will wish to kill you to benefit themselves. If one man ... the whole world are not persuaded by you, then one man ... the whole world will wish to kill you as a practitioner of dangerous tenets. If, whether persuaded or not, they wish to kill you ... you are the one who by establishing it as a norm gets yourself killed."

Mozi concludes that the doctrine of self-love is conceptually incoherent and cannot be consistently put into practice.

The debate between Mohists and Confucians are continued in the debate between contemporary consequentialists and their opponents who uphold that we have special obligations to people closely related to us. Governments and institutions have changed since the time of Mozi, but his moral philosophy has perennial relevance. More than ever before, as ethical concerns are becoming global, the universal ethics of Mozi is of vital importance in the present and future as we seek ways of resolving conflicts.

In the Confucian text, the *Great Learning*, the purpose of education is to strive for "cultivation of personal life, harmony in the family and order in the state" not as ends in themselves but as intermediate stages to peace in the world. The central tenet of Neo-Confucian thought, extension of *ren* to all beings, implies that we value the preservation of all life equally. But how are we to put this equal regard for all into action when there is a conflict of interest and disharmony? The most audacious proposal comes from Kang Youwei (1858-1927) who sought universal peace as the supreme goal of all political and personal actions and worked vigorously to bring about political and social reform. He was the leading spirit in the famed "Hundred Days of Reform," during which the emperor issued edicts of significant political reform. Kang Youwei builds on Laozi's and Zhuangzi's elimination of distinctions, Confucian cultivation of *ren*, Mozi's universal love, the compassion in Buddhism for all sentient beings and the desire to eliminate all suffering, and Zhang Zai's unity of all beings. In taking the elimination of suffering as the most important goal and putting forward love as the means to bring about the well-being of the people, Kang Youwei's starting point of seeking to eliminate the causes of suffering is similar to that of Mozi.

> My way of saving the people from these sufferings consists in abolishing these nine spheres of distinctions. First, do away with the distinction between states in order to unify the whole world. Second, do away with class distinction so as to bring about equality of all people. Third, do away with racial distinctions so there will be one universal race. Fourth, do away with the distinction between physical forms so as to guarantee the independence of both sexes. Fifth, do away with the distinction between families so men may become citizens of Heaven. Sixth, do away with the distinction between occupations so that all productions may belong to the public. Seventh, do away with the spheres of chaos so that universal peace may become the order of the day. Eighth, do away with the distinction between species so we may love all sentient beings. And ninth, do away with the sphere of suffering so happiness may reach its height.[23]

Kang Youwei's *Book of Great Unity* recaptures the insight in Confucius and in the *Great Learning* that there is a continuum from the good of the individual to the good of the world. Kang Youwei regards Confucius as the first intellectual leader and the foremost political reformer and sought to revitalize the Confucian ethics.[24] As Neo-Confucian philosophers before him, Kang Youwei interprets the classics not for the sake of preserving the tradition but as an independent source of broad and fresh insights not restricted by the pressing concerns of the present and derives from them the guidelines for political reform. In Kang Youwei's conception wisdom and love are intertwined. Wisdom consists of possessing the knowledge to accomplish the goal of love: bringing benefits to people and all things. Kang Youwei draws on the ability of human beings to develop *ren*.

> Although they differ as inner and outer and as substance and function, their constituting the Way is the same. It is love, that is all. ... All people have the mind to love each other. The word *ren* consists of one part meaning man and another part meaning many. It means that the way of men is to live together. It is the power of love.

As the range of concern for the well-being of all forms of life leads directly to extending love, to the entire universe, Kang Youwei achieves a synthesis of the Confucian *ren*, Mozi's universal love, and Zhuangzi's love without attachment. We arrive at a grand unification of love.

Zhuangzi celebrates the life of freedom and equality of all. But unless we have good reasons to have an unshakable confidence in the principle of pre-established harmony, we need to concede that subjective freedom is more frequently the cause of conflict. Zhuangzi seeks to show how authentic existence and self-development lead to the unity of the *dao* of the individual and the *dao* of man, nature, and Heaven. Zhuangzi can defend freedom not as a natural right but on the grounds of the common interests of all. Zhuangzi, in upholding individual freedom, is not a champion of anarchy of feeling and individual will. The True men are not thoughtless: citing the ancient worthies, Zhuangzi states that they all did "service for other men and sought to serve for them what they desired, not seeking their own pleasure." General well-being is possible when individuals have the possibility of full self-realization. The autonomy of the individual and the concern for the shared interests are not in conflict. Zhuangzi's aim is to bring contending positions into a comprehensive, universal and an objective point of view beyond shifting opinions. When contradictory views are in collision we need to seek out that which is found not in one isolated standpoint only but what is held in common. With the "proper light of the mind" we can find "the pivot of the *dao*." (*Zhuangzi* 2, Legge I. 183)

> Therefore the scintillations of light from the midst of confusion are indeed valued by the sagely man. Not to use one's own views and to take his position on the ordinary views is what is called using the proper light (Legge I. 187).

The sage makes the mind of the people his mind. By following one's given nature Zhuangzi does not mean following individual inclinations disregarding all else. The still point of the turning world is not the self but the point of view of Heaven. To affirm everything and to say "Yes!" to the universe – that is the knowledge of the *dao*.[25]

> A human being is a part of the whole, called by us "the universe," a part limited in time and space. He experiences himself, his thoughts and feelings, as something separate from the rest – a kind of optical delusion of his consciousness. This delusion is a kind of prison for us restricting us to our personal decisions and to affection for a few persons nearest to us. Our task must be to free ourselves by widening our circle of compassion to embrace all living creatures and the whole of nature in its beauty.[26]

These words of Einstein, who believed that "one exists for other people – first of all for those upon whose smile and well-being our own happiness is wholly dependent and then for the many unknown to us, to whose destinies we are bound by the ties of sympathy," embody the ideas of Zhuangzi.

We conclude with Zhuangzi's words on the unity of all beings. Zhuangzi regards the completion of nature as all things returning to the common origin and refers to this returning to the beginning as "vacancy." In our silence at the completion of our actions we are aligned with the original way of Heaven (*Zhuangzi* 12).

> When our nature (*xing*) is cultivated we return to the power (*de*). Having returned to the power, we become identified with the Beginning. Being thus identified, there comes pure vacancy. With this emptiness, there comes vastness. We are then like the birds who sing with their beaks closed. Being like this, we reach a union with the universe. The closing and silencing is like the union of heaven and earth at the beginning. It is the same as the Grand submission to the natural course.

Notes

Preface
[1] Durant, *Our Oriental Heritage* p.640.
[2] Peter Singer has made this observation.
[3] Jonathan Barnes in *The Presocratic Philosophers* makes this point.
[4] Wittgenstein quotes Krönberger in the *Philosophical Investigations*.

Introduction
[1] Durant, *op.cit.* p.642.
[2] Durant, op. cit. 643. *Book of History*, Tr. by W. G. Old, pp.20-21.
[3] Plato, *Republic*, Book V.
[4] Graham, *The Book of Lieh-tzu*, p.2.

Chapter 1
[1] Fung Yu-lan, *A History of Chinese Philosophy*, I, p. 45.
[2] Wilhelm, *Understanding the I Ching*, p.26.
[3] Wilhelm, *op.cit.* p.5.
[4] Wordsworth's words.
[5] Byron's words.
[6] In sharp contrast to Plato who referred to the ancient quarrel between poetry and philosophy and denigrated the poets as "the imitative tribe", initially expelling them from the *Republic*, Confucius values poetry as expanding the moral imagination. Shelly in *Defense of Poetry* puts forward the same view as Confucius.
[7] Fung Yu-lan, *op.cit.* I. pp. 31-32.
[8] Odes, 249, 256, 257. A. C. Graham, *The Disputers of the Tao*, p.19. A. Waley, *The Analects of Confucius*, p.27. Waley points out that *"ren"* in early Chinese referred to freemen as opposed to *min*, subjects or the common people.
[9] Zhuangzi goes even further in rejecting the virtues of *ren* and righteousness, urging the life of spontaneity unconstrained by moral injunctions. See Chapter 2 below.
[10] Waley's translation of *"ren"* as "Good" or "Goodness" captures the meaning of *"ren"* as a term for virtue in the inclusive sense but it is too general. Graham regards "benevolence" as inappropriate and adopts "noble," based on the historical usage of the term by the Zhou aristocracy who used it to distinguish themselves from the common people. But as Confucius' innovation was to establish *ren* as an inherent virtue in all men, retaining the term "noble" to denote the most significant moral concept for Confucius is problematic. While recognizing that Confucius is forming a new concept, Graham states that Confucius finds *ren* most fully exemplified in *junzi*, lord's son. But as Confucius characterizes *junzi* solely by the moral virtues of a person and not by

his social standing, it is misleading to relate *junzi* to the connotation of *ren* as "noble."

[11] W.-T. Chan, *A Source Book in Chinese Philosophy*, p.16.
[12] See Chapter 2.
[13] Waley, *The Way and Its Power*, pp.60-62.
[14] Fung Yu-lan, *op. cit.* I, p.38, p.68.
[15] Gernet, Jacques, *A History of Chinese Civilization*. Cambridge: Cambridge University Press, 1999, p.79.
[16] W.-T. Chan. *A Source Book in Chinese Philosophy.*
[17] Grousset, *The Rise and Splendour of the Chinese Empire*, p.31.
[18] Waley makes the observation that in the early myth, legend, and literature the qualities of the heroes are of an international type. Hou Chi, the prince of the millet, incorporated the characteristics of Asclepius, Dionysus, and Zeus – he was endowed with the knowledge to heal, to bring intoxication and to be the paradigm of power and virility.
[19] Fung Yu-lan, *op.cit.* I p.56.
[20] Fung Yu-lan, *op.cit.* I p.72.
[21] Legge, *The Works of Mencius*, p.56.
[22] In this perhaps both Legge and Gernet understate the inventive aspect of Mencius' mind. Legge, *ibid.* p.48; Gernet, *op.cit.* p.95.
[23] Legge, *The Works of Mencius*, p.278.
[24] Dawson, *The Chinese Experience*, p.9.
[25] W.-T. Chan, *op.cit.* p.78; Legge, *Shoo King*, p.292.
[26] Plato, *Crito*.
[27] This is also one of the common themes on political reform shared by different philosophers, from Mozi and Zhuangzi to Kang Youwei. See Chapters 2, 3 and 4.
[28] Waley, *The Way and Its Power*, p.49.
[29] See Chapter 2.
[30] Legge, *The Works of Mencius*, p.41.
[31] The quotations from *Xunzi* are adapted from W.-T. Chan, *op.cit.* pp. 115-134 and Burton Watson, Tr., *Hsün Tzu: Basic Writings*.
[32] W.-T. Chan, *op.cit.* p.115.
[33] *Ibid.*
[34] The Legalist philosophy is discussed in Chapter 3.
[35] Xunzi's emphasis on the necessity of the restraining and formative influence of law is clearly in sharp contrast to Zhuangzi's sweeping rejection of all laws and conventions as constraints on the natural goodness of human nature.
[36] W.-T. Chan, *op.cit.* p.127.

[37] The quoted passages are adapted from Legge, *Confucius - the Confucian Analects, the Great Learning, and the Doctrine of the Mean* and W.-T. Chan, *op.cit.* pp.84-94.

[38] Legge, *op. cit.* pp.28-33.

[39] Zhuxi's commentary.

[40] Goethe's remark in his *Theory of Colour*.

[41] The quoted passages are adapted from W.-T. Chan, *op.cit.* pp.95-114.

[42] See Chapter 5.

Chapter 2

[1] Kuanzi, quoted in Waley, *The Way and Its Power*, p.30

[2] Legge, *The Texts of Taoism*, I, p.12.

[3] *Ibid.*

[4] Waley, *The Way and Its Power*, p.30.

[5] Graham, *The Book of Lieh Tzu*, p.1.

[6] *Ibid.* p.2. This is a fair description of Confucius' approach to the *dao* which is also elucidated by R. Wilhelm.

[7] Graham, *The Book of Lieh Tzu*, p.2.

[8] To paraphrase Wittgenstein's famous fly-bottle of philosophy.

[9] Waley, Legge, Fung Yu-lan, and W.-T. Chan lean toward this view.

[10] Whitehead states that philosophy is mystical in this sense.

[11] The Duke of Wellington remarked that wining a battle was the saddest thing next to losing it. Legge, *The Texts of Taoism*, I, p.74.

[12] Contrary to Legge's view that "*ren de*" seems an inappropriate title, I interpret this section as being a significant explanation of "*ren de*". Legge, *The Texts of Taoism*, I, p.77.

[13] Graham, *The Disputers of the Tao*, p.29.

[14] Horace echoes Laozi's views: "We turn virtue upside down and want to soil a clean vessel. If honest man lives among us, we call him slow and stupid."

[15] Plato characterized thought with this phrase.

[16] In *The Defense of Poetry*, Shelley argues this forcefully.

[17] Nietzsche's phrase is appropriate here.

[18] The references to Zhuangzi are from *Zhuangzi* and adapted from Legge's *The Texts of Taoism*. I am indebted to Richard Palmer, Lauren Pfister, and Jay Goulding for their helpful comments.

[19] The immediate context of "leaping into the boundless" passage is Zhuangzi's criticism of the disputers of the world – Confucians, Mohists, the Logicians, and the Hundred Schools of Thought (These views are discussed in Chapter 3.) In putting forward an interpretation of the

conclusion of "leaping into boundless" as urging freedom and spontaneity we link Zhuangzi's discussion of knowledge with the idea of
authentic existence his moral philosophy.

[20] Waley, *Three ways of Thought in Ancient China*, p.163. Both J. Gernet and J. Legge refer to Zhuangzi simply as a genius.

[21] The *Historical Records* is the first general history of China from the
beginning to the reign of the emperor Wu (140-87 BCE) in Han dynasty. It was begun by Sima Tan (died 110 BCE) and completed by his
son Sima Qian (145-ca. 86 BCE), the Herodotus of China. Quoted in
Fung Yu-lan, *A History of Chinese Philosophy*, I, p.221.

[22] Graham, *Chuang Tzu*, p.33.

[23] W.-T. Chan, *A Source Book in Chinese Philosophy*, p.181.

[24] R. Wilhelm, *Dschuang Dsi*, p.157.

[25] Graham, *The Book of Lieh Tzu*, p.4.

[26] Dante who condemns the hypocrites to the lower circle of the Inferno
than the thieves would agree with Zhuangzi.

[27] Graham, *Chuang Tzu*, p.188.

[28] See Chapter 5 below. While Zhuangzi establishes the unity of existence on the basis of the *dao*, the Neo-Confucian thinkers build on the
analysis of the common underlying principle (*li*) of all things and the
material force (*qi*).

[29] Isaiah Berlin, "Two Concepts of Liberty" in *Four Essays on Liberty*,
Oxford University Press, 1969. Charles Taylor, "What is wrong with
Negative Liberty", *The Idea of Liberty*, Alan Ryan, ed., Oxford Univer-
sity Press, 1979.

[30] Bertrand Russell pointed this out.

[31] This phrase is originally from Sidgwick. Peter Singer develops it
further to designate an impartial point of view in ethics; see *The Expanding Circle* and *Writings on an Ethical Life*.

[32] *Meno*, 98 d-99 e.

[33] Goethe, *Faust*.

[34] G. E. Moore's discussion of goodness as a "non-naturalistic" quality
comes to mind here.

[35] Zhuangzi's ideas influenced *Chan* Buddhism significantly. To "sit in
forgetfulness" with "the fast of the mind" became the foundation of
Chan meditation. See Chapter 4.

[36] *Xunzi*, 23. Quoted in Waley, *The Way and Its Power*, p.91.

[37] Graham, *The Book of Lieh Tzu*, p.3.

[38] A statement by an advocate of law, Cicero, *De Officia,* I , 33.

[39] Cartier Bresson, *The Decisive Moment*, New York: Simon and

Schuster, 1952, 7.15.

[40] Quoted in Waley, *The Way and Its Power*, p.58.

[41] Graham, *The Book of Lieh-tzu*.

[42] Quoted in Waley, *The Way and Its Power*, p.42.

[43] Fung Yu-lan, *op.cit.* I, p.137; p.285.

Chapter 3

[1] The quotations from *Mozi* are from W.-T. Chan, *op.cit.* p.213.

[2] Fung Yu-lan, *op.cit.* , I, p. 84.

[3] *Ibid.*

[4] *Ibid.*

[5] *Mozi*, ch. 18; Fung Yu-lan, *op.cit.* I, pp.101-104.

[6] Fung Yu-lan, *op. cit.* I, p.95.

[7] W.-T. Chan, *op. cit.* p.227.

[8] Fung Yu-lan, *op. cit.* I, p.96.

[9] W.-T. Chan, *op. cit.* p.220.

[10] Fung Yu-lan, *op. cit.* I, p.99.

[11] W.-T. Chan, *op.cit.* p.220.

[12] Fung Yu-lan, *op. cit.* I, p.93.

[13] *Ibid.*

[14] W.-T. Chan, *op.cit.* p.214.

[15] We know too well that our love does not ensure that we are loved in return. Shakespeare knew this well. In *A Midsummer Night's Dream*, Hermia says "I frown upon him, yet he loves me still ... I give him curses, yet he gives me love... The more I hate, the more he follows me." Then we have Helena who has the converse affliction: "The more I love, the more he hateth me."

[16] Fung Yu-lan, *op.cit.* I, p.95. Peter Singer's views on our moral responsibility to alleviate suffering has a close affinity with Mozi's views. See his *Practical Ethics* and *Writings on an Ethical Life*.

[17] Fung Yu-lan, *op.cit.* I, pp.91-92.

[18] W.-T. Chan, *op. cit.* p.214.

[19] *Mozi*, ch.33. Fung Yu-lan, *op. cit.* I, pp.85-86.

[20] Fung Yu-lan, *op.cit.* I, p.92.

[21] *Ibid.* p.85.

[22] Fung Yu-lan, *op. cit.* I, p.92.

[23] W.-T. Chan, *op. cit.* p.212. It has been remarked that "it was inherently weak because it was largely motivated by the benefits it would bring." (Dubs, "The Development of Altruism in Confucianism," *Phi-*

losophy East and West, C. A. Moore, ed., 48-55.

[24] See Chapter 5.

[25] "*Metus improbos, compescit, non clementia.*" Syrus, *Maxims*.

[26] Quoted in Waley, *The Way and Its Power*, p.75.

[27] Fung Yu-lan, *op.cit.* I, p.312.

[28] Grousset, *op.cit.* p.37.

[29] *Hanfeizi*, W.-T. Chan, *op.cit.* pp.252-258.

[30] *Hanfeizi*, p.50. Quoted in Waley, *The Tao and Its Power*, p.75.

[31] Sima Qian remarks that Hanfeizi was influenced by Laozi.

[32] W.-T. Chan, *A Source Book in Chinese Philosophy*, pp.260-1.

[33] *Ibid.*

[34] Graham, *The Disputers of the Tao*, p.74.

[35] Fung Yu-lan, *op.cit.* I, p.193.

[36] Graham, *The Disputers of the Tao*, p.78. *Zhuangzi*, 33.

[37] *Ibid.* W.-T. Chan, *op.cit.* pp.233-235.

[38] Graham, *Chuang Tzu*, p.284. W.-T. Chan, *op.cit.* pp.233-235.

[39] Graham, *The Disputers of the Tao*, p.81.

[40] *Ibid.* p.80.

Chapter 4

[1] Oliver Leaman, *Key Concepts in Eastern Philosophy*, London: Routeledge, 1999, p.11.

[2] *Ibid.* p.29.

[3] This is Hegel's remark regarding Kant's idea of the "thing-in-itself."

[4] Ninian Smart, *World Philosophies*, London: Routeledge, 1999, p.49.

[5] Oliver Leaman, *op.cit.* p.11.

[6] I am indebted to Paul Mustacchio for his explication of Hegel.

[7] The quotations are from the *Pure Land Sutra* are from D. Sommer, ed., *Chinese Religion: An Anthology of Sources*, pp.121-4.

[8] E. A. Burtt, ed., *The Teachings of the Compassionate Buddha*, p.205.

[9] In this discussion of Buddhism I have drawn from K. Ch'en, *Buddhism in China, A Historical Survey*, p.342.

[10] Waley, *The Way and its Power*, p.43.

[11] Fung Yu-lan, *A History of Chinese Philosophy*, II, p.353.

[12] Niels C Nielson, Jr., ed., *Religions of the World*, New York: St. Martins Press, 1993, p.170.

[13] Ninian Smart, *op.cit.* p.82.

[14] *Ibid.* p.320.

[15] *Ibid.* p.311.

[16] K. Ch'en, *Buddhism in China, A Historical Survey*, p.303.

[17] W.-T. Chan, *op.cit.* p.397. *Mencius,* 6. 2.12.

[18] Ninian Smart, *op.cit.* p.80.

[19] Fung Yu-lan, *op.cit.* II, p.383.

[20] *Ibid.* p.355.

[21] *Ibid.*

[22] This is a paraphrase of N. Smart's characterization of the *gongan op.cit.* p.85.

[23] Peter Harris, ed., *Zen Poems,* New York: A. Knopf, Inc., 1999, p.30.

[24] *Ibid.*

[25] *Ibid.* p.41.

[26] Ch'en, *op.cit.* pp. 480-1. Rene Groussett, *Chinese Art and Culture,* New York, 1959, p. 250.

[27] Bruno Snell, *The Discovery of the Mind,* p.174.

Chapter 5

[1] W.-T. Chan, *A Source Book in Chinese Philosophy,* p.461.

[2] All quotations from the *Diagram of the Supreme Ultimate* are from Fung Yu-lan, *A History of Chinese Philosophy,* II. p. 435-437.

[3] F. Cornford, Tr., "Sophist" in *Plato: The Collected Dialogues,* E. Hamilton, ed., Princeton: Princeton University Press, 1961, p.958.

[4] Fung Yu-lan, *op.cit.* II, p.478.

[5] *Ibid.* p.466.

[6] *Ibid.* p.471.

[7] *Ibid.* p.466.

[8] *Apology,* 25 e–26 a, *Plato: The Collected Dialogues,* p.12.

[9] Fung Yu-lan, *op.cit.* II, pp.466-7.

[10] *Penetrating the Book of Changes,* W.-T. Chan, *op.cit.* p.479.

[11] All quotations from "The Western Inscription", *Correct Discipline for Beginners* are from Fung Yu-lan, *op.cit.* II, pp. 493 -491.

[12] *The Record of Origins from Yi-lo,* 6.53-67, Fung Yu-lan, *op.cit.* II, p. 478.

[13] *The Complete Works of the Two Chengs,* W.-T. Chan, *op.cit.* p.523.

[14] *History of the Sung Dynasty,* cited in Fung Yu-lan, *op.cit.* , II, p. 499.

[15] *Ibid.*

[16] *Zhuangzi,* Book 22. W.-T. Chan, *op.cit.,* pp.525-6.

[17] K. Ch'en, *Buddhism in China, A Historical Survey,* p.472.

[18] The quoted selections are from *Selected Sayings,* 1, 3a. pp.527-529.

[19] Plato illuminates the idea of the Good by comparing it to the sun.

[20] *Conversations of Zhuxi,* 12.8. W.-T. Chan, *op.cit.,* p.559.

[21] The quotations from Lu's *Complete Works,* are from Fung Yu-lan,

op.cit. II, pp.573-581.

[22] This is Peter Singer's objection.

[23] Fung Yu-lan, *op.cit.* , II, p. 602.

[24] *Ibid.* p.169. Fung Yu-lan, *op.cit.* II, p. 609. C.A. Moore ed., *Philosophy: East and West*, p.63.

[25] *The Philosophy of Wang Yang-Ming*, F. G. Henke, Tr. Chicago: Open Court, 1916, p.50

[26] *Ibid.* p.62

[27] *Ibid.*

[28] Nivison airs this objection in *The Ways of Confucianism*, p.172.

[29] *Record of Instructions*, pp.53-55. Fung Yu-lan, *op.cit.* II, p.604.

[30] *Ibid.*

[31] *Ibid.*

[32] The quotations from the *Record of Instructions* are from Fung Yu-lan, *op.cit.* II, pp. 602-604.

[33] The quotations from the *Questions on the Great Learning* are from Fung Yu-lan, *op.cit.* , II, p.601.

[34] *Record of Instructions*, pp.114-116. Fung Yu-lan, *op.cit.* II, p.616.

[35] *Ibid.*

[36] *Ibid.*

[37] Fung Yu-lan, *op.cit.* II. p.616.

[38] *Ibid.* p.605.

[39] *Ibid.* p.601. *Questions on the Great Learning*, pp.204-208.

[40] *Ibid.* p.613.

Chapter 6

[1] Weiss wie Lilien, reine Kerzen,
Sternen gleich, bescheidener Beugung,
Leuchtet aus dem Mittelherzen,
Rot gesäumt, die Glut der Neigung.

So frühzeitige Narzissen
Blühen reihenweis im Garten.
Mögen wohl die Guten wissen,
Wen sie so spaliert erwarten.

(*Goethe, Selected Verse*, D. Luke, ed. Harmondsworth: Penguin, 1981.)

[2] *Ibid*, p.639.

[3] *Ibid*.

[4] Dawson makes this comparison in *The Chinese Experience*, p.9.

[5] Legge, *The Works of Mencius*, p.106.

[6] Graham, *Disputers of the Dao*, p.315; p.317.

[7] A. Waley, *The Way and Its Power*, p.12.

[8] J. Gernet, *op.cit.* p.681.

[9] Montaigne's warning is in the spirit of Laozi.

[10] Kitto's explanation of the Greek mind also characterizes the philosophical thought in China. *The Greeks*, p.169.

[11] Peter Singer has pointed this out. *How are We to Live?* p.230.

[12] For a summary of philosophy in China in the twentieth century, see W.-T. Chan's "Philosophy of China" in *Twentieth Century Philosophy*, ed. D. D. Runes. New York: Philosophical Library, 1943, 54-57.

[13] "Famine, Affluence and Morality", reprinted in *Writings on an Ethical Life*. New York: The Ecco Press, 2000. *Practical Ethics*. Cambridge: Cambridge University Press, 1993, pp.223-228. Jonathan Bennett, James Rachels, and Michael Tooley have also denied that there is a distinction between acts and omissions.

[14] Rene Grousset, *The Rise and Splendour of Chinese Empire*, p.9.

[15] Some elements of the early art appear to have come from Mesopotamia and Turkestan.

[16] This point is made by Dawson in *The Chinese Experience*, p.17. Jacques Gernet's discussion *A History of Chinese Civilization*, p.106.

[17] *Lectures on the History of Philosophy* I, Tr. E. S. Haldane and Frances H. Simson, New Jersey: Humanities Press, 1983, p.121.

[18] Quoted in Julia Ching, "Chinese Ethics and Kant." *Philosophy East and West* 28:2 (April) pp.161-172.

[19] Kant, "Perpetual Peace: A Philosophical Sketch"; "Idea for a Universal History from a Cosmopolitan Point of View." *Kant, Selections*, L. W. Beck, ed. New York: Macmillan, 1988, pp. 430-457, pp. 415-425.

[20] *Crito*, 49 b-e

[21] See Chapter 3. Peter Singer has noted that Confucius' reply is compatible with Robert Axelrod's strategy of "Tit for Tat." See Singer's discussion in *How are We to Live?* Chapter 7.

[22] Graham, *The Disputers of the Dao*, pp.61-62.

[23] The quotations are from the *Book of Great Unity* are from W.-T. Chan, *op.cit.* , pp.725-736.

[24] Derk Bodde's commentary in Fung Yu-lan, *op.cit.* II. p. 676.

[25] Graham, *Chuang Tzu*, p.60.

[26] Einstein, Albert, *Ideas and Opinions*.

Bibliography

Chan, Wing-Tsit. *A Source Book in Chinese Philosophy*. Princeton: Princeton University Press, 1973.

Ch'en, Kenneth. *Buddhism in China, A Historical Survey*. Princeton: Princeton University Press, 1964.

Cheng Chung-ying. *New Dimensions of Confucian and Neo-Confucian Philosophy*. Albany: State University of New York Press, 1991.

Confucius. Tr. by James Legge. *Confucius – Confucian Analects, The Great Learning, and The Doctrine of the Mean*. New York: Dover 1971.

Confucius. Tr. by Arthur Waley. *Analects of Confucius*. London: Allen & Unwin, 1938.

Confucius. Tr. by D. C. Lau. *Confucius: The Analects*. Harmonsworth, Middlesex: Penguin Classics, 1979.

Confucius. Tr. by Ezra Pound. *The Great Digest, The Unwobbling Pivot, The Analects*. New York: New Directions, 1969.

Creel, Herrlee G. *What is Taoism?* Chicago: University of Chicago Press, 1970.

Dawson, Raymond. *The Chinese Experience*. London: Phoenix Press, 1978.

Durant, Will. *The Story of Civilization: Our Oriental Heritage*. New York: MJF Books, 1963.

Fingarette, Herbert. *Confucius: The Secular as Sacred*. New York: Harper Torchbooks, 1972.

Fung Yu-lan. *A History of Chinese Philosophy*. Tr. by Derk Bodde. Princeton: Princeton University Press, 1952.

Fung Yu-lan. *A Short History of Chinese Philosophy*. Tr. by Derk Bodde. New York: Macmillan & Co., 1958.

Fung Yu-lan. *The Spirit of Chinese Philosophy*. Tr. by E. R. Hughes. London: Routledge and Kegan Paul, 1962.

Gernet, Jacques. *A History of Chinese Civilization*. Cambridge: Cambridge University Press, 1999.

Graham, A. C. *Disputers of the Tao, Philosophical Argument in Ancient China*. Chicago: Open Court Publishing Co., 1997.

Grousset, René. *The Rise and Splendour of the Chinese Empire*. Berkeley: University of California Press, 1953.

Hall, David L. and Ames, Roger T. *Thinking Through Confucius*. Albany: State University of New York Press, 1987.

Hansen, Chad. *Language and Logic in Ancient China*. Ann Arbor:
University of Michigan Press, 1983.
Höchsmann, Hyun. *On Chuang Tzu*. Belmont: Wadsworth Publishers,
2001.
I Ching, Book of Changes. Tr. by James Legge. New York:
Bantam Books, 1969.
I Ching or Book of Changes. Tr. by Richard Wilhelm
London: Routledge & Kegan Paul, 1968.
Laozi. *Tao Te Ching: The Book of Meaning and Life*. Richard Wilhelm.
Harmondsworth: Penguin Books, 1989.
Laozi. Tr. by James Legge. *The Texts of Taoism, The Tao Te Ching of
Lao Tzu, The Writings of Zhuangzi*. New York: Dover, 1962.
Laozi. Tr. by Arthur Waley. *The Way and its Power*. London:
Allen & Unwin, 1934.
Laozi. Tr. by D. C. Lau. *Lao Tzu, Tao te ching*. Harmondsworth,
Middlesex: Penguin, 1963.
Maspero, Henri. *Taoism and Chinese Religion*. Tr. by F. A. Kieman, Jr.
Amherst, MA: University of Massachusetts Press, 1981.
Mencius, *Mencius*. Tr. by D. C. Lau. Harmondsworth,
Middlesex: Penguin, 1970.
Mencius. *The Works of Mencius*, Tr. by James Legge, New York,
Dover, 1970.
Mozi. Tr. by Y. Mei. *The Ethical and Political Works of Mo-tse*.
London: Arthur Probsthain, 1929.
Mozi. Tr. by Burton Watson, *Mo Tzu: Basic Writings*. New York:
Columbia University Press, 1963.
Needham, Joseph. *Science and Civilization in China*.
Cambridge: Cambridge University Press, 1954.
Nivison, David. *The Ways of Confucianism*. Chicago:
Open Court, 1996.
Rosemont, Henry, Jr. ed. *Chinese Texts and Philosophical
Contexts*. La Salle, IL: Open Court, 1990.
Schipper, Kristofer. *The Taoist Body*. Tr. by Karen C. Duval.
Berkeley: University of California Press, 1993.
Schwartz, Benjamin I. *The World of Thought in Ancient China*.
Cambridge, MA: Harvard University Press, 1985.
Shih Ching. (The Book of Odes) Tr. by Bernhard Karlgren. Stockholm:
Museum of Far-Eastern Antiquities, 1950.
Shoo King (Book of History), The Chinese Classics. Tr. by James
Legge. New York: Dover, 1990

Singer, Peter. *How Are We to Live?* Melbourne: Text Publishing, 1993.
Singer, Peter. *Practical Ethics.* Cambridge: Cambridge University Press, 1993
Singer, Peter. *Writings on an Ethical Life.* New York: The Ecco Press, 2000.
Sommer, Deborah. ed. *Chinese Religion: An Anthology of Sources.* New York: Oxford University Press, 1995.
Sun Tzu. *The Art of Warfare.* Tr. by Roger Ames. New York: Ballantine Books, 1993.
Tu Wei-Ming. *Neo-Confucian Thought in Action: Wang Yangming's Youth (1472-1509).* Berkeley: University of California, 1976.
Waley, Arthur. *Three Ways of Thought in Ancient China.* London: Allen & Unwin, 1939.
Waley, Arthur. Tr. *Chinese Poems.* London: Unwin Books, 1946.
Waley, Arthur. Tr. *The Book of Songs.* New York: Grove Press, 1978.
Wilhelm, Helmut, and Richard Wilhelm. *Understanding the I Ching.* Princeton: Princeton University Press, 1995.
Wilhelm, Helmut. *Change: Eight Lectures on the I Ching.* Tr. by Carey F. Baynes. New York: Pantheon Books, 1960.
Wilhelm, Helmut *Heaven, Earth and Man in the Book of Changes.* Seattle, WA: University of Washington Press, 1977.
Wilhelm, Richard. *Lectures on the I Ching.* Tr. by Irene Eber. Princeton, NJ: Princeton University Press, 1979.
Wright, Arthur, ed. *Confucianism and Chinese Civilization.* Stanford: Stanford University Press, 1964.
Wright, Arthur. *Buddhism in Chinese History.* Stanford: Stanford Stanford University Press, 1959.
Xunzi. Tr. by H. H. Dubs. *The Works of Hsuntze.* London: Arthur Probsthain, 1928.
Xunzi. Tr. by Burton Watson. *Hsün Tzu: Basic Writings.* New York: Columbia University Press, 1963.
Zhuangzi. Tr. by A. C. Graham. *Chuang-Tzu: The Inner Chapters* Indianapolis: Hackett, 2001.
Zhuangzi. Tr. by James Legge. *The Texts of Taoism, The Tao Te Ching of Lao Tzu, The Writings of Chuang Tzu.* New York: Dover, 1962.
Zhuangzi. Tr. by Burton Watson. *The Complete Works of Chuang Tzu.* New York: Columbia University Press, 1968.
Zhuangzi. Tr. by Richard Wilhelm. *Dschuang Dsi, Das Wahre Buch vom südlichen Blütenland.* München: Eugen Diederichs, 1996.